Forest Plants
OF
Northeastern
ONTARIO

Forest Plants
OF
Northeastern
ONTARIO

Written by
Karen Legasy

Illustrated by
Shayna LaBelle-Beadman

Edited by
Brenda Chambers

The Publisher
Lone Pine Publishing

206, 10426-81 Ave.	202A-1110 Seymour Street	16149 Redmond Way, #180
Edmonton, Alberta	Vancouver, British Columbia	Redmond, Washington
Canada T6E 1X5	Canada V6B 3N3	USA 98052

Canadian Cataloguing in Publication Data

Legasy, Karen L.
    Forest plants of northeastern Ontario

Includes bibliographical references and index.
ISBN 1-55105-064-1

1. Forest plants—Ontario, Northern—identification. I. LaBelle-Beadman, Shayna. II. Chambers, Brenda, 1953– III. Title
QK203.O6L43 1995   581.9713'13   C95-910544-1

The Authors

Karen Legasy	*Northeast Science & Technology, Ontario Ministry of Natural Resources*
Shayna LaBelle-Beadman	*Northeast Science & Technology, Ontario Ministry of Natural Resources*
Brenda Chambers	*Central Region Science & Technology, Ontario Ministry of Natural Resources*

Editors: Jennifer Keane, Roland Lines, Nancy Foulds
Botanical Editor: Linda Kershaw
Design: Bruce Timothy Keith
Layout: Greg Brown, Bruce Timothy Keith
Separations: Elite Lithographers Co. Ltd., Edmonton, Alberta, Canada
Printing: PrintWest Communications, Saskatoon, Saskatchewan, Canada
Front & Back Cover Photos: Graeme Oxby

Funding for the development and printing of this publication has been made available in part through the Northern Ontario Development Agreement, Northern Forestry Program (NODA).

	Natural Resources Canada	Ressources naturelles Canada
	Canadian Forest Service	Service canadien des foret
	Ministry of Natural Resources	Ministère des Richesses naturelles

This field guide to the forest plants of Northeastern Ontario is a co-publication of Northeast Science & Technology and Lone Pine Publishing. This guide was developed in partnership with Central Region Science & Technology unit of the Ontario Ministry of Natural Resources.

The publisher gratefully acknowledges the assistance of Alberta Community Development, the Department of Canadian Heritage, and the Canada/Alberta Agreement on the Cultural Industries.

This guide is dedicated
to a gentle man of wisdom and laughter
who was always willing to lend a hand.

Gerry Boissoneau
(1948-1995)

Acknowledgments

The producers of this guide would like to acknowledge the continued support,
expertise and commitment of the following people:

*Dr. Irwin Brodo, Research Scientist, Lichenology, Canadian Museum of Nature;
Dr. Bill Crins, Regional Ecologist, Central Region, OMNR, Huntsville;
Louise Clément, Secretary, Northeast Science & Technology, Cochrane;
Albert Dugal, Collections Specialist, Vascular Plants, Canadian Museum of
Nature; Trevor Howard, Systems Analyst, Central Region Science &
Technology, OMNR, North Bay; Dr. Robert Ireland, Bryologist, Ottawa;
Neil Mauer, Remote Sensing Specialist, Northeast Science & Technology,
OMNR, Timmins; Dr. John Morton, Professor Emeritus, Biology Department,
University of Waterloo, Waterloo; Steve Newmaster, Consultant, Wawa;
Doug Skeggs, Communications Specialist, Northeast Science & Technology,
OMNR, Timmins; Kimberly Taylor, Forest Ecologist, Northeast Science &
Technology, OMNR, Cochrane; John E. Thompson, Life Science Biologist,
Northeast Provincial Parks, OMNR, Cochrane; Al Willcocks, Manager,
Northeast and Northwest Science & Technology, OMNR, Timmins.*

Thanks must also be given to the following people who have helped along the
way and to anyone we might have missed:

*Ken Baldwin, Wally Bidwell, Gerry Boissoneau, Céline Boisvenue,
Rob D'Eon, Jim Finnigan, Sara Forsyth, Marianne Hendry, Joanne Hallarn,
Leith Hunter, Sylvain Levesque, Wayne Lewis, Alison Luke, Dr. Brian Naylor,
Sue Pickering, Bruce Richard, Lisa Spracklin, Jane Stringer, Peter Uhlig,
Judy Venn and Diane Wahlman.*

We acknowledge the use of plant specimens from the Forestry Canada
Herbarium in Sault Ste. Marie for photographic purposes.

TABLE OF CONTENTS

REFERENCES

Andrus, R.E. 1980. *Sphagnaceae (Peat Moss Family) of New York State*. Univ. of the State of New York, Albany, N.Y. 89 pp.

Arnup, R., B. Dowsley, L. Buse, and W. Bell. 1995. Pocket Guide to Autecology of Selected Crop Trees and Competitor Species in Northeastern Ontario. OMNR.

Bailey, L.H. 1963. *How Plants Get Their Names*. Dover Publications Inc., New York, N.Y.

Baldwin, K.A., and R.A. Sims. 1989. *Field Guide to the Common Forest Plants in Northwestern Ontario*. OMNR, Toronto, Ont. 344 pp.

Baldwin, W.K.W. 1958. *Plants of the Clay Belt of Northern Ontario and Quebec*. National Museum of Canada, Ottawa, Ont., Bulletin No. 156. 304 pp.

Banfield, A.W.F. 1974. *The Mammals of Canada*. National Museum of Natural Sciences, Univ. of Toronto Press, Toronto, Ont. 438 pp.

Bell, F.W. 1991. *Critical Silvics of Conifer Crop Species and Selected Competitive Vegetation in Northwestern Ontario*. Forestry Canada, OMNR, COFRDA Rep. 3310/NWOFTDU Tech. Rep. 19. 177 pp.

Bentley, C.V., and F. Pinto. 1994. *The Autecology of Selected Understory Vegetation in Central Ontario*. CRST, OMNR, North Bay, Ont. 169 pp.

Bergen, J.Y. 1908. *Essentials of Botany*. The Athenaeum Press, Boston, Mass. 267 pp.

Blouin, G. 1984. *Weeds of the Woods: Small Trees and Shrubs of the Eastern Forest*. Goose Lane Editions, Fredericton, N.B. 125 pp.

Bowles, J.M. 1983 (unpublished). *Field Guide to the Common Forest Plants of the Clay Belt Region of Northern Ontario*. OMNR, Timmins, Ont.

Brown, L. 1979. *Grasses: An Identification Guide*. Houghton Mifflin Co., USA. 240 pp.

Bunney, S. 1992. *The Illustrated Encyclopedia of Herbs: Their Medicinal and Culinary Uses*. Chancellor Press, London, Eng. 320 pp.

Cadman, M.D., P.F.J. Eagles, and F.M. Helleiner. 1987. *Atlas of the Breeding Birds of Ontario*. Federation of Ontario Naturalists, Univ. of Waterloo Press, Waterloo, Ont. 617 pp.

Case, F.W. Jr. 1964. *Orchids of the Western Great Lakes Region*. Cranbrook Institute of Science, Bloomfield Hills, Mich. 147 pp.

Cobb, B. 1963. *A Field Guide to the Ferns and their Related Families*, Peterson Field Guide Series. Houghton Mifflin Co., Boston, Mass. 281 pp.

Conard, H.S. 1956. *How to Know the Mosses and Liverworts*. Wm. C. Brown Co. Publ., Dubuque, Iowa. 226 pp.

Corns, I.G.W., and R.M. Annas. 1986. *Field Guide to Forest Ecosystems of West-Central Alberta*, Northern Forestry. Centre, Canadian Forestry Service, Edmonton, Alta. 251 pp.

Crum, H.E. 1983. *Mosses of the Great Lakes Forest*, 3rd edition. Univ. of Mich. Press, Ann Arbor, Mich. 417 pp.

D'Eon, R., and R. Watt. 1994. *A Forest Habitat Suitability Matrix for Northeastern Ontario*. NEST, OMNR, Timmins, Ont. 83 pp.

DeGraaf, R.M., and D.D. Rudis. 1986. *New England Wildlife: Habitat, Natural History, and Distribution*. USDA, Forestry Service, Broomall, Pa.. 491 pp.

Dore, W.G., and J. McNeil. 1980. *Grasses of Ontario*., Agr. Can., Que. 566 pp.

Densmore, F. 1974. *How Indians Use Wild Plants for Food, Medicine and Crafts*. Dover Publications, Inc., New York, N.Y. 397 pp.

Erichsen-Brown, C. 1979. *Use of Plants for the Past 500 Years*. Breezy Creeks Press, Aurora, Ont. 510 pp.

Fernald, M.L. 1979. *Gray's Manual of Botany*, 8th edition. Van Nostrand Publ. Co., N.Y. 1632 pp.

Fleurbec. 1993. *Fougères, prèles et lycopodes*. Fleurbec, Saint-Henri-de-Levis, Que. 511 pp.

———. 1987. *Plantes sauvages des lacs, rivières et tourbières*. Flourbec, Saint-Augustin, Que. 399 pp.

Foster, S., and J.A. Duke. 1990. *A Field Guide to Medicinal Plants: Eastern and Central North America*. Houghton Mifflin Co., Boston, Mass. 366 pp.

Frankton, C., and G.A. Mulligan. 1971. *Weeds of Canada*. Can. Dept. Agric. Publ. 948. 217 pp.

Gibbins Bryan, R., and M. Newton-White. 1978. *Wildflowers of the North*. Highway Book Shop, Cobalt, Ont. 215 pp.

Gleason, H.A. 1952. *The New Britton and Brown Illustrated Flora of the Northern United States and Adjacent Canada*, Vols. I, II, and III. Hafner Press, N.Y. 1732 pp.

Glime, J.M. 1993. *The Elfin World of Mosses and Liverworts of Michigan's Upper Peninsula and Isle Royale*. Isle Royale Natural History Association, Houghton, Mich. 148 pp.

Grieve, M., and C.F. Level. 1992 (revised ed.) *A Modern Herbal*. Tiger Books Int., London, Eng. 912 pp.

Hale, M.E. 1979. *How to Know the Lichens*, 2nd edition. William C. Brown Co. Publ., Dubuque, Iowa. 246 pp.

Hosie, R.C. 1969. *Native Trees of Canada*. Canadian Forestry Service, Ottawa, Ont. 291 pp.

Klinda, K., *et al.* 1989. *Indicator Plants of Coastal British Columbia*. Univ. of B.C. Press, Vancouver, B.C. 288 pp.

Krussmann, G. 1976. *Manual of Cultivated Broad-Leaved Trees & Shrubs*, Vols I, II, & III. Timber Press, Beaverton, Ore. 1403 pp.

Lackschewitz, K. 1991. *Vascular Plants of West-Central Montana: Identification Guidebook*. USDA, Forestry Service, Intermountains Research Station, GT Rep. INT-277. 648 pp.

Lamoureux, G., et collaborateurs. 1988. *Plantes sauvages printanières*. Fleurbec, Saint-Augustin, Que. 7th edition. 247 pp.

Lellinger, D.B. 1985. *A Field Manual of the Ferns and Fern-allies of the United States and Canada*. Smithsonian Inst. Press, Washington, D.C. 389 pp.

MacKinnon, A., and J. Pojar. 1994. *Plants of Coastal British Columbia*. Lone Pine Publishing, Edmonton, Alta. 527 pp.

MacKinnon, A., J. Pojar, and R. Coupé. 1992. *Plants of Northern British Columbia*. Lone Pine Publishing, Edmonton, Alta. 338 pp.

Marie-Victorin, Frère. *Flore Laurentienne*. Les Presses de l'Université de Montréal, Montréal, Qué. 2nd Edition. 923 pp.

McCarthy, T., *et al.* 1994. *Field Guide to Forest Ecosystems of Northeastern Ontario*. Draft. NEST Field Guide FG-001.

McKay, S., and P. Catling. 1979. *Trees, Shrubs and Flowers to Know in Ontario*. Alger Press, Oshawa, Ont. 208 pp.

McQueen, C.B. 1990. *Field Guide to the Peat Mosses of Boreal North America*. University Press of New England, Hanover. 138 pp.

Meades, W.J., and L. Moores. 1989. *Forest Site Classification Manual: A Field Guide to the Damman Forest Types of Newfoundland*. Ministry of Supply and Services Canada, and Newfoundland Dept. of For. and Agr.

Morton, J., and J. Venn. 1990. *A Checklist of the Flora of Ontario Vascular Plants*. Dept. of Biol., Univ. of Waterloo, Ont. 218 pp.

Newmaster, S., and A. Lehela. 1995. *Ontario Plant List*. OMNR, Ontario Forest Research Institute FRP128, Queen's Printer.

Niering, W., and N. Olmstead. 1979. *The Audubon Society Field Guide to North American Wildflowers: Eastern Region*. Alfred A. Knopf, Inc., N.Y. 887 pp.

Peterson, L.A. 1977. *A Field Guide to Edible Wild Plants*. Houghton Mifflin Co., Boston, Mass. 330 pp.

Peterson, R.T. and M. McKenny. 1968. *A Field Guide to Wildflowers of Northeastern and North-Central North America*. Houghton Mifflin Co., Boston, Mass. 420 pp.

Robuck, O.W. 1985. *The Common Plants of the Muskegs of Southeast Alaska*. Pacific Northwest Forest and Range Experiment Station, U.S. Dept. of Agric., Portland, Ore.

Rouleau, R. 1990. *Petite flore forestière du Québec*. Les Publications du Québec, Québec, Qué. 2nd Edition. 250 pp.

Semple, J.C., and S.B. Heard. *The Asters of Ontario: Aster L. and Virgulus Raf. (Compositae: Asteraceae)*. Univ. of Waterloo, Waterloo, Ont. 88 pp.

Semple, J.C., Ringius, G.S. 1992. *Goldenrods of Ontario: Solidago and Euthamia*. Univ. of Waterloo, Waterloo, Ont. 82 pp.

Soper, J.H., and M.L. Heimburger. 1982. *Shrubs of Ontario*. Royal Ont. Mus., Publ. in Life Sci., Toronto, Ont. 495 pp.

Van Allen Murphey, E. 1959. *Indian Uses of Native Plants*. Mendocino County Historical Society, Fort Bragg, Ca. 81 pp.

Vitt, D., J. Marsh, and R. Bovey. 1988. *Mosses, Lichens & Ferns of Northwest North America*. Lone Pine Publishing, Edmonton, Alta. 296 pp.

Westbrooks, R.G., and J.W. Preacher. 1986. *Poisonous Plants of Eastern North America*. Univ. of South Carolina Press, Columbia, S.C. 226 pp.

White, J.H. (revised by R.C. Hosie). 1973. *The Forest Trees of Ontario*. OMNR, Toronto, Ont. 119 pp.

Whiting, R.E., and P.M. Catling. 1986. *Orchids of Ontario: An Illustrated Guide*. Canacoll Foundation, Ottawa, Ont. 169 pp.

Wilkinson, K. 1990. *Trees and Shrubs of Alberta*. Lone Pine Publishing, Edmonton, Alberta. 191 pp.

INTRODUCTION

The boreal forest is a wide forest zone that extends from Alaska–Yukon in the northwest of North America to Newfoundland in the east. *Forest Plants of Northeastern Ontario* has been developed for anyone who wants to explore our part of the boreal forest and recognize the plants within it—field naturalists, resource managers, hikers, campers and armchair adventurers.

This guide contains descriptions of 310 plants common to the upland and lowland ecosystems of the boreal forest of northeastern Ontario. The majority of species described are characteristic of undisturbed forests; however, several introduced species found along roadsides and in other disturbed habitats are included.

Regional Overview

The northeast region of Ontario has a mosaic of forest ecosystems: coniferous treed wetlands on deep peats, upland mixed forests on bedrock-controlled terrain, extensive jack pine forests on sandy soils, sphagnum–black spruce bogs with acid-loving plants, rich fens and cedar swamps. It extends from the Ontario–Quebec border west to the Manitouwadge area. Its southern boundary extends from Wawa, dipping to the south of Chapleau, Gogama and Kirkland Lake. Its northern boundary extends into the Hudson Bay lowlands. The species described in this guide grow outside of these administrative boundaries, but this is the area referred to in the text as 'our region.'

Our region sits in the narrowest band of the boreal forest, with the cold, year-round influence of Hudson Bay to the north and the warmer, moderating effects of the Great Lakes to the south. The region can be broadly divided into two areas: the Clay Belt to the north and the Height of Land area to the south and west.

The Clay Belt

The Clay Belt is characterized by flat to gently undulating plains, with deep, stone-free clay till or varved lake deposits. The fine-textured soils were derived from soft calcareous rocks to the north, in the Hudson Bay lowland area. Extensive peat deposits have formed in poorly drained, cool areas, supporting ecosystems dominated by black spruce, sphagnum and feathermosses, and many members of the heath family, including Labrador-tea, blueberry and leatherleaf. Eastern white cedar and larch commonly grow with black spruce in these lowland areas. Warm, moist sites host balsam poplar, black ash and white elm, as well as a fascinating shrub and herb-rich flora. Better-drained upland sites support white and black spruce, balsam fir, trembling aspen, white birch and diverse understories of tall shrubs such as mountain maple and beaked hazel, along with a host of herbaceous species. The coarser, drier, sandy to gravelly soils typical of landforms created by glacial meltwaters, including outwash plains, eskers and kames are dominated by jack pine forests, with their associated heath shrubs, feathermosses and lichens. White and red pine, tree species characteristic of the Great Lakes–St. Lawrence Forest to the south, are scattered relics of a warmer period in post-glacial times.

The Height of Land Area

The Height of Land area is dominated by bedrock-controlled terrain of the Precambrian Shield, with varying depths of often stony, sandy to silty till material. Ecosystem pattern is a result, in part, of local climate and soil factors, and many of the plant species present in the Clay Belt also occur across the Height of Land area. In the southernmost part of our region are several types of transitional Great Lakes–St. Lawrence forest stands, including red maple mixedwoods, sugar maple and yellow birch. The understorey of these transitional stands lacks the many spring ephemeral species present in Great Lakes–St. Lawrence stands south of our region.

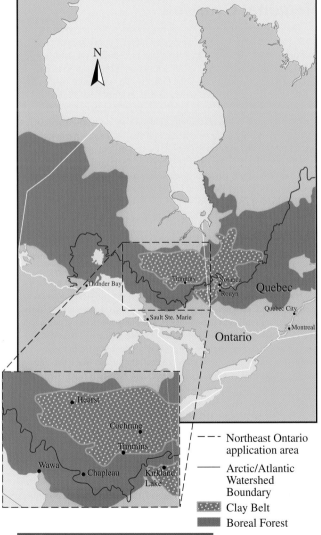

- - - Northeast Ontario application area
— Arctic/Atlantic Watershed Boundary
Clay Belt
Boreal Forest

Climate

The climate in our region can be described as modified continental, with mean annual temperatures typically below the freezing mark, ranging from -1.1 to 1.7°C, and a growing season from 140–169 days long. The Clay Belt experiences the coldest temperatures and shortest growing season within our region. Climate in the Height of Land area varies greatly, with differences in the topographic pattern of the land. The topography remains rugged toward Lake Superior, but the climate is modified, and longer growing seasons there are characteristic.

Disturbance

The overall pattern of forest ecosystems on the landscape is a result of differences in climate, soil texture, moisture regime, topography and the pervasive influence of disturbance. Fire has played a significant role in the pattern, stability and diversity of boreal forest ecosystems. From the tree layer to the mosses on the forest floor, many plant species and their ecosystems have evolved in the face of repeated fire disturbances. Human activities have had a major influence on forest ecosystem pattern through settlement, logging, mining and agriculture. These activities have also introduced non-native species into our region.

Organization of This Guide

The plants are divided into sections according to their growth form, as follows: trees, shrubs, herbs, grasses, sedges and rushes, ferns and fern allies (horsetails and clubmosses), liverworts, mosses and lichens. The sections are divided into species groups, and most sections begin with a chart or key which outlines the groupings.

Each species is accompanied by a detailed line drawing, a colour photograph (when available) and descriptive text. The text for the plant descriptions is based on a review of available taxonomic literature and is written in plain English with a minimal use of technical terms. Each entry begins with a general description of the plant; detailed descriptions of the leaves, flowers and fruit (where applicable) and habitat follow the general description. Information about similar species and distinguishing features is provided in the Notes sections, which also describe historical, aboriginal, nutritional and medicinal uses of the plants, and their importance to the wildlife of the region.

> *Caution: We are NOT RECOMMENDING the use of any of these plants for medicinal, healing or food value purposes. We also caution that many of the plants in our region are poisonous or harmful and may cause adverse reactions if consumed or used externally. The information about food and medicinal values of plants is provided for interest's sake and historical value only. The information has been compiled from other books and its accuracy has not been tested.*

How to Use This Guide

When trying to identify a plant in the field, go to the appropriate section of the guide by identifying the growth form—is it a tree, a shrub, an herb or another form? When a chart or key is available, begin by refering to it, and match your specimen's characteristics (e.g., leaf shape, toothed or toothless margins) with those listed. If there is no chart or key, or it doesn't lead you to the correct species, try to match the unknown specimen against the photos and line drawings. When you find a photo of a species you think might match your specimen, refer to the text for more specific information. If the photo, line drawing and text match the unknown species, you have made a field identification. If you are not able to make a match, a more comprehensive reference should be consulted. (Note that some photos in this guide are of herbarium specimens. Because these plants have been dried, they will differ in colour and shape from plants growing in the field.)

A glossary is included for users who may be unfamiliar with some of the technical terms used in the plant descriptions, and a pictorial glossary provides further clarity.

Plant Names

Common names, in English and French, are provided whenever possible.

The nomenclature for this guide follows *The Ontario Plant List* (Newmaster and Lehela, 1995) and *A Checklist of the Flora of Ontario* (Morton and Venn, 1990).

Habitat information was obtained from the Northeast Forest Ecosystem Classification dataset and from existing literature.

—*Brenda Chambers*

Pine Family (Pinaceae)

General: Conifer; evergreen; up to 15 m or more tall; trunk slightly tapered and usually covered with dead branches that persist for years; 30–60 cm in diameter; symmetrical with a narrowly pyramid-shaped crown; roots shallow; young bark greyish, smooth and has raised 'blisters' filled with aromatic resin or gum, older bark has irregular, brownish scales; twigs greenish and smooth or slightly hairy; buds waxy and have rounded tips.

Leaves: Needle-like; spirally arranged; single but appear to be in 2 rows (making the needled branch or spray appear flat); stalkless; flat with rounded or notched tip; 2–4 cm long; upper surface shiny and dark green with 2 white bands or lines on underside; margins toothless.

Karen Legasy

Flowers: Cones; male flowers small, cone-like, yellowish-red or purplish-tinged, short-lived and hang from axils of previous year's leaves; female flowers erect, purplish to greenish cones about 5–10 cm long; male and female flowers on same tree.

Fruit: Winged seeds eventually released from female cones.

Habitat: Fresh to moist sites; all upland soil types, all stand types; often grows with black spruce, white spruce, trembling aspen and white birch; abundant.

Notes: Balsam fir's wood is soft, light, odourless and white. It is used for lumber or pulpwood. Balsam fir has long been a Christmas tree favourite for its balsamic fragrance and long-lasting needles. The resin or gum from the 'blisters' is used to make turpentine, and the resin has historically been used in remedies for colds, sores and wounds. See caution in Introduction. • This tree has a high wildlife value. It provides browse for moose. Red squirrels, other small mammals and songbirds such as crossbills and chickadees eat the seeds. Balsam fir provides cover for moose, snowshoe hare, white-tailed deer, ruffed grouse, small mammals and songbirds. • See notes on ground hemlock (*Taxus canadensis*).

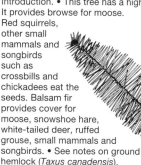

1 cm

LARCH ◆ *Larix laricina*
MÉLÈZE LARICIN

Pine Family (Pinaceae)

Karen Legasy

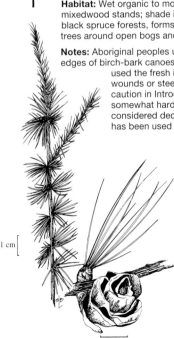

1 cm

1 cm

General: Deciduous; evergreen; up to 18 m tall; trunk straight with little taper; 30–60 cm in diameter; crown small, narrow, open and cone-shaped; roots shallow but wide-spreading; young bark grey, thin and smooth, becomes reddish-brown and scaly, inner bark dark reddish-purple; twigs orange-brown, slender and hairless; buds dark red, small, rounded and smooth.

Leaves: Needle-like; spiral; single, in clusters of 10–20 on elongated twigs or dwarf twigs; stalkless; triangular in cross-section, slender; 2–3 cm long; soft and flexible; light green, turn golden-yellow and shed in fall; margins toothless.

Flowers: Male small, cone-like and short-lived; female light-brown, upright, rounded cones 1–2 cm long; male and female on same tree; often stay on tree over winter and throughout following summer; appear in May.

Fruit: Winged seeds; released from female cones in fall.

Habitat: Wet organic to moist upland sites; conifer mixedwood stands; shade intolerant; frequent in boggy black spruce forests, forms a characteristic area of stunted trees around open bogs and is rarely in pure stands.

Notes: Aboriginal peoples used larch roots to sew the edges of birch-bark canoes and to weave baskets, and used the fresh inner bark as a poultice for wounds or steeped it for a medicinal tea. See caution in Introduction. • Larch wood is somewhat hard, heavy and oily and is considered decay-resistant even in water. It has been used to make railway ties, poles, fence posts and crates, and the curved roots have been used in shipbuilding. • Spruce grouse feed on expanding buds. Chickadees, crossbills, the red-breasted nuthatch and red squirrels eat the seeds, and larch provides browse for the snowshoe hare and porcupine. • Larch is also known as 'tamarack.'

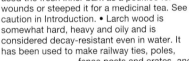

Pine Family (Pinaceae)

General: Conifer; evergreen; up to 24 m tall, but may be as tall as 40 m; trunk noticeably tapered; up to 120 cm in diameter; crown cone-shaped, spreading to slightly drooping branches extend down to base or ground except in dense stands with heavy shade where lower branches are gradually shed; roots shallow but widespread; bark light greyish-brown, thin and scaly, inner bark silvery-white; twigs whitish-grey to yellowish and usually hairless; buds have blunt tips and pointed outer scales.

Leaves: Needle-like; spiral; single; stalkless; linear and straight with blunt ends, 4-sided or squarish in cross-section; around 2 cm long; green to dull bluish-green with a whitish powdery covering (bloom); stiff and thick; margins toothless; often have a skunk-like fragrance when crushed.

Karen Legasy

Flowers: Male small, pale red, cone-like, on branch ends, short-lived; female slender, cylindrical, reddish to light-brown cones 5–7 cm long open in fall and drop from tree during fall or winter; male and female on same tree.

Fruit: Winged seeds; released from female cones in fall.

Habitat: Moist to dry upland sites; conifer and hardwood mixedwoods and transition tolerant hardwood stands; common in well-drained sites along river valleys; rarely forms pure stands.

Notes: White spruce is a commercially important tree species for lumber and pulpwood. It is also used to manufacture musical instruments such as guitars and violins. • Aboriginal peoples used the pliable roots to sew birch-bark canoes and to make baskets and snowshoes, and used the inner bark to make a poultice for wounds or swellings. See caution in Introduction. • White spruce has a high wildlife value. Red squirrels and other small mammals eat the seeds, as do songbirds such as chickadees, crossbills, and nuthatches. Spruce grouse eat the needles. The snowshoe hare and porcupine use white spruce for browse and it provides cover for moose, white-tailed deer, caribou and songbirds. See notes on black spruce (*Picea mariana*).

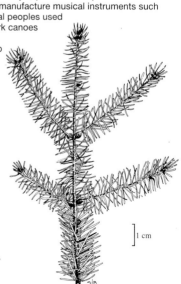

1 cm

1 cm

BLACK SPRUCE ♦ *Picea mariana*
ÉPINETTE NOIRE

Pine Family (Pinaceae)

Karen Legasy

General: Conifer; evergreen; 5–18 m tall; trunk straight with little taper and without branches for much of its length, branches drooping with ends turned upward; averages 15–25 cm in diameter; narrow crown often club-shaped at top; roots shallow; bark dark greyish-brown, thin and scaly, inner bark deep olive-green; twigs dark brown and covered with dense, short, rusty hairs; buds have finely hairy outer scales with long, slender, hair-like points that extend to above the tip.

Leaves: Needle-like; spirally arranged, giving branchlets a cylindrical appearance; single; stalkless; linear with blunt ends and 4-sided or squarish in cross-section; 0.5–1.5 cm long; dull, dark bluish-green; thick and stiff; margins toothless.

Flowers: Male small, cone-like, dark red, at branch ends and short-lived; female purplish to dark-brown, egg-shaped cones 2–3 cm long that become rounded when open and often remain on tree for 20–30 years; male and female on same tree.

Fruit: Winged seeds gradually released from female cones throughout winter (some seeds may remain in cones for a number of years).

Habitat: All moisture regimes and soil textures, pure stands and conifer and hardwood mixedwoods and transition tolerant hardwood stands; common in sphagnum bogs and on moist, acidic sites; forms pure stands or grows with jack pine, white spruce, balsam fir, trembling aspen, larch or white birch; the main forest tree of low-lying, poorly drained areas; abundant.

Notes: When young, black and white spruce may be difficult to distinguish in the field. A key distinguishing feature is the buds. Black spruce buds are hairy at the tips while white spruce's are not.

• Black spruce, with its long, strong fibres, is a commercially important pulpwood species used for manufacturing newsprint and other paper products. The roots were used for sewing birch-bark canoes. The gum or resin of black spruce was histori-cally used as a chewing gum.

• Black spruce has a high wildlife value. Red squirrels and songbirds eat the seeds, and spruce grouse feed on the needles. It provides cover for moose and songbirds and browse for snowshoe hare.

1 cm

Pine Family (Pinaceae)

General: Conifer; evergreen; 12–18 m tall, sometimes up to 30 m; trunk straight, slender and has little taper; 20–30 cm or possibly more in diameter; crown shape highly variable, branches spreading to upward-growing; roots moderately deep and wide-spreading; young bark reddish-brown to grey and thin, becomes dark brown and flaky; twigs yellowish-green and slender, become dark greyish-brown; buds pale reddish-brown and rounded.

Karen Legasy

Leaves: Needle-like; spiral; in spreading pairs; straight or slightly curved with sharp point and a papery sheath at base; 2–4 cm long; yellowish-green; stiff; margins minutely toothed.

Flowers: Male yellowish, small, about 1 cm long, cone-like, short-lived and clustered at branch ends; female cones yellowish-brown, variable in shape from oblong to cone-shaped and straight to strongly curved inward, 2.5–7.5 cm long, often whorled on branches, and often remain closed and stay on tree for a number of years; male and female on same tree.

Fruit: Winged seeds enclosed in female cones; seeds black and often ridged.

Habitat: Dry to fresh, rocky to sandy to coarse-loamy sites, pure stands or conifer and hardwood mixedwood stands; abundant.

Notes: Requiring a temperature of about 50°C or more for the female cones to open and release their seeds, pure stands of natural jack pine are usually of fire origin. Jack pine is used for lumber and pulpwood. • Aboriginal peoples dug up the long roots, split them in half, rolled them up and soaked them in water to loosen and remove the bark, then used them for sewing things like canoe seams. • Jack pine has a very high wildlife value. Songbirds, red squirrels and other small mammals eat the seeds, and spruce grouse eat the needles. Young stands provide cover for the snowshoe hare.

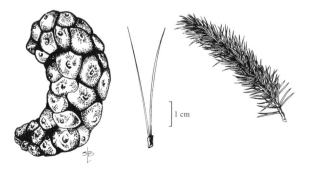

1 cm

Pine Family (Pinaceae)

General: Conifer; evergreen; 20–30 m tall; trunk straight, limbless and has little taper; diameter is 30–60 cm but may be as much as 90 cm; crown usually oval; roots moderately deep and wide-spreading; bark reddish to pinkish and scaly, older bark is furrowed or grooved with long, flat, scaly ridges; twigs orange to reddish-brown, thick and shiny; buds have sharp, pointed tips and loosely overlapping, hairy scales.

Karen Legasy

Leaves: Needle-like; in clusters; paired; slender, straight and flexible, flattened on inside of clusters, rounded on outside, with sharp, pointed tips and papery sheaths at base; 10–15 cm long; dark green and shiny; margins minutely toothed.

Flowers: Male small, cone-like and short-lived; female egg-shaped cones, about 4–7 cm long, release seed in fall and usually drop from tree the following spring; male and female on same tree.

Fruit: Winged seeds enclosed in female cones.

Habitat: Dry, sandy sites; minor component in pure conifer and hardwood mixedwood stands; frequent in the southern part of our region, occasional and rare northward.

Notes: Red pine has 2 needles in every cluster; this distinguishes it from white pine (*Pinus strobus*), which has 5. • Red pine is often used for lumber, telephone poles and railway ties. • Its reddish bark helps to explain the common name. • Aboriginal peoples used the sap or resin to make a tar for waterproofing the seams on birch-bark canoes and roofs. • Red pine has a very high wildlife value. Songbirds such as the crossbill, chickadee, grosbeak and siskin eat the seeds, as do red squirrels and other small mammals. Snowshoe hare browse red pine, and songbirds take cover in it.

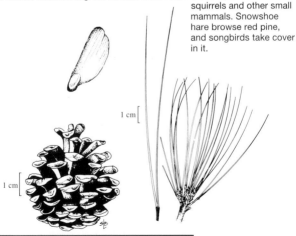

1 cm

1 cm

Pine Family (Pinaceae)

General: Conifer; evergreen; 30–40 m tall; trunk has little taper, is often branchless for over 1/2 its height, branches are wide-spreading and often at right angles to trunk near midsection and upward-growing toward top; usually up to about 90 cm in diameter; crown widely oval to irregular with wide-spreading branches; roots moderately deep and wide-spreading; young bark greyish-green, thin and smooth, older bark dark greyish-brown with deep longitudinal furrows; twigs green and downy, become orange-brown and hairless; buds reddish-brown, slender, with pointed tips and overlapping scales.

Karen Legasy

Leaves: Needle-like; about 7–12 cm long, slender; in clusters of 5; soft and flexible; bluish-green; margins finely toothed; no sheaths at base.

Flowers: Male and female on same tree; male small, cone-like and short-lived; female cylindrical and often curved cones about 8–20 cm long, on stalks about 1 cm long, green in summer, dark brown in fall when they open, drop from tree during late fall or winter.

Fruit: Winged seeds enclosed in female cones; released in fall.

Habitat: Fresh to moist, rocky to coarse-loamy sites; a minor component in mixedwood stands; frequent in the southern part of our region, occasional and rare northward.

Notes: White pine is the tallest conifer in eastern Canada. When growing in the open, branches on mature trees are often angled east because of prevailing westerly winds. • White pine is valued for its lumber, which is used to make furniture, panelling, window frames and doors, among other things. The British Navy used white pine for shipbuilding. The tall, straight trunks were used for ship masts. • Aboriginal peoples used white pine gum in a sore-throat remedy and the bark in a cold remedy. See caution in Introduction. • White pine has a very high wildlife value. Red squirrels, other small mammals and songbirds such as crossbills, chickadees, grosbeaks and siskins eat the seeds. Snowshoe hare browse white pine, and songbirds, white-tailed deer and moose use it for cover. Ospreys and eagles use it for nesting and roosting.

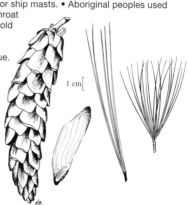
1 cm

WHITE CEDAR ♦ *Thuja occidentalis*
CÈDRE

Cypress Family (Cupressaceae)

Karen Legasy

General: Conifer; evergreen; 15–20 m tall; trunk rapidly tapers, is often twisted and looks rugged; about 30 cm in diameter; crown narrow, cone-shaped and extends to ground; roots shallow and wide-spreading; bark reddish-brown, thin and shreds, older bark forms narrow, flat ridges; twigs yellowish-green and form wide, fan-shaped sprays; buds green and minute.

Leaves: Scale-like and tightly overlapping; opposite; in pairs; stalkless; upper and lower leaves flat with pointed tips and a prominent yellowish resin spot, side leaves folded and clasp bases of upper and lower leaves; dull yellowish-green; 2–4 mm long; margins toothless.

Flowers: Tiny male flowers short-lived, at branchlet tips; female flowers are oval, woody cones about 1 cm long, with 10–12 scales in opposite pairs; male and female on same tree.

Fruit: Seeds with 2 wings; enclosed by the scales of the female cone; released a year after cone develops.

Habitat: Wet organic to fresh, fine- to coarse-loamy upland sites; conifer and hardwood mixedwoods; often grows in limestone-based areas; does not form large pure stands in our region; frequent along shores of rivers and lakes and in wet black spruce forests.

Notes: If cedar oil is ingested in quantity, it can cause abnormally low blood pressure, convulsions and death. Cedar has historically been taken internally as a diuretic and used externally for skin diseases and as an insect repellent. See caution in Introduction. • The soft wood is light and not overly strong, but it is somewhat decay-resistant and has been used for items such as posts, poles and shingles, and in canoe- and boat-building. The cedar boughs were used as brooms, and the sweeping action deodorized the house with cedar fragrance. • Cedar swamps are habitat for many songbirds, including the Canada warbler and golden-crowned kinglet. In winter, white-tailed deer 'yard up' in cedar swamps and porcupines chew through the outer bark to eat the inner bark.

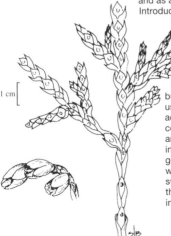

1 cm

Willow Family (Salicaceae)

General: Hardwood; deciduous; 15–25 m tall; trunk short and tapered; usually 30–60 cm in diameter; crown oval but often uneven with a few coarse, irregular branches; roots shallow; young bark pale green to yellowish-grey and usually orange-tinged, older bark dark grey and furrowed; twigs brownish-grey, dull, often slightly hairy and stout; buds have greyish, downy hairs.

Leaves: Broad-leaved; alternate; on flattish stalks; simple; egg-shaped to widely oval or almost rounded, tip blunt to pointed, base wedge-shaped to rounded; 4–12 cm long; upper surface dark green, underside paler and downy when leaves are unfolding; margins have large, irregular, wavy or rounded teeth; easily tremble or quiver in the slightest breeze.

Flowers: In cone-like catkins; male catkins about 5–10 cm long, female 7.5–12.5 cm long when in fruit; appear before leaves; male and female on separate trees.

MNR Photo

Fruit: Capsules; cone-shaped; about 6 mm long; split open to release tiny seeds covered with silky hairs; May–June while leaves are expanding.

Habitat: Dry to fresh, well-drained sandy to loamy areas; shade intolerant; often grows in mixed stands with trembling aspen, white birch, white pine and red pine; frequent only in the southern part of our region.

Notes: Largetooth aspen can be recognized in the spring by the downy hair covering its twigs and buds and later by the large teeth on its leaf margins. • The wood is used to make pulp, plywood, veneer and matches. • The scientific name *Populus* means 'people' and most likely was chosen because poplar species were often planted in public squares where people congregated.

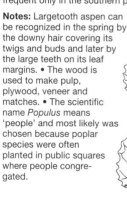

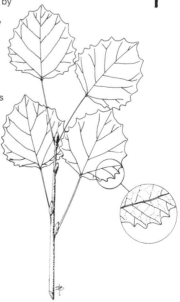

1 cm

TREMBLING ASPEN ♦ *Populus tremuloides*
PEUPLIER FAUX-TREMBLE

Willow Family (Salicaceae)

Karen Legasy

General: Hardwood; deciduous; 12–20 m tall; trunk cylindrical with little taper and branch-free for most of its length; usually 20–25 cm in diameter; crown short and rounded; roots shallow and wide-spreading; young bark pale green to almost white, smooth and waxy, older bark grey with long furrows or ridges; twigs brownish-grey, round in cross-section, slender and shiny; end buds small, shiny and dark reddish-brown, with pointed tips, not sticky or fragrant.

Leaves: Broad-leaved; alternate; on flat stalks usually longer than the blade; simple; widely egg-shaped to rounded, tip pointed and base flat to rounded or slightly heart-shaped; 2–8 cm long, 1.8–7 cm wide; upper surface deep green, underside paler; hairless; margins have fine, irregular teeth.

Flowers: In drooping, cone-like catkins; male and female on separate trees; appear in early spring before leaves.

Fruit: Capsules or pods; narrowly cone-shaped; hairless; split open to release tiny seeds covered with long, white, cottony hairs.

Habitat: Moist clayey to dry sandy sites; pure stands and conifer and hardwood mixedwoods; a component of transition tolerant hardwood stands; abundant.

Notes: Trembling aspen is considered an invasive species after a forest disturbance such as a fire or clearcut. • The common name refers to the way the leaves 'tremble' or quake in the slightest breeze. • As a member of the willow family, trembling aspen contains salicylic acid, a main ingredient for aspirin. See caution in Introduction. • This tree is used to make pulp, plywood, veneer, wooden matches and chopsticks. Aspen reproduces mainly by root suckers.

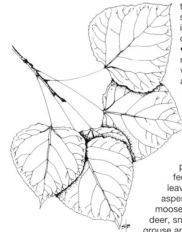

• Trembling aspen is a primary food source for moose, white-tailed deer, beaver, snowshoe hare and porcupines. Black bears feed on the expanding leaves in spring. Trembling aspen provides cover for moose, beaver, white-tailed deer, snowshoe hare, ruffed grouse and songbirds.

1 cm

Willow Family (Salicaceae)

General: Hardwood; deciduous; up to 30 m tall; trunk long, straight and cylindrical; usually 30–60 cm in diameter; crown narrow and open with a few stout, upward-growing branches; roots shallow; young bark greenish-brown and smooth; older bark dark greyish and furrowed with irregular, V-shaped crevices; twigs reddish-brown, round in cross-section, stout and hairless; end buds reddish-brown, slender with long, pointed tips, sticky and fragrant.

NWO FEC Photo

Leaves: Broad-leaved; alternate; on stalks round in cross-section; simple; egg-shaped, tapering to point at tip and tapered to rounded at base; 5–12 cm long; upper surface shiny and dark green, underside paler and often has rusty or brownish resin blotches; margins finely serrated with rounded teeth that turn inward at the tips.

Flowers: Greenish or reddish; on drooping catkins; minute; numerous; appear in early spring before leaves.

Fruit: Capsule; egg-shaped, hairless and thick-skinned; opens to release numerous minute seeds with long, white, cotton-ball-like hairs; matures in spring or early summer.

Habitat: Moist to fresh, clayey to medium-loamy soils; rich pure hardwood stands and hardwood mixedwoods.

Notes: Balsam poplar is used for plywood and pulp. Pieces of the lower bark were used as floats for fishing nets or lines. Aboriginal peoples used the buds to make an ointment for cuts and wounds and rubbed the buds inside their nostrils to help relieve congestion. See caution in Introduction.
• Balsam poplar provides browse for moose, snowshoe hare and beaver. Small mammals occasionally eat the seeds.

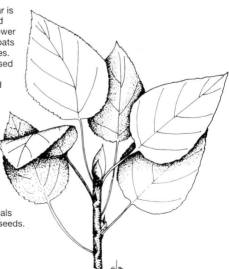

1 cm

WHITE BIRCH ♦ *Betula papyrifera*
BOULEAU BLANC

Birch Family (Betulaceae)

Karen Legasy

General: Hardwood; deciduous; about 15–25 m tall; trunk slender, often curves and extends almost to top of crown; up to 60 cm in diameter; in the forest, crown consists of many upward-growing branches ending in clusters of fine branchlets, in the open, crown is pyramid-shaped with an irregularly rounded outline; young bark reddish-brown, thin and smooth, older bark creamy-white, papery and peels easily to expose a reddish-orange inner layer that turns black with age; twigs dark reddish-brown, slender, sometimes hairy and without wintergreen taste; buds greenish-brown, darker on tips of scales, have blunt to occasionally pointed tips and often are sticky.

Leaves: Broad-leaved; alternate; on slender stalks; simple; egg-shaped to triangular with sharply pointed tip and flattish to rounded or slightly heart-shaped base; 5–10 cm long; upper surface dull green, underside paler and slightly hairy; margins singly to doubly toothed from tip to about 1.5 cm from leafstalk.

Flowers: In catkins; male catkins cylindrical, in drooping clusters and elongate up to 10 cm long in May before leaves; female catkins single or in pairs, erect and elongate to about 5 cm long.

Fruit: Nutlets; rounded; winged; shed in early fall.

Habitat: Dry to moist upland sites, conifer and tolerant hardwood stands, occasional in pine stands; shade intolerant; abundant.

Notes: One of the best-known traditional uses of birch by aboriginal peoples is the construction of birch-bark canoes. Aboriginal peoples also used birch bark as a waterproof layer on wigwams and to make items such as torches, funnels, splints, spoons, dishes, and artwork. Birch bark was often wrapped around foodstuffs and sometimes even bodies to prevent their decay. In emergency situations, birch bark can be used to protect eyes from damage that may be caused by the extreme brightness of the sun reflecting on snow. Placing strips of birch bark over the eyes protects them while allowing for some visibilty through the natural openings in the bark. • White birch has a very high wildlife value. Songbirds such as the pine siskin eat white birch seeds, as do ruffed grouse and, occasionally, small mammals. White birch is a primary food source for moose, porcupines, caribou, beaver and the snowshoe hare. See notes on yellow birch (*Betula alleghaniensis*).

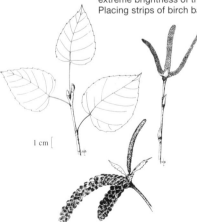

1 cm

Birch Family (Betulaceae)

General: Hardwood; deciduous; 18–30 m tall; in stands, trunk branch-free for more than half its height and has very little taper; 60–120 cm in diameter; in the forest, crown is short and irregularly rounded, in the open it is long and wide-spreading; roots deep and wide-spreading; young bark dark reddish and shiny to yellowish or bronze, becomes darker with age and breaks into large, raggedy pieces; does not peel easily; twigs brown, slightly hairy and have a wintergreen taste when broken; buds chestnut brown and have sharply pointed tips.

Karen Legasy

Leaves: Broad-leaved; alternate; on stalks; simple; oval, gradually tapering to a sharp, pointed tip and narrow, often slightly heart-shaped base; 8–12 cm long, 2.5–5 cm wide; upper surface deep yellowish-green, underside paler and has soft down on veins; 12 or more pairs of veins each extend to 1 of the large teeth on margin; margins finely to sharply toothed; turn yellow in fall.

Flowers: Catkins; male catkins 7.5–12.5 cm long and present during winter; female catkins about 1.5 cm long and develop from buds in spring.

Fruit: Cone-like; oval; about 3 cm long, 1.5 cm wide; erect on branches, contain numerous small, winged seeds.

Habitat: Fresh, coarse-loamy to silty upland sites; transition tolerant hardwood stands; infrequent.

Notes: One way to distinguish yellow birch from white birch (*Betula papyrifera*) is the taste of the twigs. Yellow birch twigs have a distinctive wintergreen taste; white birch twigs do not. The inner bark has historically been considered edible, and a tea was made with the twigs. See caution in Introduction. • Aboriginal peoples mixed yellow birch sap with maple sap, and used yellow birch saplings for wigwam poles. The wood is used for furniture, cabinets, moulding, flooring, doors, veneer, plywood and other products.

• Yellow birch has a very high wildlife value. It provides browse for beaver, moose, white-tailed deer and snowshoe hare. Songbirds and (occasionally) red squirrels and other small mammals eat the seeds.

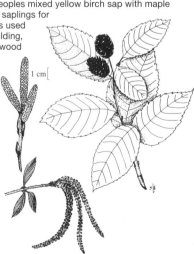

1 cm

WHITE ELM ♦ *Ulmus americana*
ORME D'AMÉRIQUE

Elm Family (Ulmaceae)

Emma Thurley

General: Hardwood; deciduous; commonly 18–24 m tall; trunk usually straight and forks above into a few large, ascending limbs; diameter up to 1.3 m; crown vase- or umbrella-like and gracefully spreading; roots shallow and wide-spreading; bark dark greyish-brown with wide, deep, intersecting ridges or often scaly; twigs greyish-brown, slightly hairy or hairless and zigzag; buds pale reddish-brown with slightly hairy scales and pointed tips.

Leaves: Broad-leaved; deciduous; alternate; on stalks; simple; oval to inversely egg-shaped, tip pointed, base blunt or rounded and unequal; 5–15 cm long; upper surface dark green and smooth to slightly rough (sandpapery), underside paler and slightly hairy or hairless; margins coarsely double-toothed.

Flowers: Small; on slender and undivided stalks about 1.25 cm long.

Fruit: Winged (samara); egg-shaped to oval; about 0.5 cm wide; wing deeply notched at tip and hairless except for a fringe of hairs around edge.

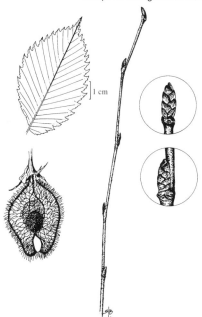

1 cm

Habitat: Wet to rich, moist sites; often in river flats; common in the southern part of our region in farmlands, on lakeshores and in woods with ash; occasional northward.

Notes: White elm is often used as an ornamental tree, and its wood is used to make furniture, panelling, barrels, boxes, caskets, crates and boats. • Deer mice eat the winged fruit (samara), and wood ducks, purple finches, rose breasted grosbeaks and red squirrels eat the seeds. • Dutch elm disease, a fungus spread by a beetle, has decimated this species.

Maple Family (Aceraceae)

General: Hardwood; deciduous; large at maturity, 24–30 m tall; trunk straight, 60–90 cm in diameter; crown narrow and round; roots wide-spreading and relatively deep; bark dark grey with irregular strips that usually curl outward; twigs reddish-brown, shiny and hairless; buds reddish-brown with sharp-pointed tips and numerous pairs of minutely hairy scales.

Leaves: Broad-leaved; opposite; on stalks; simple; 3–5 lobes, usually 5, top lobe nearly square, tapers to slender point and separated from 2 side lobes by wide notches that are rounded at

Brenda Chambers

the bottom; 9–15 cm wide; upper surface yellowish-green, underside paler and hairless; margins have a few irregular, wavy teeth; yellow to brilliant orange and scarlet in the fall.

Flowers: Yellowish; without petals; freely suspended in tassel-like clusters 5–10 cm long; appear with leaves in April and May.

Fruit: Paired and winged (keys); wings nearly parallel; seeds plump; on slender stalks usually longer than the fruit; 2.5–4 cm long; matures in fall.

Brenda Chambers

Habitat: Fresh, coarse-loamy to silty upland sites; transition tolerant hardwood stands; infrequent; shade tolerant.

Notes: Sugar maple is Canada's national tree. It is the chief source for maple syrup and sugar, which contain vitamin B, phosphorus, calcium and enzymes. See caution in Introduction. • The wood is valued for its strength and used for furniture, flooring, plywood and other lumber products. • Sugar maple has a very high wildlife value. Beaver, moose, white-tailed deer and snowshoe hare browse it, and ruffed grouse, songbirds, red squirrels and other small mammals eat the seeds. The least flycatcher and other songbirds are known to nest in sugar maple.

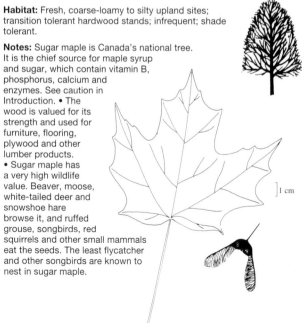

]1 cm

RED MAPLE ♦ *Acer rubrum*
ÉRABLE ROUGE

Maple Family (Aceraceae)

Karen Legasy

Brenda Chambers

General: Hardwood; deciduous; up to about 16 m high or sometimes higher; when growing in the forest, the trunk is usually branch-free for half its length and when in the open, the trunk divides or branches nearly to the ground; up to 1.2 m in diameter; crown short and narrow; roots shallow and widely spreading; young bark light-grey and smooth, older bark dark greyish-brown with scaly ridges; twigs red, shiny and hairless, turn greyish with age; buds reddish, shiny, smooth and have blunt tips.

Leaves: Broad-leaved; opposite; on reddish stalks; simple; 3–5 sharply pointed lobes with shallow, V-shaped crevices (sinuses) between lobes, base heart-shaped; 5–15 cm wide; surface bright green, underside whitish; usually hairless when mature; margins coarsely and irregularly double-toothed; turn deep red or scarlet in fall.

Flowers: Red to yellowish or orange; in dense clusters; on slender stalks; appear before the leaves; May.

Fruit: In winged pairs (keys); reddish; individuals about 2 cm long; June–July.

Habitat: Fresh, coarse-loamy to silty upland sites; transition tolerant hardwood-dominated mixedwood stands.

Notes: Red maple is named for the reddish colour of its buds, leafstalks, flowers and fruit and the deep-red colour of its leaves in fall.
• The bark was boiled and used as a dye or to produce a black 'ink.' Its sap, though not as sweet as sugar maple's (*Acer saccharum*), was historically used to make syrup and sugar. See caution in Introduction. • Red maple is used for furniture, veneer, plywood, crates and other items, but it is not considered an important commercial species for timber. • Red maple has a very high wildlife value. It is preferred browse for moose, white-tailed deer, snowshoe hare and beaver. Ruffed grouse, red squirrels, chipmunks and other small mammls eat the seeds.

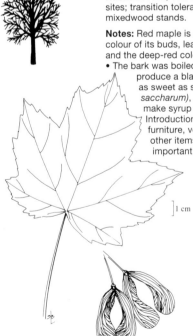

] 1 cm

Olive Family (Oleaceae)

General: Hardwood; deciduous; up to 25 m tall; trunk slender and sometimes leaning or bent and extends almost to top of crown; 30–60 cm in diameter; crown open with coarse, upward-growing branches; roots shallow and wide-spreading; bark pale grey and flaky (may be tight as well), develops cork-like ridges which are easily rubbed off; twigs light grey, stout, round in cross-section, dull and hairless; end buds blackish, side buds small.

Karen Legasy

Leaves: Broad-leaved; opposite; on stalks; compound, 7–11 leaflets; leaf 30–40 cm long; leaflets stalkless, oblong to lance-shaped, tapering to long, slender point at tip and rounded or slightly tapered at base, 7–10 cm long, 1.5–3 cm wide, dark green and hairless; margins finely toothed; rust-coloured tufts of hairs present where young leaflets join main leafstalk.

Flowers: Small, inconspicuous, with no petals; in dense clusters; appear in early spring before leaves.

Fruit: Seed enclosed in a flat, narrowly oblong, single wing rounded or blunt at both ends; 2.5–4 cm long, 6–10 mm wide; ripens in fall and remains on tree for most of winter.

Habitat: Mineral or organic sites; moist to wet, low or swampy areas; forms small, pure, localized stands or grows with speckled alder, eastern white cedar and/or red maple, balsam poplar, elm, and other conifers such as white spruce; low, wet shores; occasional.

Notes: Aboriginal peoples used the inner bark in a remedy for internal ailments. See caution in Introduction.
• Ash was believed to have the power to ward off snakes. Aboriginal peoples wove baskets out of layers of wood stripped off black ash, and used black ash bark to cover wigwams.

1 cm

SHRUBS

The illustrations below show examples of leaf arrangements of shrubs in this section.

simple alternate leaves
shown: *Alnus viridis* ssp. *crispa*
Green alder

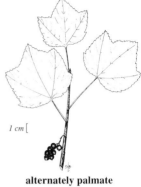

alternately palmate
shown: *Ribes triste*
Wild red currant

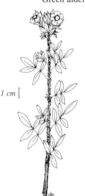

alternately compound
shown: *Potentilla fruticosa*
Shrubby cinquefoil

simple opposite leaves
shown: *Cornus stolonifera*
Red osier dogwood

oppositely palmate
shown: *Viburnum edule*
Mooseberry

oppositely compound
shown: *Sambucus canadensis*
Canada elderberry

Yew Family (Taxaceae)

General: Evergreen; low and spreading or straggling; rarely over 2 m high; branchlets green, slender and become scaly and brownish with age; branches up to 2 m long, spread from base of plant for about 1/3 of their length, then curve upward and form flat sprays (needle arrangement makes branches appear flat).

Leaves: Alternate, spirally arranged but twisted and flattened in 2 rows, on short, twisted stalks; simple; flat, narrow and needle-like with a short, sharp tip and narrowed base; 1–2.5 cm long, 1–3 mm wide; upper surface dark green, underside paler.

Brenda Chambers

Flowers: Male and female flowers in leaf axils; tiny female flowers solitary (or paired) at tip of short, scaly stalk; May.

Fruit: Bright red; berry-like with a hole or opening at tip; pulpy; about 0.75 cm long; 1 brown, bony seed; July.

Habitat: Fresh to moist, sandy to clayey upland sites to wet organic sites; conifer to hardwood mixedwoods and transition tolerant hardwood stands; shady areas; occasional.

Notes: The branchlets, leaves and seeds are considered poisonous. The berry-like fruit, with its reportedly sweet taste but slimy texture, has historically been considered edible. See caution in Introduction. • Ground hemlock may be confused with shrubby growth forms of balsam fir (*Abies balsamea*), but it can be distinguished by its bright-red fruit and the short, pointed tips of its needle-like leaves (balsam fir needles are blunt or notched). • Moose occasionally eat ground hemlock, and white-tailed deer eat it in winter. • This shrub is also known as 'Canada yew.'

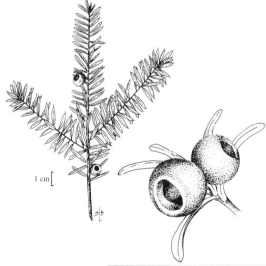

1 cm

Cedar Family (Cupressacae)

Brenda Chambers

General: Evergreen; low, erect or spreading; up to 1.5 m high (rarely higher); branchlets greenish and smooth, older branchlets become pale- to dark-brown with ridges and scaly bark; branches curved upward to erect and typically lack a main stem (leader); forms large patches that usually die off from centre first.

Leaves: Needle-like; mostly in whorls of 3; stalkless; awl-shaped with tapered, slender, spine-like, pointed tip and rounded base; 5–15 mm long, up to 2 mm wide; have a wide, bluish-white strip along centre of upper surface; stiff and erect on younger branches, become more open on older branches; prickly.

Flowers: In tiny cones that grow from leaf axils of previous year's growth; May–June.

Fruit: Round, berry-like cone 6–10 mm wide; bluish-black; fleshy; covered with a fine, bluish-white, waxy powder; contains 1–3 seeds.

Habitat: Sandy to rocky areas; open forests, clearings and fields; shorelines; uncommon.

Notes: There is little documentation of the raw berries being eaten and they are said to be **toxic to livestock**. Common juniper oil has historically been used to flavour gin. The berries were used to make a beer and as a pepper substitute. See caution in Introduction.
• Common juniper was burned to fumigate a sick person's room.

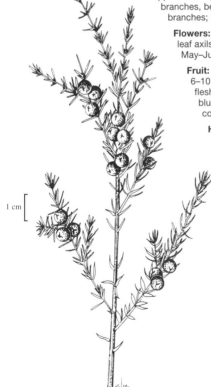

1 cm

S|B

Willow Family (Salicaceae)

General: Deciduous; numerous species within family vary in appearance, range from ground-hugging, dwarf shrubs to taller bushy shrubs and tree-like forms.

Leaves: Mainly alternate, stalked, simple, range from long and narrow with parallel margins and pointed tips to rounded with blunt tips; many species have tiny leaf-like stipules at base of leafstalks; stipules fall off early or persist.

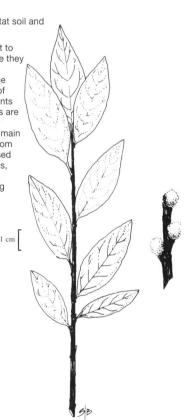

Karen Legasy

Flowers: In catkins; appear before leaves, with leaves or after leaves, depending on species; male catkins erect to spreading or drooping; female catkins usually erect or spreading; stalkless or stalked, often on short lateral branches with small leaves; buds covered with single, hood-shaped scale.

Fruit: Capsules; split open to release seeds; seeds have tufts of silky hair.

Habitat: Variety of forest habitat soil and site conditions.

Notes: Willows can be difficult to distinguish in the field because they frequently hybridize with each other, and there is often a large difference in the appearance of young sprouts and mature plants of the same species. • Willows are pollinated mainly by insects. • Acetylsalicylic acid (ASA), the main ingredient of aspirin, comes from willows. Aboriginal peoples used willow for a variety of purposes, ranging from making cold and headache remedies to weaving baskets and smoking meat. See caution in Introduction. • Willows have a high wildlife value. Songbirds eat the seeds early in the season, and willow is a primary food source for moose, white-tailed deer, caribou, beaver, small mammals, ruffed grouse and other birds.

1 cm

AUTUMN WILLOW ♦ *Salix serissima*
SAULE TRÈS TARDIF

Willow Family (Salicaceae)

General: Deciduous; medium-sized; about 2–4 m high; branchlets yellowish-brown to reddish-brown, smooth, hairless and shiny; older branches greyish-brown.

Leaves: Alternate; on stalks 4–10 mm long; simple; oval to oblong, tapering to a point at tip and pointed to rounded base; blades 4–10 cm long, 1–3 cm wide; upper surface dark green, smooth and shiny, underside paler with a whitish powder (bloom) and prominent, fine network of veins; margins finely toothed with glandular-tipped teeth.

Brenda Chambers

Flowers: In short-cylindrical to nearly spherical catkins; male catkins 1–3.5 cm long; female catkins 1.5–4.5 cm long and up to 2 cm wide.

Fruit: Capsules; narrowly cone-shaped; olive- to light-brown; 7–10 mm long; hairless; open late summer or autumn.

Habitat: Moist to wet areas; boggy openings and clearings; wet sedge meadows; occasional.

Notes: Of the willows, autumn willow is the last in the season to flower. The dead female catkins remain attached to the stems during the following winter.
• The heather vole eats the bark and buds in winter. Willow is habitat for birds such as the American woodcock, alder flycatcher, sedge wren and the Tennessee, Wilson's and orange-crowned warblers.

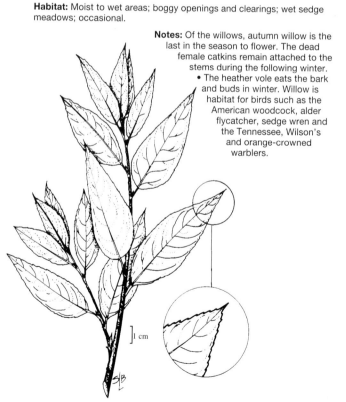

1 cm

Willow Family (Salicaceae)

General: Deciduous; medium-sized; usually 2–3 m high; branchlets yellowish to olive, smooth and shiny, older branches dark purplish-red to greyish-brown.

Leaves: Alternate; on slender stalks 0.5–2 cm long; simple; oval to egg- or pear-shaped with pointed tip and rounded to heart-shaped base; blade 3–8 cm long, 2–4 cm wide; upper surface deep green and smooth, underside bluish-green to whitish with

Bill Crins

prominent veins; margins slightly glandular-toothed; young leaves often purplish-red when unfolding and very thin to almost transparent, mature leaves firmer.

Flowers: In catkins; female catkins 3–8 cm long, 2–4 cm wide; male catkins 2–5 cm long; appear with the leaves.

Fruit: Capsules; hairless; 5–8 mm long; small leaves (bracts) at base of capsules are reddish-brown and have long, white hairs.

Habitat: Moist to wet areas; bogs and swamps; sandy shorelines and ditches; frequent.

Notes: Crushing the buds and foliage releases a strong, balsam-like fragrance. • Aboriginal peoples used the bark in a fever and headache remedy. See caution in Introduction.
• Willow is a food source for moose, ruffed grouse, beaver, muskrat, red squirrel, deer and snowshoe hare.

1 cm

**SLENDER WILLOW ♦ *Salix petiolaris*
SAULE PÉTIOLÉ**

Willow Family (Salicaceae)

Brenda Chambers

General: Deciduous; low to medium-sized with upward-growing to erect branches; 1–3 m high; branchlets yellowish-green to olive brown, slender and slightly hairy; older branches smooth, hairless and dark-brown to almost black; often forms clumps.

Leaves: Alternate; on yellowish stalks 3–10 mm long; simple; lance-shaped with pointed tip and base; 2–7 cm long, 0.5–1.5 cm wide; upper surface green, normally smooth and satiny, underside slightly waxy or with thin, silky hairs; slightly silky when young; margins finely toothed.

Flowers: In catkins; male catkins round to egg-shaped, 1–2 cm long; female catkins 1.5–2.5 cm long, loosely flowered and up to 4 cm long when in fruit; catkins appear with the leaves in May–June.

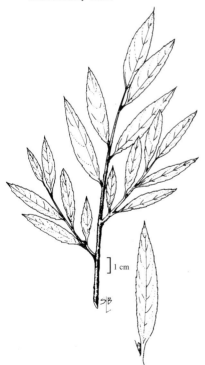

1 cm

Fruit: Capsule; egg-shaped to oblong with elongated, slender beak; slightly hairy; 5–7 mm long.

Habitat: Dry to wet areas; swamps, depressions, fields and ditches; shorelines and roadsides; may also occur in upland forest areas such as jack pine stands.

Notes: Slender willow bark and roots were historically used in a remedy to control hemorrhaging, and aboriginal peoples used the bark in a fever and headache remedy. See caution in Introduction. • Moose, ruffed grouse, beaver, muskrat, red squirrel, deer and snowshoe hare all eat willow.

Willow Family (Salicaceae)

General: Deciduous; low with upward-growing to erect branches; 0.3–1 m high; lower branches often root; branchlets yellowish to olive-green, hairless, older branches reddish to purplish and greyish.

Leaves: Alternate; on stalks 2–6 mm long; simple; narrowly oval to lance-shaped and widest above middle, with rounded to blunt or pointed tip and rounded to tapered base; 1–5 cm long, 0.5–2.5 cm wide; upper surface dark green, hairless, underside paler to whitish or waxy; firm or leathery; margins toothless and usually rolled downward; with a network of veins (reticulate) and a prominent, pale- or reddish-brown midrib.

Flowers: In catkins; at top of leafy branches; male catkins 0.5–2 cm long; female catkins 1–3 cm long.

Fruit: Capsules; yellow to brown; 4–7 mm long; hairless; on slender stalks 2–4 mm long.

BC MOF/Frank Boas

Habitat: Wet areas; sphagnum bogs; along edges of swamps and marshes.

Notes: Aboriginal peoples used the bark in remedies for stomach trouble. See caution in Introduction. • Bog willow's distinguishing features are its low height (1 m or less), the prominent network of veins on its leaves and the fact that it usually grows in bogs.

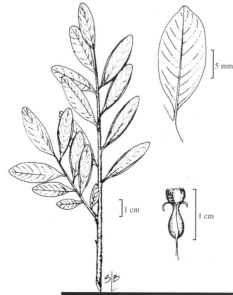

GREEN ALDER ♦ *Alnus viridis* ssp. *crispa*
AULNE CRISPÉ

Birch Family (Betulaceae)

Brenda Chambers

General: Deciduous; tall, up to 3 m high; pith triangular in cross-section; winter buds stalkless with sharp, pointed, curved tips; branchlets brown, hairy and sticky with pale, cork-like spots or lines; older branches reddish-brown to grey, hairless.

Leaves: Alternate; on stalks 6–12 mm long; simple; rounded oval to egg-shaped with blunt or pointed tip and rounded or slightly heart-shaped base; 4–9 cm long, 2.5–5 cm wide; upper surface bright green, underside paler; margins have numerous regularly spaced, fine, sharp-pointed teeth; thin; sticky when young.

Flowers: Male flowers appear in late summer as a group of long-stalked, slender, scaly catkins about 1 cm long which lengthen the following spring to about 5–8 cm; female catkins cone-like, 1–2 cm long, on long stalks in small clusters, appear in spring.

Fruit: Winged nutlets shed from woody scales on female cones (catkins) in late summer to fall.

Habitat: Dry to fresh, very shallow to deep upland sites; jack pine stands, conifer and hardwood mixedwoods; gravelly shores, roadsides; disturbed areas; forms thickets around sandy lakes; common.

Notes: You can distinguish green alder from speckled alder (*Alnus incana* ssp. *rugosa*) by the leaf margins and cones. Speckled alder's leaf margins are double-toothed and more coarsely toothed, whereas green alder's have fine, regularly spaced teeth. Also, speckled alder's cones are short-stalked while green alder's have longer stalks. • Aboriginal peoples applied fresh alder leaves to tumours and inflamed areas, and the leaves were also wrapped around people with a high fever. See caution in Introduction. • Songbirds such as the American goldfinch and pine siskin eat the seeds. • See speckled alder for additional notes.

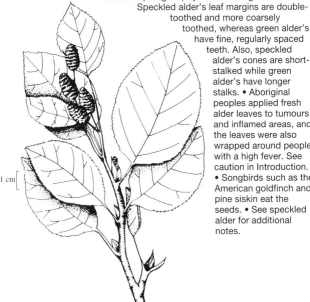

1 cm

Birch Family (Betulaceae)

General: Deciduous; coarse and spreading; up to 5 m tall; branchlets light reddish-brown and covered with fine, soft hairs; pith triangular in cross-section; buds dark reddish-brown with blunt tips; bark smooth, reddish-brown with cork-like, orange to whitish markings or speckles.

Leaves: Alternate; on stalks 1–2 cm long; egg-shaped to oval, usually pointed at tip and rounded at base; 6–10 cm long, 3–6 cm wide; upper surface dark green, smooth, dull and often wrinkled, underside has fine hairs along straight, prominent veins; margins double-toothed, wavy, with sharply and finely toothed edges.

Karen Legasy

Flowers: Male flowers appear as group of stalked catkins 1–2.5 cm long in late summer and lengthen the following spring to become drooping tails 5–8 cm long; female catkins smaller and appear in late summer at branch tips in clusters that aren't expanded, mature to become cone-like, about 1 cm long, with woody scales, on short stalks or stalkless.

Fruit: Wingless nutlets shed in fall from female cones.

Habitat: Wet organic sites to moist clayey to medium-loamy upland sites, black spruce stands and conifer and hardwood mixedwoods; along edges of streams, rivers and lakes; swamps; abundant.

Notes: Aboriginal peoples used the inner bark to make a yellow to reddish dye. • Alder roots and leaves have nitrogen-fixing nodules, which help to fertilize soil. • Songbirds, ruffed grouse and small mammals eat the seeds, moose and white-tailed deer browse speckled alder, and it serves as cover for ruffed grouse. Alders provide habitat for birds such as the American woodcock, alder flycatcher, pine siskin, veery, Philadelphia vireo and the Tennessee and Wilson's warblers. See notes on green alder (*Alnus viridis* ssp. *crispa*).

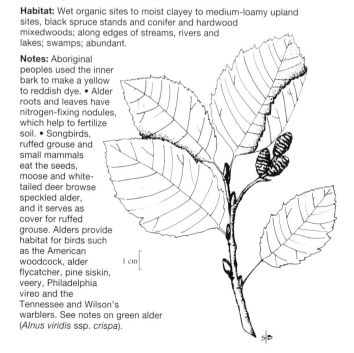

1 cm

DWARF BIRCH ♦ *Betula pumila*
BOULEAU NAIN

Birch Family (Betulaceae)

Karen Legasy

General: Deciduous; erect, slender and much-branched; 0.5–3 m high; branchlets usually have fine hairs but mature to become hairless, dotted with glands; older stems have smooth, dark-grey to reddish-brown bark with pale, cork-like spots (lenticels).

Leaves: Alternate; on stalks 3–6 mm long; simple; circular or kidney- to egg-shaped, widest above middle, with blunt to rounded tip and rounded to tapered base; 1–4 cm long, 1–2 cm wide; upper surface dark green, underside paler to whitish; hairless, dotted with yellow glands; margins coarsely toothed with rounded or blunt to pointed teeth; 4–5 pairs of veins more prominent on underside.

Flowers: Male flowers in hanging, slender catkins 12–20 mm long; female flowers in erect, cone-like catkins 12–25 mm long and about 6 mm thick, with numerous overlapping, papery scales; catkins develop in late summer and open the following spring in May–June.

Fruit: Rounded, flattened, winged nutlet.

Habitat: Wet organic black spruce stands, bogs; shorelines; boggy clearings; abundant.

Notes: Aboriginal peoples used the catkins in an aromatic incense to remedy inflamed mucous membranes. Historically, women drank a tea made from the cones during their menstrual cycles and to regain strength after childbirth. See caution in Introduction. • The twigs were used to make basket ribs. • Dwarf birch provides browse for moose, snowshoe hare and beaver. Ruffed grouse, small mammals and songbirds eat the seeds.

1 cm

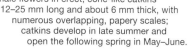

Birch Family (Betulaceae)

General: Deciduous; 3–4 m high; often grows in dense clumps; branchlets hairless to sparsely hairy; bark smooth, pale brown to grey.

Leaves: Alternate; on stalks 8–18 mm long; simple; egg-shaped to oval with pointed tips and rounded or heart-shaped base; 5–12 cm long, 2.5–7 cm wide; upper surface bright green, underside paler, often hairy; irregular margins coarsely double-toothed.

Flowers: Male flowers in beige catkins up to 5 cm long; tiny female catkins concealed by scales; crimson, hair-like stigmas protruding; open in April or May.

MNR Photo

Fruit: Round, hard-shelled nut enclosed in a bristly husk with a thin, bristly, tube-like beak 3–4 cm long that is open and narrowly lobed at the tip; nuts light brown; ripen August–September.

Habitat: Dry to moist upland sites; hardwood to mixedwood stands; clearings and along the forest edge; often associated with mountain maple; common in open woods.

Notes: Beaked hazelnuts are rich in protein and oil and low in carbohydrates. Oil from the nuts was historically used as a remedy for toothache. See caution in Introduction. • Aboriginal peoples made brooms with the twigs and drumsticks with the stems. • Beaked hazel provides browse for moose, snowshoe hare and beaver. Red squirrel and ruffed grouse eat the seeds, and the eastern chipmunk eats the hazelnuts.

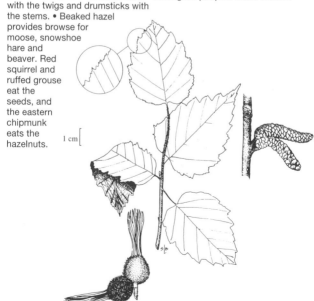

1 cm

SWEET FERN ♦ *Comptonia peregrina*
COMPTONIE VOYAGEUSE

Bayberry Family (Myricaceae)

Karen Legasy

General: Deciduous; erect, low and much-branched; up to 1 m tall; branchlets hairy and have gland dots; bark reddish-brown to grey or blackish; from long, spreading underground stems (rhizomes); forms dense patches or thickets.

Leaves: Alternate; on stalks up to 6 mm long; simple; long and narrow, tapered at tip and base; 6–12 cm long, 0.5–1 cm wide; upper surface dark green, underside paler; hairy and with resin dots; margins lobed, fern-like; pairs of tiny leaf-like stipules at base of leafstalks are slightly heart-shaped with long, pointed tips.

Flowers: Inconspicuous; male flowers in slender, dry, scaly catkins 2.5 cm or less long clustered near ends of branches; female flowers in small catkins at ends of short branches; late April–May.

Fruit: In round, burr-like, bristly catkins about 2.5 cm across; numerous smooth, rounded nutlets about 4–5 mm long; June-July.

Habitat: Sandy to gravelly or rocky soils, dry areas; often associated with jack pine; common.

Notes: Sweet fern's sweet fragrance is especially noticeable when the leaves and young branches are crushed. • Aboriginal peoples used sweet fern as a toothache remedy, and also used it in cures for diarrhea and skin irritations such as that caused by poison ivy. They lined blueberry-picking containers with sweet fern, and covered the berries with it so they would not spoil. A 'diet drink' tea was historically made from sweet fern. See caution in Introduction. • Small mammals, white-tailed deer and ruffed grouse infrequently use sweet fern for browse and cover.

1 cm

Bayberry Family (Myricaceae)

General: Deciduous; upward-growing and much-branched; 0.3–2 m tall; branchlets dark brown, gland-dotted, hairy and fragrant; bark is dark-greyish to reddish-brown with small, pale, cork-like spots (lenticels).

Leaves: Alternate; on short stalks; simple; lance-shaped, usually widest above middle with rounded and toothed tip and wedge-shaped base; up to 6 cm long and 2 cm wide; upper surface dark green to greyish, hairless, underside paler and smooth to hairy; margins toothless from base to above middle but rounded tip distinctly toothed; covered with tiny, bright-yellow glandular dots; fragrant.

Flowers: In small catkins; male catkins linear to oblong, 1–2 cm long, crowded in elongated clusters, dark brown; female catkins egg-shaped to oblong with blunt top, brownish, cone-like, 8–10 mm long.

Karen Legasy

Fruit: Nutlets; egg-shaped; 2–3 mm long; overlapping, winged at base, resinous and with gland dots.

Habitat: Moist to wet areas; forms thickets along shores, edges of marshes and swamps; shallow water and wet clearings; common.

Notes: Sweet gale oil was believed to strengthen hair and cause it to grow more. Crushed sweet gale was historically used to dry boils and stop nosebleed. The leaves were added to broth to make it tastier, and the dried leaves have been used to make a tea. See caution in Introduction. The seeds were used to dye yarn yellow.

**MOUNTAIN-HOLLY ◆ *Nemopanthus mucronatus*
FAUX HOUX**

Holly Family (Aquifoliaceae)

Karen Legasy

General: Deciduous; erect, much-branched; 0.3–3 m tall; terminal branchlets purplish and slender with distantly spaced leaves, lateral branchlets on short spurs, with crowded leaves that often look whorled; bark grey or ashy and mainly smooth with many pale, cork-like markings (lenticels).

Leaves: Alternate; on purplish, slender stalks about 1 cm long; simple; narrowly egg-shaped, usually wider above the middle, with short, pointed tip and tapered to rounded base; up to 7 cm long and 2.5 cm wide; upper surface bright green, underside paler; margins usually toothless or may have a few scattered teeth.

Flowers: Small; either male or female, but both sexes on same plant; solitary or males in clusters of 2–4; on thread-like stalks about 2.5 cm long from leaf axils; late May.

Fruit: Red, berry-like drupe; about 6 mm in diameter; on slender stalks; with 4–5 slightly ribbed nutlets; August–September.

Habitat: Dry to fresh, rocky to medium-loamy sites; conifer mixedwood stands and transition tolerant mixed hardwood stands; swamps and moist forest areas; edges of sphagnum bogs; frequent in thickets on rocky or sandy shores and in damp forest openings and clearings; uncommon.

Notes: You can recognize mountain holly by its purplish leafstalks.
• Aboriginal peoples made a tonic from the branches and used it for a variety of ailments. Some sources report the berries to be poisonous while others say they are edible. They apparently have a strong, bitter taste that makes them unpalatable. See caution in Introduction.

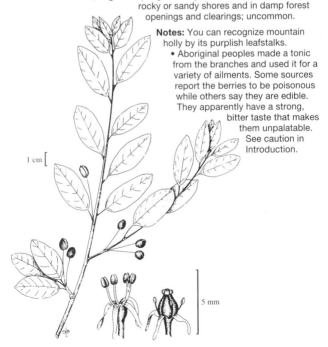

1 cm

5 mm

Gooseberry Family (Grossulariaceae)

General: Deciduous; low with spreading and upward-growing branches; up to 1 m tall; branchlets pale brown, minutely hairy, ridged and covered with slender, sharp prickles and longer thorns or spines at nodes; older branches have greyish, peeling bark and an exposed, often blackish inner layer.

Karen Legasy

Leaves: Alternate; stalks slightly hairy; simple; 3–5 lobes pointed, deeply cut, again irregularly lobed; base heart-shaped to squared; 4–8 cm long and just as wide; upper surface dark green, underside paler; usually hairless, sometimes with scattered hairs; margins have rounded, coarse teeth.

Flowers: Greenish-purple; saucer-shaped with 5 petals; individuals tiny, each petal about 1.3 cm long; in drooping, slender, elongated clusters; May–June.

Fruit: Purple-black, round berry; bristly with gland-tipped hairs; 0.8 cm in diameter; ripen late July–August.

Habitat: Wet organic to fresh medium-loamy sites; rich conifer and hardwood mixedwoods; nitrogen-rich soils; swamps and shady to open areas; common.

Notes: Aboriginal peoples ate the berries fresh or cooked, but they are not very palatable. See caution in Introduction.
• Be careful when touching this shrub; the sharp prickles can give a painful stab.

1 cm

WILD RED CURRANT ♦ *Ribes triste*
GADELLIER AMER

Gooseberry Family (Grossulariaceae)

Karen Legasy

General: Deciduous; low, spreading, straggling or reclining on ground with stems often rooting; up to about 1 m tall; stems lacking prickles; branchlets grey to brownish, ridged and minutely hairy; bark peels off older branches to reveal an often reddish-purple to blackish layer.

Leaves: Alternate; on sparsely hairy stalks 2.5–6 cm long; simple; maple-leaf-like with 3–5 wide lobes cut less than halfway to leaf base and pointed to rounded at tips; leaf bases shallowly heart-shaped to squared; 2 sides of leaf are almost parallel; 4–10 cm long, 5–10 cm wide; upper surface dark green and almost hairless, underside paler and usually hairy; margins have rounded to abruptly pointed teeth.

Flowers: Greenish-purple; saucer-shaped, 5 petals; small, less than 6 mm wide; in elongated, drooping clusters from scaly buds in leaf axils; on slender stalks with scattered, gland-tipped hairs; June.

Fruit: Bright-red berry; smooth; 6–9 mm in diameter; in drooping clusters; ripens July–August.

Habitat: Wet organic to fresh, coarse-loamy sites; rich conifer and hardwood mixedwoods and black spruce stands; moist soil along streams; common.

Notes: Historically, the berries have been used to make jams, jellies and pies, but they are apparently very sour when raw. See caution in Introduction. • In addition to the different berry colours, you can distinguish wild red currant from northern wild black currant (*Ribes hudsonianum*) by their stems and leaves. Wild red currant has spreading to reclining stems that often root and its maple-like leaves have no yellow resin dots on the underside, while northern wild black currant is upward-growing to erect and its leaves have yellow resin dots on the underside.

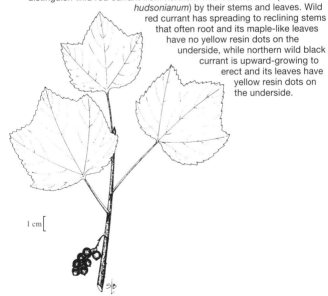

1 cm

Gooseberry Family (Grossulariaceae)

General: Deciduous; low with stiff, upright or upward-growing branches; 60–90 cm tall; stems lack prickles; branchlets have scattered yellowish glandular dots, are minutely hairy and somewhat angled; outer greyish bark peels from older stems to reveal a dark-purplish or blackish layer.

Brenda Chambers

Leaves: Alternate; on stalks with fine hairs and glandular dots, 2.5–4.5 cm long, base slightly wider with long hairs; simple; kidney- to egg-shaped with 3–5 blunt to pointed lobes that are cut less than halfway to leaf base; base prominently heart-shaped; 5–9 cm long, 6–13 cm wide; upper surface dark green, hairless or with a few scattered hairs, underside greyish to whitish, hairless to hairy with scattered yellow glandular dots; margins coarsely toothed.

Flowers: Whitish; bell-shaped with 5 petals; small, less than 6 mm long; about 6–12 in upward-growing to erect clusters; on thread-like stalks; late May–early June.

Fruit: Rounded, black berries; about 9 mm in diameter; in clusters; smooth with a few glandular dots; ripen late July–August.

Habitat: Moist areas; swamps, thickets, low forest areas; shorelines; scarce in our region.

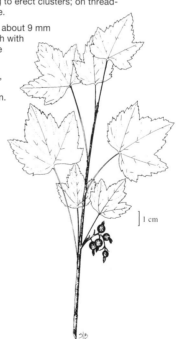

Notes: You can recognize northern wild black currant in the field by the way its stem lacks prickles and by the way its 3- to 5-lobed leaves are cut to less than half their length and have yellow resin dots on the underside.
• Some people consider the berries edible, but others say they have a very bitter and disagreeable taste. See caution in Introduction.
• Aboriginal women drank northern wild black currant in a tea mixture, believing it would help them conceive.
• See notes on wild red currant (*Ribes triste*).

] 1 cm

SKUNK CURRANT ♦ *Ribes glandulosum*
GADELLIER GLANDULEUX

Gooseberry Family (Grossulariaceae)

General: Deciduous; stems low and trailing to upward-growing; less than 1 m tall; branchlets brown to purplish-grey, minutely hairy to hairless and somewhat ridged or angled; older branches often blackish and smooth as outer bark peels off; plant has a distinctive, skunk-like odour when crushed; lacks prickles.

Leaves: Alternate; on finely hairy leafstalks 3–5.5 cm long; simple; maple-leaf-like with 3–5 (sometimes 7) egg-shaped, pointed lobes and a deeply heart-shaped base; 4–8 cm wide (wider than long); upper surface dark green, hairless, underside paler with fine hairs; margins doubly toothed.

Brenda Chambers

Flowers: Yellow-green to purplish; saucer-shaped, with 5 petals; small, less than 6 mm wide; in loose, elongated, upright clusters 2.5–6 cm long; flowerstalks and tiny leaf-like bracts at base of flower have gland-tipped hairs; June.

Fruit: Red berries bristly with glandular hairs; about 6 mm in diameter; July–August.

Habitat: Wet organic to fresh, sandy upland sites; hardwood-dominated and conifer mixedwoods; shorelines and streambanks; often occurs with bristly black currant; common.

Notes: You can distinguish skunk currant in the field by crushing some of its leaves and smelling its distinctive, skunk-like odour. The berries have a disagreeable taste.
• Aboriginal peoples used the roots in a remedy for back pain. See caution in Introduction. • *Ribes* spp. are an occasional food source for small mammals and birds.
• See notes on northern wild black currant (*Ribes hudsonianum*).

]1 cm

Gooseberry Family (Grossulariaceae)

General: Deciduous; low with upward-growing to erect branches; up to 90 cm tall; branchlets greyish, often have scattered prickles and 1–3 slender, sharp spines 3–8 mm long where leafstalks join branches; greyish outer bark on older stems eventually peels away to reveal a smooth, reddish-brown to blackish layer.

Leaves: Alternate; on stalks 1–3 cm long, simple; 3–5 lobes with pointed tips, base wedge- to heart-shaped; 2.5–6 cm long and just as wide; upper surface dark green, hairless to slightly hairy, underside paler and hairy; margins hairy and coarsely toothed.

Karen Legasy

Flowers: Greenish-yellow to purplish; narrowly bell-shaped with 5 petals; small, 6–9 mm long; 2–3 in loose clusters from leaf axils; on short, usually hairless stalks; tiny leaf-like bracts at base of flower, fringed with long hairs; June.

Fruit: Smooth, round, bluish-black berry; 8–12 mm in diameter; ripens July–August.

Habitat: Wet organic to fresh, silty upland sites; conifer and hardwood mixedwoods; rocky shores; frequent around open bog edges, riverbanks and clearings.

Notes: The sour-tasting berries have been used to make jams and preserves. See caution in Introduction. • Wild goose-berry is hybridized with cultivated European species to make cultivated gooseberries. • This shrub has a high wildlife value. Songbirds and small mammals eat the berries, and moose occasionally browse the leaves, twigs and bark.

] 1 cm

SERVICEBERRY ◆ *Amelanchier* spp.
AMÉLANCHIER

Rose Family (Rosaceae)

Karen Legasy

General: Deciduous; small trees or shrubs, erect; may be as tall as 10 m, usually about 2–3 m; stems mainly slender and lacking prickles; sometimes forms clumps through suckering or patches from trailing stems (stolons).

Leaves: Alternate; on stalks; simple; conspicuously veined; margins finely to coarsely toothed.

Flowers: White; with 5 parts or petals; often in showy clusters; usually appear May–June.

Fruit: Round, berry-like pomes; reddish to purplish or blackish; fleshy; with 5–10 seeds; ripen July–August.

Habitat: Dry to fresh sites, all upland soil types, jack pine stands, conifer and hardwood mixedwoods; along shores or ridges; peat bogs and swamps, thickets, fields, openings; abundant.

Notes: There are several species of serviceberry, but their tendency to hybridize makes accurate field identification to the species level very difficult. • The berry-like pomes have historically been considered edible and were often referred to as 'pears.' Aboriginal peoples gathered serviceberries and dried them for winter food. See caution in Introduction. • Serviceberries have a very high wildlife value. Red fox, ruffed grouse, songbirds, black bear, red squirrel and other small mammals eat the berries. Serviceberries provide browse for beaver, moose and snowshoe hare, and small mammals, ruffed grouse, songbirds and other birds use them for nesting. The American goldfinch usually builds its nest in the terminal forks of serviceberries.

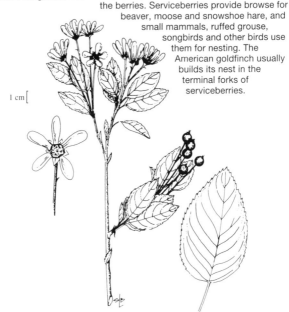

1 cm

Rose Family (Rosaceae)

General: Deciduous; erect and slender; to about 2 m tall; often growing in clumps; branchlets purplish, smooth and mainly hairless.

Leaves: Alternate; on hairless or silky-hairy stalks 2–10 mm long; simple; narrowly egg-shaped to oblong with blunt to pointed tip and tapered base; 3–5 cm long, 1–2.5 cm wide; upper surface green, underside paler; hairless; margins have fine, sharp teeth close together, often tinged purplish-red when unfolding.

Karen Legasy

Flowers: White; 5 petals 6–10 mm long; individual flowers about 2 cm in diameter; solitary or in small clusters of 2–4 from tops of branches and axils of upper leaves; on hairless stalks; May–June.

Fruit: Round, berry-like pomes; purplish-black; longer than wide, 1–1.5 cm long; on stalks 1–2 cm long; July–August.

Habitat: Dry to moist sites, all upland soil types, conifer and hardwood mixedwood stands; sandy shorelines; bogs and swamps; more frequent on wetter sites than are other serviceberries; openings, clearings and shore thickets.

Notes: You can distinguish mountain juneberry in the field by the fine, close and sharp teeth on its leaves and by its small clusters of 1–4 flowers.
• The fruit has historically been considered edible. See caution in Introduction.

1 cm

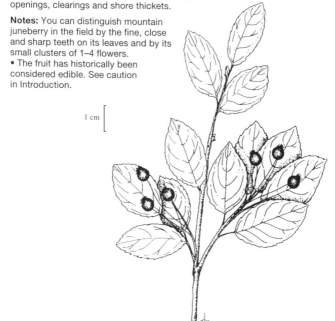

Rose Family (Rosaceae)

Karen Legacy

General: Deciduous; slender and erect; up to 12 m tall; branchlets smooth, dark reddish-brown, with small, scattered, pale-brown, cork-like markings (lenticels); bark on older stems and branches peels in horizontal papery strips.

Leaves: Alternate; stalks 1–3 cm long, usually with glands near the blade; simple; oblong to lance-shaped or narrowly egg-shaped with short to long, pointed tip and blunt to rounded base; 4–11 cm long, 1–3 cm wide; upper surface bright green and shiny, underside paler; hairless; margins have fine, irregular, blunt to rounded, gland-tipped teeth.

Flowers: White; small, 1.2–1.5 cm wide, have 5 petals, on stalks 1–2 cm long; in small, flat-topped clusters from leaf axils or crowded at tips of small branches; May–early June.

Fruit: Bright-red, round, juicy cherries 5–7 mm in diameter, single pit or stone in centre; ripen August–September.

Habitat: Fresh to dry, sandy to silty upland sites; jack pine and conifer and hardwood mixedwoods; transition tolerant mixed hardwood stands; burned or disturbed areas; roadsides, shores and trails; common.

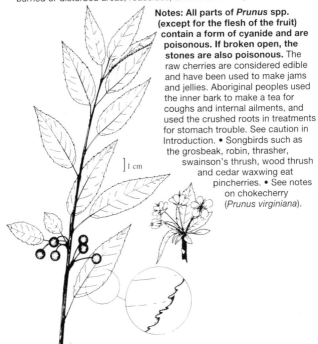

] 1 cm

Notes: All parts of *Prunus* spp. (except for the flesh of the fruit) contain a form of cyanide and are poisonous. If broken open, the stones are also poisonous. The raw cherries are considered edible and have been used to make jams and jellies. Aboriginal peoples used the inner bark to make a tea for coughs and internal ailments, and used the crushed roots in treatments for stomach trouble. See caution in Introduction. • Songbirds such as the grosbeak, robin, thrasher, swainson's thrush, wood thrush and cedar waxwing eat pincherries. • See notes on chokecherry (*Prunus virginiana*).

Rose Family (Rosaceae)

General: Deciduous; erect, large, 2–3 m tall (sometimes up to 10 m tall and tree-like); spreads from shoots and often forms thickets; branchlets reddish-brown to purplish-grey, hairless to minutely hairy, have a strong, unpleasant odour when bruised.

Karen Legasy

Leaves: Alternate; on stalks 0.5–2 cm long with 1 or several glands at or near base of blade; simple; widely oval to egg-shaped, often widest above middle, usually short pointed at tip and tapered or rounded at base; 4–12 cm long, 2–6 cm wide; upper surface hairless, underside hairless to downy; margins have sharp, fine teeth.

Flowers: White; small (8–10 mm wide), with 5 petals, on stalks 4–8 mm long; 10–25 in elongated clusters 5–15 cm long at branch ends; May–June.

Fruit: Deep red or crimson, ripening blackish, round cherries 8–10 mm in diameter; large stone or pit in centre; juicy; August–September.

Habitat: Moist to fresh, clayey to medium-loamy, hardwood mixedwoods and transition tolerant hardwood stands; shorelines, roadsides and edges of forests or swamps; clearings or disturbed areas; common.

Notes: All parts of chokecherry, except the flesh of the fruit, are poisonous to humans. The bitter, sour-tasting berries are considered edible and have been used to make jelly and wine. Aboriginal peoples used the fresh bark in a diarrhea remedy. See caution in Introduction. • You can distinguish chokecherry from pincherry (*Prunus pensylvanica*) by the following characteristics: chokecherry has elongated flower clusters while pincherry has more or less flat-topped flower clusters; chokecherry's leaves are usually widest above the middle and have a short-pointed tip, while pincherry's leaves are usually widest below the middle and often have a tapered point at the tip; chokecherries are deep-red to usually blackish when ripe, while ripe pincherries are bright red. • Songbirds, ruffed grouse and small mammals eat chokecherries.

] 1 cm

NARROW-LEAVED MEADOWSWEET ♦ *Spiraea alba*
SPIRÉE BLANCHE

Rose Family (Rosaceae)

Karen Legasy

General: Deciduous; erect, often with numerous branches and twigs; up to 1.5 m tall; branchlets yellowish-brown, hairless to minutely hairy, angled or ridged, older branches' purplish-grey bark peels off in papery-thin, narrow strips.

Leaves: Alternate; on short stalks 2–6 mm long; simple; narrowly lance-shaped to oblong with pointed tip and base; 3–6 cm long, 1–2 cm wide; upper surface dark green, hairless, underside paler and sometimes with fine hairs along veins; firm; margins finely and sharply toothed; many, often crowded.

Flowers: White; 5 rounded petals and 5 small sepals; small, 5–8 mm wide; numerous in dense, narrow, elongated and slightly pyramid-shaped clusters at branch tips; short stalks and branches of flower clusters are finely hairy; June–September.

Fruit: Capsules; small, smooth, shiny and papery, splitting open along 1 side; few (usually 4) narrow seeds; in clusters of 5–8.

Habitat: Moist to wet areas; fields, swamps, ditches; roadsides and shorelines; frequent.

Notes: Aboriginal peoples made what was reportedly one of the best-tasting tea substitutes from the leaves. See caution in Introduction. • The finely hairy branches and stalks of the flower clusters give them a sort of 'fuzzy' appearance.

1 cm [

Rose Family (Rosaceae)

General: Deciduous; low and herbaceous; branches erect, unbranched, lacking prickles and have 1–3 leaves near top; 10–30 cm tall; from a slender, woody extensively creeping underground stem (rhizome).

Leaves: Alternate; on long stalks (2–8 cm long); simple; rounded to kidney-shaped with 5–7 shallowly cut and rounded lobes; 4–11 cm wide; leathery; margins blunt-toothed.

Flowers: White; 5 spreading petals; 2–3 cm wide; solitary,

NWO FEC Photo

on long terminal stalks either male or female; June–July.

Fruit: Reddish, becoming orange or yellowish; raspberry-like; 1–2 cm in diameter; soft when ripe; ripens late August–September.

Habitat: Wet organic to moist, medium-loamy sites; black spruce and mixed conifer stands; sphagnum mats and hummocks; occasional.

Notes: The berries are high in vitamin C and taste like baked apples. People eat cloudberries raw and use them in jellies and pies. See caution in Introduction.

] 1 cm

NORTHERN DWARF RASPBERRY ♦ *Rubus acaulis*
RONCE ACAULE

Rose Family (Rosaceae)

Jim Pojar

General: Deciduous; low and herbaceous; 5–10 cm tall; stems erect, slender, lacking prickles, finely hairy, woody toward base and unbranched to sparingly branched; flowering branches erect, have 2–3 leaves and solitary terminal flower.

Leaves: Alternate; stalks finely hairy and usually longer than leaf; compound with 3 leaflets; leaflets widely diamond-shaped to inversely egg-shaped, terminal leaflet on short stalk and 2 side leaflets almost stalkless, 1–4.5 cm long and 0.5–3.5 cm wide; upper surface hairless, underside minutely hairy; leathery and shiny; margins coarsely and irregularly toothed to slightly lobed.

Flowers: Pink; solitary or sometimes 2 at top of flowerstalks; petals 10–20 mm long; June–August.

Fruit: Red, rounded raspberry; about 1 cm in diameter; ripens July–September.

Habitat: Moist to wet areas; open bogs; moist streambanks and riverbanks; sedge meadows; wet, open black spruce-larch forests; occasional.

Notes: *Rubus acaulis* has been called *Rubus arcticus*. Northern dwarf raspberry's shiny and leathery leaves distinguish it from dwarf raspberry (*R. pubescens*). The fruit is eaten raw or used to make jams and jellies. See caution in Introduction.

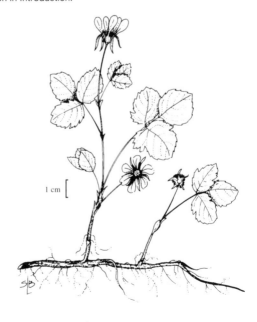

1 cm

Rose Family (Rosaceae)

General: Deciduous; low, trailing or creeping and slender; stems have soft hairs with erect, leafy flowering branches; long, trailing shoots taper to slender, whip-like rooting tips.

Leaves: Alternate; compound; 3 and rarely 5 egg-shaped to vaguely diamond-shaped leaflets; 2–10 cm long, 1–4.5 cm wide; central leaflet tapers to point at base and tip, lateral leaflets rounded to tapered at base and taper to pointed tip; smooth, usually hairless; margins sharply toothed.

Karen Legasy

Flowers: White to pale pink; about 1 cm wide; 5 petals; in loose terminal clusters or 1 or 2 flowers in leaf axils; May–June.

Fruit: Dark-red to purple raspberry; juicy; not easily picked or separated from its core; July–September.

Habitat: All moisture regimes, soil and stand types; abundant.

Notes: Dwarf raspberry is quite easy to distinguish from wild red raspberry (*Rubus idaeus* ssp. *melanolasius*). Dwarf raspberry is a low, trailing plant with whip-like runners, whereas wild red raspberry is a bristly, erect shrub up to 2 m tall. Dwarf raspberry usually has 3 leaflets per compound leaf while wild red raspberry has 3–7 (often 5), and wild red raspberries are easier to pick than dwarf raspberries. See notes on wild red raspberry.

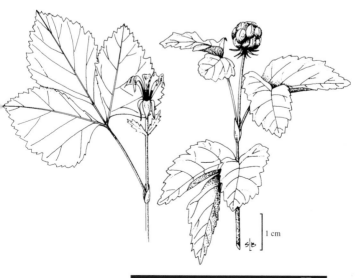

1 cm

WILD RED RASPBERRY ♦ *Rubus idaeus*
FRAMBOISIER ssp. *melanolasius*

Rose Family (Rosaceae)

Karen Legasy

General: Deciduous; stems erect, arching, spreading, woody and prickly or bristly; up to 2 m tall; young branches sparsely to densely bristly and usually with slender, gland-tipped hairs; older stems brownish, smoother and shed their papery bark.

Leaves: Alternate; on bristly hairy stalks; compound, 3–5, rarely 7 leaflets; leaflets egg-shaped to oblong with sharp, pointed tip and rounded to tapered base; 5–10 cm long; upper surface dark-green, smooth to slightly hairy, underside greyish- or whitish-hairy; margins toothed; when there are 5 leaflets, the middle 2 are closer to the top leaflet than to the bottom 2.

Flowers: White to greenish-white; 5 petals; at branch ends in small clusters of 2–5; June–July.

Fruit: Red or amber raspberry; usually drop from their cores intact; July–August.

Habitat: All moisture regimes and soil textures; conifer and hardwood mixedwood stands; open areas; disturbed ground or burn areas; abundant.

Notes: The berries were an important food source for aboriginal peoples, who ate them fresh, dried them for winter use or made them into jelly. These peoples made an eyewash with the bark of roots. See caution in Introduction. • Songbirds such as the pine grosbeak and veery eat the berries, as do the black bear, ruffed grouse and small mammals such as the eastern and least chipmunks, deer mouse, meadow jumping mouse, woodland jumping mouse and American marten. Snowshoe hare browse it. • See notes on dwarf raspberry (*Rubus pubescens*).

1 cm

1 cm

s|b

Rose Family (Rosaceae)

General: Deciduous; low and bushy; up to about 1 m tall, usually less; branchlets reddish and covered with many straight, slender prickles 3–4 mm long; thorns persist on older branches and are often present to base of stem.

Leaves: Alternate; stalkless or on short stalks with a pair of small, leaf-like stipules at base; compound; 5–7 leaflets egg-shaped to oval with a blunt to pointed tip and rounded to slightly heart-shaped

Brenda Chambers

base, 2–5 cm long; upper surface dull green, hairless, underside paler and minutely hairy; margins sharply toothed.

Flowers: Pink; saucer-shaped; 5 petals 2–3 cm long; usually solitary or sometimes a few, near branch tips; June–July.

Fruit: Bright-red, fleshy rosehips; rounded to egg-shaped; about 2 cm long; smooth; many stiff-hairy achenes; August–September.

Habitat: All moisture regimes, soil textures and stand types; fields, clearings and open forests; roadsides and dry shorelines; common in openings on drier forest sites.

Notes: The rosehips are high in vitamin C and have been used to make jelly and tea. The petals have historically been used in salads and the dried leaves were used to make a tea substitute. Rose plants were also used in diarrhea remedies. See caution in Introduction. • Songbirds, ruffed grouse and small mammals eat the rosehips, and snowshoe hare browse the bark, leaves and twigs. • See notes on smooth wild rose (*Rosa blanda*) for distinguishing features.

1 cm

SMOOTH WILD ROSE ♦ *Rosa blanda*
ROSIER INERME

Rose Family (Rosaceae)

Karen Legasy

General: Deciduous; erect and low; up to 1.5 m tall; stems lacking prickles or with a few straight, slender prickles; branchlets reddish-purple and lacking prickles or with a few straight, slender prickles toward the base, vigorous shoots often densely prickly near base, upper leafy flowering branches smooth and almost lacking prickles.

Leaves: Alternate; on stalks; compound, with 5–7 (sometimes 9) leaflets and a pair of small leaf-like stipules at base of leafstalk; leaflets oval to egg-shaped with widest part above the middle, pointed to rounded tip and rounded to wedge-shaped base, 1–4.5 cm long; margins sharply toothed to below middle.

Flowers: Pink; saucer-shaped; 5 petals, 2–3 cm long; solitary or a few in terminal clusters; May–early July.

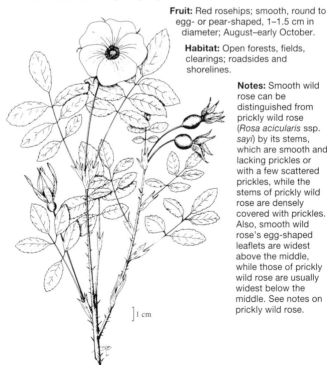

Fruit: Red rosehips; smooth, round to egg- or pear-shaped, 1–1.5 cm in diameter; August–early October.

Habitat: Open forests, fields, clearings; roadsides and shorelines.

Notes: Smooth wild rose can be distinguished from prickly wild rose (*Rosa acicularis* ssp. *sayi*) by its stems, which are smooth and lacking prickles or with a few scattered prickles, while the stems of prickly wild rose are densely covered with prickles. Also, smooth wild rose's egg-shaped leaflets are widest above the middle, while those of prickly wild rose are usually widest below the middle. See notes on prickly wild rose.

]1 cm

Rose Family (Rosaceae)

General: Deciduous; small tree or shrub; up to 10 m tall; branchlets greenish-brown to reddish with pale, cork-like, elongated spots (lenticels), usually hairless, older branches reddish-brown; bark scaly; winter buds sticky.

Leaves: Alternate; stalked; compound, 11–17 leaflets; leaflets lance-shaped to narrowly oblong, tapering to pointed tip; 5–10 cm long, 1–2.5 cm wide

Brenda Chambers

(3–5 times as long as wide); upper surface yellowish-green, hairless, underside paler; margins finely and sharply toothed.

Flowers: White; in dense, round clusters 5–15 cm in diameter; saucer-shaped; about 7 mm in diameter; 5 petals; June–July.

Fruit: Bright-red, round berries about 7 mm in diameter; in clusters; ripen August–September.

Habitat: All moisture regimes, soil textures and stand types; moist forest openings; shorelines; clearings; rock outcrops; frequent.

Notes: The leaves contain cyanide and are poisonous. The berries have historically been considered edible, but not very palatable. Repeatedly freezing the berries will apparently give them a more pleasant taste. Aboriginal peoples ate the leaves to induce vomiting. See caution in Introduction. • The wood was used to make canoe ribs and snowshoe frames. • The berries are a food source for songbirds, black bear and ruffed grouse. Beaver eat the bark, and moose and snowshoe hare browse winter twigs. • See notes on showy mountain ash (*Sorbus decora*).

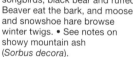

1 cm[

]1 cm

SHOWY MOUNTAIN ASH ♦ *Sorbus decora*
SORBIER DES MONTAGNES

Rose Family (Rosaceae)

Karen Legasy

General: Deciduous; small tree or shrub; up to 10 m tall; branchlets greenish-brown to reddish with pale, cork-like, elongated spots (lenticels), normally hairless, older branches reddish-brown; bark scaly; winter buds sticky.

Leaves: Alternate; on stalks; compound, 11–17 leaflets; leaflets narrowly oval to oblong; blunt to rounded tip has a short, abrupt point; 3.5–8 cm long, 1.5–3 cm wide (2–3 times as long as wide); upper surface bluish-green, underside paler to whitish and slightly hairy; margins finely to sharply toothed.

Flowers: White; saucer-shaped; 5 petals, 4–5 mm long, rounded; in dense, round clusters 6–16 cm in diameter; June–July.

Fruit: Bright-red or scarlet, round berries 8–10 mm in diameter; in dense clusters; ripen August–September.

Habitat: All moisture regimes, soil textures and stand types; open forests and thickets; rocky areas along shores of rivers and lakes; frequent.

Notes: One way to distinguish showy mountain ash from American mountain ash (*Sorbus americana*) is by their leaflets. Showy mountain ash leaflets are 2–3 times longer than wide, with a relatively round, short point, whereas American mountain ash leaflets are 3–5 times longer than wide with a longer, more slender point. Also, the flowers and fruit of showy mountain ash are slightly larger and showier than those of American mountain ash.
• Songbirds, black bear and ruffed grouse eat the berries, and moose and snowshoe hare browse showy mountain ash. •
See notes on American mountain ash.

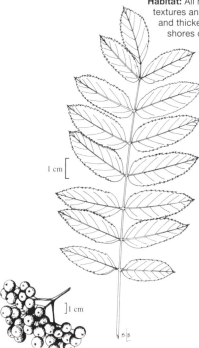

1 cm

]1 cm

Rose Family (Rosaceae)

General: Deciduous; low, much-branched and erect to spreading; up to 1 m tall; branchlets pale brown to purplish-red and have long, white, silky hairs; older branches brown to greyish-black with peeling bark.

Bill Crins

Leaves: Alternate; hairy stalks 1–2 cm long have a pair of small, papery, leaf-like stipules at base; compound, 5 leaflets (sometimes 7), 3 upper leaflets often joined at base; leaflets oblong with pointed tip and base, 1–2 cm long and 2–7 mm wide; upper surface dark green, underside paler, with silky hairs; margins toothless and usually rolled downward; numerous.

Flowers: Yellow; 5 petals, nearly round; buttercup-like; 1.5–3 cm wide; solitary or in small terminal clusters; June–September.

Fruit: Small, dry, hard, single-seeded (achene); densely hairy; in compact clusters; mature in late summer to fall, often remain on plant over winter.

Habitat: Sandy to gravelly or rocky soils; dry to wet areas along rocky or sandy riversides and lakeshores; fens or marshes.

Notes: Shrubby cinquefoil is often used as an ornamental shrub. • Cinquefoil means 'five leaves' and refers to the 5 leaflets of each compound leaf. • The heather vole eats cinquefoil.

1 cm

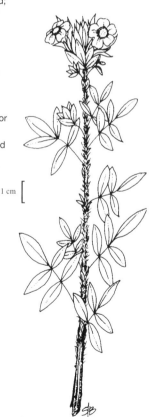

THREE-TOOTHED CINQUEFOIL ♦ *Potentilla tridentata*
POTENTILLE TRIDENTÉE

Rose Family (Rosaceae)

Brenda Chambers

General: Evergreen; tufted, erect, 10–20 cm tall, from slender, woody, extensively creeping underground stems; stems reddish-brown, from a woody base; flowering stems upward-growing to erect; 5–20 cm tall.

Leaves: Alternate; on stalks up to 3 cm long; compound, with 3 leaflets; leaflets triangular to oblong, widest above middle, usually with 3-toothed tip and tapered base, 10–25 mm long; upper surface dark green, shiny and usually hairless, underside paler and hairless or with short, yellowish hairs; leathery; margins smooth except for the 3 teeth at tip.

Flowers: White; 5 petals, 8–10 mm wide; 1–6 in loose and usually flat-topped clusters; June–July.

Fruit: Small, densely hairy, dry, hard, single-seeded (achene); in small, hairy clusters; July–August.

Habitat: Sand, gravel or rock; dry, exposed areas; along ridges.

Notes: Cinquefoil plants were historically used in remedies for fever, sore throat and piles. They were also used in a mouthwash and a lotion. See caution in Introduction.

1 cm

Cashew Family (Anacardiaceae)

General: Deciduous; erect and bushy; less than 1 m tall; branches erect to upward-growing; branchlets minutely hairy, later become hairless, ridged, brownish-grey and with wart-like markings; usually grows in patches from creeping underground stems.

Leaves: Alternate; on stalks 5–25 cm long; compound, 3 leaflets, egg-shaped with a short to tapered tip and narrowed to rounded base, 5–15 cm long and 2.5–6 cm wide, terminal leaflet on a distinct stalk, 2 side leaflets on short stalks or almost stalkless;

Karen Legasy

margins toothless to irregularly toothed or lobed; upper surface smooth, hairless, dark green and dull to shiny, underside paler, with minute hairs along veins.

Flowers: Greenish-white to yellowish; tiny, 2–3 mm long; 5 petals; in dense clusters from leaf axils; June–July.

Fruit: Whitish, round and berry-like; 5–6 mm wide; dry; contains a white seed; often stays on plant through winter; late July–August.

Habitat: Sandy to gravelly or rocky and loamy clay soils; dry to moist areas; forest areas, ravines or thickets; uncommon.

Notes: Eating poison ivy leaves or fruit can be fatal. Poison ivy contains a toxic chemical that can cause a severe allergic reaction that takes the form of an itchy rash, swelling or even blisters. If you come into contact with poison ivy, wash the affected area with a strong soap. Consult a physician if a severe reaction is experienced. • Aboriginal peoples dried poison ivy leaves and fruit and added them to fire pits which were lit when an enemy was approaching. Burning poison ivy releases its poisonous toxin through tiny droplets that settle on ashes and dust particles that spread through the air. • A vine-like form of poison ivy (*Rhus radicans* var. *radicans*) can be found in parts of southern Ontario. • The berries are an important winter food for the yellow-bellied sapsucker during prolonged periods of subfreezing weather. The yellow-rumped warbler also eats the berries in winter.

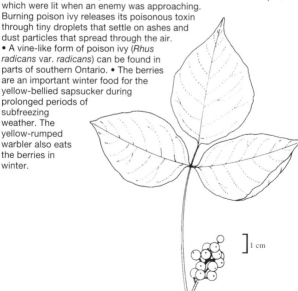

] 1 cm

ALDER-LEAVED BUCKTHORN ♦ *Rhamnus alnifolia*
NERPUN À FEUILLES D'AULNE

Buckthorn Family (Rhamnaceae)

Karen Legasy

General: Deciduous; upright to spreading; usually less than 1 m tall; often forms loose clumps; sparsely branched; branchlets green and minutely hairy, mature to become purplish-red to greyish and finely ridged.

Leaves: Alternate; on grooved stalks 6–12 mm long; simple; oval to egg-shaped with a short to tapered point at tip and narrowed base; up to 10 cm long and 5 cm wide, larger near branch ends; upper surface green, underside paler; margins have rounded to sharply pointed teeth; 6–7 pairs of prominent, almost straight veins curve toward tip near margins.

Flowers: Yellowish-green; 5 petal-like sepals; tiny, about 3 mm wide; on short stalks; in small clusters of 1–5 from axils of lower leaves; late May–early June.

Fruit: Purplish-black, rounded and berry-like; about 6–8 mm in diameter; with 3 flat nutlets; on short stalks; ripen August–September.

Habitat: Wet organic to coarse-loamy upland sites; black spruce, conifer and hardwood mixedwood stands; forms thickets along shores; wet clearings; roadsides; common.

Notes: The berries are poisonous. Alder-leaved buckthorn can be recognized by its prominent, almost straight veins that curve upward near the margins.

] 1 cm

Heath Family (Ericaceae)

General: Evergreen; 5–15 cm tall; stems trailing or spreading on ground with upward-growing branches, often several metres long; branchlets reddish-brown, finely hairy and sometimes with glands; older branches reddish-brown to greyish-black, hairless or hairy and have papery, peeling bark.

Leaves: Alternate; on short stalks; simple; egg- to spoon-shaped, widest above middle with blunt to rounded tip and tapered base; 1–3 cm long, 6–12 mm wide; upper surface dark green and shiny, underside slightly hairy and paler; leathery and firm; margins toothless and flat to slightly rolled downward.

Flowers: White to pinkish or with pink tips; urn-shaped with 5 very short, rounded lobes; about 5 mm long; in crowded terminal clusters; late May–June.

NWO FEC Photo

Fruit: Round and berry-like; red; pulpy, dry; single stone or pit has 5–10 more or less fused nutlets; ripens August.

Habitat: Dry, sandy jack pine stands; dry, rocky clearings.

Notes: Bearberry leaves were historically used in a tobacco mixture. The berries, considered too dry and tasteless for eating raw, were roasted. A liquid mixture was made from bearberry and eaten to remedy sore and sprained backs. Bearberry was also used in a remedy to ease pain caused by kidney stones. See caution in Introduction. • Black bear, gapper's red-backed vole, heather vole and grouse eat the berries. During winter, gapper's red-backed vole eats the leafstalks, twigs and winter buds and the heather vole eats the bark and buds.
• See notes on mountain cranberry (*Vaccinium vitis-idaea* ssp. *minus*).

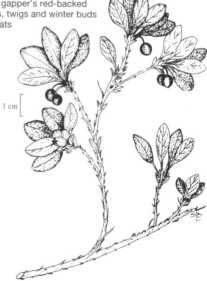

1 cm

TRAILING ARBUTUS ♦ *Epigaea repens*
ÉPIGÉE RAMPANTE

Heath Family (Ericaceae)

Brenda Chambers

General: Evergreen; stems prostrate and creeping or trailing, sparingly branched; stems wiry and covered with bristly, brown hairs.

Leaves: Alternate; on hairy stalks; simple; oval to broadly egg-shaped with blunt or slightly pointed tip and rounded or slightly heart-shaped base; 2.5–7.5 cm long, 1–4 cm wide; upper surface mostly hairless, underside hairy; margins toothless and fringed with brownish hairs.

Flowers: White to pinkish; funnel-shaped with 5 spreading lobes; 1–2 cm long; appear waxy; in clusters from leaf axils or branch tips; early spring.

Fruit: Small, round capsule surrounded by hairy calyx; contains many dark-brown seeds; late summer.

Habitat: Dry to fresh, rocky to medium-loamy sites; conifer and conifer mixedwood stands; common.

Notes: The flowers have historically been eaten in salads. See caution in Introduction. • Aboriginal peoples used the leaves in remedies for urinary tract illnesses. • Trailing arbutus is the provincial flower of Nova Scotia. • The flowers are spring food for the spruce grouse, and heather voles feed on the twigs.

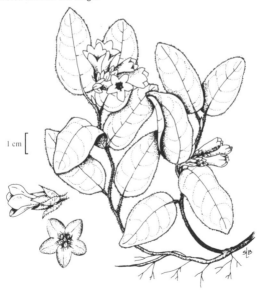

1 cm

Heath Family (Ericaceae)

General: Evergreen; often matted; stems prostrate and trailing or creeping, 20–40 cm long, slightly woody, covered with flat-lying, brownish hairs.

Leaves: Alternate; on very short stalks; simple; nearly round to egg-shaped with pointed tip and tapered base; small, 2–10 mm long; upper surface dark green to brownish, underside paler with flat-lying, bristly, brown hairs; firm; margins toothless and curled downward.

Flowers: White; bell-shaped with 4 lobes; tiny, 2–3 mm long; hidden among the leaves; solitary from leaf axils; early summer.

Fruit: Rounded berry; white; mealy; 5–7 mm in diameter; July–August.

Habitat: All moisture regimes, soil types and most stand types (except transition tolerant hardwood and rich hardwood stands); forms large, trailing mats in sphagnum bogs, conifer stands and on decaying logs or stumps; one of the most frequent plants of poorly drained black spruce forests.

MNR Photo

Notes: The white berries have historically been eaten and reportedly have a wintergreen taste. Aboriginal peoples made a tea from the leaves. See caution in Introduction.

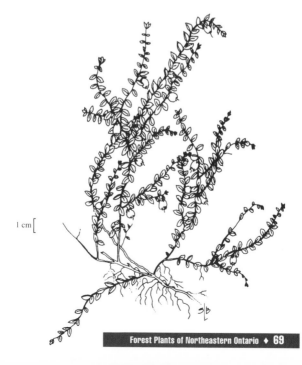

1 cm

Heath Family (Ericaceae)

General: Evergreen; low, 5–15 cm tall; stems slender, creeping on or just below the surface; branches leafy at tips, erect, single or in clumps; mostly hairless.

Leaves: Alternate, crowded near tips of erect branches; on short stalks; simple; oval to inversely egg-shaped with rounded to pointed tip and narrowed base; 1–5 cm long; upper surface dark green and shiny, underside paler; margins have obscure, bristle-tipped teeth and are rolled slightly downward; young leaves are tender, mature to become firm and leathery.

Flowers: White; urn-shaped with 5 small lobes at tip; small, 5–8 mm long; usually solitary in leaf axils; nodding below leaves, on curved or drooping stalks; June.

Karen Legasy

Fruit: Round, berry-like capsule; red; fleshy; about 10 mm in diameter; ripens September and often stays on plant throughout winter.

Habitat: Dry to fresh, sandy to coarse-loamy sites; pure conifer and conifer mixedwood stands; common.

Notes: The berries have historically been eaten and are reported to taste best after having spent a winter on the plant. The berries and leaves have a distinctive wintergreen flavour. The leaves were used in remedies for rheumatism, colds, stomach ailments and to restore strength or 'make one feel good.' The berries were used to flavour beer. Wintergreen leaves were wrapped around sore teeth as a remedy for toothache and children chewed the roots to help prevent tooth decay. See caution in Introduction. • Small mammals such as the eastern chipmunk and woodland jumping mouse eat the berries.

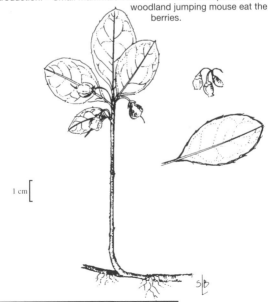

1 cm

Heath Family (Ericaceae)

General: Deciduous; erect with many spreading and upward-growing branches; up to 60 cm, but usually less than 35 cm tall; branchlets greenish-brown, hairless or finely hairy and have tiny, warty dots; older branches reddish-brown to blackish, smooth, hairless and have flaky, ridged bark; form large patches.

Brenda Chambers

Leaves: Alternate; leafstalk very short; simple; oval or narrowly lance-shaped, tapered at base and tip; 1–3 cm long, 4–10 mm wide; bright green and smooth on both sides except for a few hairs on underside along veins; margins with minute, bristle-tipped teeth (use hand lens).

Flowers: White to pale pink; bell-shaped with 5 small lobes; less than 6 mm long; nodding in crowded clusters; May–early June.

Fruit: Blueberry; 6–12 mm diameter; June–August.

Habitat: All moisture regimes, soil and stand types; forms extensive patches following fire; abundant.

Karen Legasy

Notes: Low sweet blueberry can be distinguished from velvet-leaf blueberry (*Vaccinium myrtilloides*) by its leaves. Low sweet blueberry's leaves are mainly hairless and their margins are minutely toothed, while velvet-leaf blueberry's leaves are velvety and have toothless margins. See notes on velvet-leaf blueberry. • The berries are edible raw or cooked. Aboriginal peoples dried the flowers, placed them on hot stones and inhaled the fumes as a remedy for 'craziness.' See caution in Introduction. • Low sweet blueberry has a very high wildlife value. Ruffed grouse, small mammals, black bear, red fox and songbirds eat the fruit and seeds.

**VELVET-LEAF BLUEBERRY ♦ *Vaccinium myrtilloides*
AIRELLE FAUSSE-MYRTILLE**

Heath Family (Ericaceae)

Brenda Chambers

Karen Legasy

General: Deciduous; low with spreading or upward-growing branches; up to 50 cm tall; branchlets greenish-brown, densely velvety with whitish hairs, older branches reddish to brown with peeling bark and wart-like dots; spreads to form large patches.

Leaves: Alternate; on short, hairy stalks; simple; oval to oblong with pointed tip and base or somewhat rounded base; 2.5–5 cm long, 1–2.5 cm wide; upper surface dark green, hairless to downy or velvety, underside paler and downy; margins toothless and with fine hairs.

Flowers: Whitish to pinkish; cylindrical to bell-shaped with 5 small lobes; less than 6 mm long; in crowded clusters at branch tips; May–June.

Fruit: Blueberry; usually with a whitish powder (bloom); 4–7 mm wide; ripens late July–August.

Habitat: All moisture regimes, soil and stand types; common.

Notes: See notes on low sweet blueberry (*Vaccinium angustifolium*). • Black bears, songbirds, ruffed grouse, caribou, white-tailed deer and small mammals such as the southern bog lemming, gapper's red-backed vole, heather vole, meadow jumping mouse, American marten and rock vole eat the berries.

1 cm

Heath Family (Ericaceae)

General: Evergreen; delicate, prostrate and trailing with slender, wiry stems; upward-growing or erect flowering branches up to 20 cm tall; branchlets light- to reddish-brown and minutely hairy, outer bark on older stems peels in pale strips and exposes a smooth, dark inner bark.

Leaves: Alternate; stalkless; simple; narrowly oblong or egg-shaped with a pointed tip and rounded base; less than 1 cm long; upper surface dark green and shiny, underside whitish; margins toothless and curled downward; widely spaced.

Karen Legasy

Flowers: Pink; 4 petals bend back toward base, 5–8 mm long; shooting-star-like; on slender stalks from leaf axils near stem tips; late spring and summer.

Fruit: Round cranberry; about 1 cm across; pale red or pinkish and speckled; ripens August–September.

Habitat: Wet organic to moist upland sites; black spruce stands; open sphagnum bogs; occasional.

Notes: Small cranberry may be confused with creeping snowberry (*Gaultheria hispidula*), but creeping snowberry's leaves are rounder and have brown, coarse bristles underneath. Creeping snowberry's white berries are hidden among the leaves while small cranberry's speckled, reddish berries are often in the open. • Small cranberries have been used in preserves, juices, jellies and tarts. See caution in Introduction. • Small cranberry was formerly known as *Oxycoccus microcarpon*.

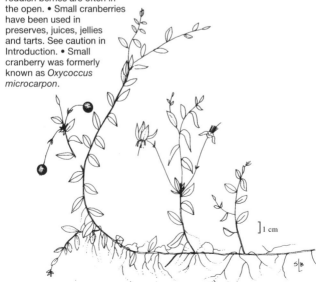

]1 cm

LARGE CRANBERRY ♦ *Vaccinium macrocarpon*
AIRELLE À GROS FRUITS

Heath Family (Ericaceae)

MNR Photo

General: Evergreen; prostrate with a trailing, elongated and much-branched, intertwining, slender and cord-like stem often 1 m or more long; branches upright-growing and usually less than 20 cm tall; branchlets light- to reddish-brown and minutely hairy, bark on older branches peels in papery outer layers to reveal a smooth, dark inner layer.

Leaves: Alternate; on very short stalks; simple; oblong to elliptic with blunt to rounded tip and blunt base; 5–15 mm long, 2–5 mm wide; upper surface dark green, underside paler; leathery; margins toothless and rolled under.

Flowers: Light- or pale-pink to whitish; shooting-star-like; nodding; slender, long-stalked; 4 petals or segments spreading to curved backward; solitary or in clusters of 2–6; about 8–10 mm wide; July.

Fruit: Red, oblong to round cranberry; about 1–2 cm in diameter; often remains on plant over winter; ripens late August–September.

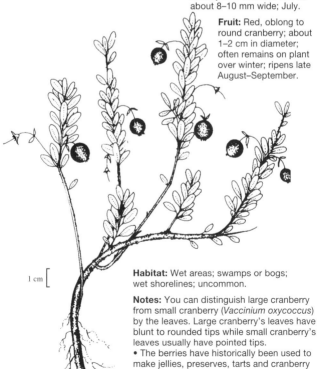

1 cm

Habitat: Wet areas; swamps or bogs; wet shorelines; uncommon.

Notes: You can distinguish large cranberry from small cranberry (*Vaccinium oxycoccus*) by the leaves. Large cranberry's leaves have blunt to rounded tips while small cranberry's leaves usually have pointed tips.
• The berries have historically been used to make jellies, preserves, tarts and cranberry sauce. See caution in Introduction.

Heath Family (Ericaceae)

General: Evergreen; creeping or trailing, forms mats; low, less than 15 cm tall; branching stems slender and erect; branchlets greenish-brown to reddish and almost hairless or have short, white hairs, older branches brown to blackish with peeling bark.

Linda Kershaw

Leaves: Alternate; on crispy-hairy stalks 1–2 mm long; simple; narrowly egg-shaped to oval with widest part above middle; blunt to rounded tip and tapered base; 0.5–2 cm long, 3–15 mm wide; upper surface dark green, smooth and shiny, underside paler with erect, black glands; leathery; margins toothless and rolled under.

Flowers: Pinkish to reddish or whitish; bell-shaped with 4 lobes; nodding, on short stalks; in small clusters at branch tips; June–July.

Fruit: Dark-red cranberries; about 8–10 mm in diameter; remain on plant over winter; ripen August–September.

Habitat: Dry to wet areas; a variety of soil and site conditions; sphagnum bogs; large rocks or moss-covered stumps.

Notes: You can distinguish mountain cranberry from bearberry (*Arctostaphylos uva-ursi*) by the blackish, bristly dots on the underside of mountain cranberry's leaves. Mountain cranberry's leaves are shorter than those of bearberry. • The sour berries have been used to make pies, tarts, jelly and cranberry sauce, and are apparently more palatable after being exposed to frost. See caution in Introduction.

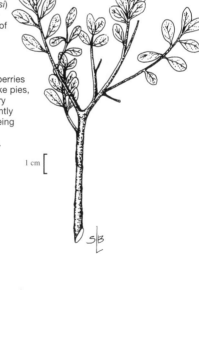

1 cm

BOG ROSEMARY ◆ *Andromeda polifolia* ssp. *glaucophylla*
ANDROMÈDE GLAUQUE

Heath Family (Ericaceae)

MNR Photo

General: Evergreen; erect or trailing; 30–60 cm tall; few branches; branchlets brownish, smooth, hairless and round in cross-section; older stems grey to blackish.

Leaves: Alternate; on very short stalks or stalkless; simple; narrowly oblong with tiny, pointed to rounded tip, tapered base; 2–5.5 cm long, 3–10 mm wide; upper surface bluish-green to dark green, underside whitened by fine, erect hairs when young; leathery and firm; margins toothless and curled toward underside.

Flowers: White to pinkish; bell- or urn-shaped with 5 lobes; less than 6 mm long; in drooping clusters at branch tips; May–June.

Fruit: Small, rounded capsule with long, persistent style; bluish to brown; about 6 mm in diameter; contains numerous light-brown seeds; July–August.

Habitat: Wet organic sites, black spruce stands, open bogs; often forms thickets on margins of boggy lakes; common.

Notes: Bog rosemary contains an **andromedotoxin**, which, if ingested, can lower blood pressure and cause breathing problems, dizziness, cramps, vomiting and diarrhea. • Bog rosemary's rounded stems help to distinguish it from bog laurel (*Kalmia polifolia*), which has flattened stems. Another distinguishing feature is the leaves. Bog rosemary's leaves are alternate, bluish-green and have impressed nerves while those of bog laurel are opposite, dark shiny green and smooth. • Aboriginal peoples used the young leaves to brew a tea, but, because of the andromedotoxin, this is not advised. See caution in Introduction. • Small mammals occasionally eat the fruit.

] 1 cm

s|B

Heath Family (Ericaceae)

General: Evergreen; low and spreading; up to 1 m tall; branchlets densely covered with woolly brown hairs, older stems smooth, hairless, and greyish to purplish or reddish-brown.

Leaves: Alternate; on short stalks; simple; narrowly oval to oblong with blunt tip and rounded or tapered base; 2–5 cm long, 5–20 mm wide; upper surface dark green, hairless and often wrinkled, underside with brown or rusty woolly hairs; leathery, firm; margins toothless and rolled under; fragrant when crushed.

Karen Legasy

Flowers: White; 5 petals less than 6 mm long; small, about 1 cm wide; on slender stalks; in dense, rounded, showy clusters at branch tips; spring and early summer.

Fruit: Small capsules 5–6 mm long; slender, persistent style at tip; split from bottom upward to release numerous seeds; empty capsules can remain on plant for a number of years; late July–August.

Habitat: All moisture regimes and soil types; conifer and conifer mixedwood stands; the most frequent and abundant plant of wet black spruce forests.

Notes: Aboriginal peoples made a tea from the leaves to drink and use for medicinal purposes. See caution in Introduction. They also used the leaves as a tobacco substitute. A brown dye was made from Labrador-tea. • Ruffed grouse and songbirds occasionally eat the fruit and seeds.

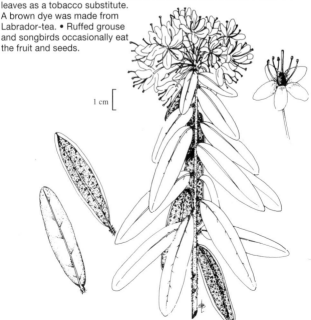

1 cm

LEATHERLEAF ♦ *Chamaedaphne calyculata*
CASSANDRE CALICULÉ

Heath Family (Ericaceae)

MNR Photo

General: Evergreen; low, erect and much-branched; up to 1 m tall; often growing in dense patches; branchlets brownish, with minute hairs or small, flaky scales; older stems greyish with shredding outer bark and a smooth, reddish inner bark.

Leaves: Alternate; on a very short stalk; simple; oval to oblong with short-pointed or rounded tip and slightly rounded or tapered base; 1–4.5 cm long, 3–15 mm wide; upper surface hairless and dull green, underside paler and covered with rusty or white scales; leathery; margins toothless or with minute, rounded teeth; smaller toward tip of flowering branches.

Flowers: White; somewhat urn-shaped, 5-lobed; 5–6 mm long; hanging from axils of reduced leaves in 1-sided, elongated terminal clusters on spreading branches; spring–early summer.

Fruit: Round capsule; brownish; less than 6 mm in diameter; slender style persisting; contains numerous minute seeds.

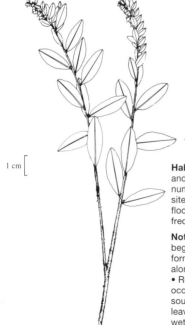

1 cm

Habitat: Wet organic black spruce and mixed conifer stands, sphagnum bogs and fens, highly acidic sites; along streams and lakeshores; flooded wetlands; abundant, frequently forms dense thickets.

Notes: Leatherleaf can indicate the beginning of bog development by forming floating mats when growing along lakeshores or pond edges.
• Ruffed grouse and songbirds occasionally eat the seeds. The southern bog lemming eats the leaves and twigs, and peaty wetlands with leatherleaf are habitat for the sandhill crane.

Heath Family (Ericaceae)

General: Evergreen; low and straggling; less than 1 m tall; very few branches; branchlets pale- to dark-brown or blackish and 2-edged.

Leaves: Opposite; stalkless; simple; narrowly oval or lance-shaped with blunt tip and rounded to tapered base; 1–4 cm long, 6–12 mm wide; upper surface dark green, shiny and hairless, underside whitened with a powdery covering and short hairy; leathery; margins toothless and curled under.

Flowers: Pink; saucer-shaped with 5 lobes; about 10–15 mm across; on slender, long stalks; in terminal clusters.

Fruit: Round to oval capsule with long, slender, persistent style; brown; less than 6 mm in diameter; contain numerous seeds; in erect clusters; July–August.

MNR Photo

Habitat: Wet organic to moist upland sites; black spruce stands; sphagnum bogs; common.

Notes: Bog-laurel contains a poisonous toxin that may cause severe illness to humans and animals if ingested. See notes on bog rosemary (*Andromeda polifolia* spp. *glaucophylla*).

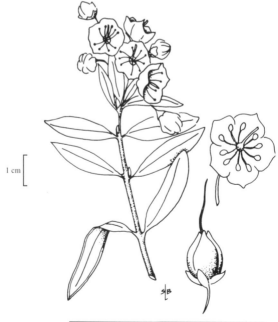

1 cm

SHEEP-LAUREL ◆ *Kalmia angustifolia*
KALMIA À FEUILLES ÉTROITES

Heath Family (Ericaceae)

Karen Legasy

General: Evergreen; branches erect and slender; 60–100 cm tall; branchlets brownish and minutely downy, round in cross-section, older branches greyish, hairless.

Leaves: Opposite or in whorls of 3; on stalks 3–10 mm long; simple; oblong to oval or elliptic with rounded, blunt or sometimes pointed at tip and narrowed at base; 1.5–5 cm long, 5–20 mm wide; upper surface dark green, underside lighter; smooth and mainly hairless; firm, leathery; margins toothless and slightly rolled under.

Flowers: Deep pink to crimson; saucer-shaped with 5 lobes; 0.6–1 cm wide; on long stalks in lateral clusters from leaf axils of previous year's growth; not at branch tips; June–July.

Fruit: Round capsules; small, up to 6 mm in diameter; contain many small seeds; slender, long, persistent style (almost as long as capsule) at tip; often remain on plant for a number of years; late July–August.

Habitat: All moisture regimes and soil textures; conifer and conifer mixedwood stands; around bogs and in moist coniferous stands; characteristic of sandy jack pine forests; forms extensive thickets; common.

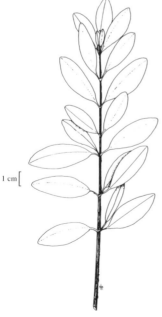

1 cm

Notes: Sheep-laurel is considered poisonous and should not be ingested. • The species name *angustifolia* means 'with narrow leaves.' • Aboriginal peoples used sheep-laurel to make a remedy for colds and sore backs, and also used it in a tonic that was taken in small amounts to remedy bowel ailments. A poultice was made from crushed leaves and applied to the head as a headache remedy. See caution in Introduction.

Wintergreen Family (Pyrolaceae)

General: Evergreen; low and slightly woody; up to 25 cm tall; slender stems (rhizomes) creeping at or just below ground level and freely rooting; flowering stems upright, leafy and single or in groups; branchlets greenish to brownish, smooth, hairless and have fine longitudinal ridges.

Brenda Chambers

Leaves: Mainly in whorls on the stem; on short, grooved stalks; simple; inversely lance-shaped with blunt or pointed tip and tapered base; 3–7 cm long, 1–2 cm wide; upper surface dark green, smooth, shiny and with impressed veins, underside slightly paler with prominent veins; leathery; margins prominently toothed, especially near tip, and slightly rolled under.

Flowers: White to rose-pink; saucer-shaped with 5 petals; 10–15 mm wide; 3–10 in clusters that extend above leaves; on erect or recurved stalks; late June– August.

Fruit: Capsules; round; 4–8 mm in diameter; usually erect; splitting from tip down; with numerous, minute seeds; August–September.

Habitat: Dry, rocky, sandy or coarse-loamy areas, coniferous and mixedwood forests and clearings; usually on well-drained sites; scarce.

Notes: Prince's-pine was historically used in remedies for cold in the bladder, consumption, smallpox, kidney stones and stomach troubles. It was also used to purify blood. See caution in Introduction. • Prince's-pine is also called 'pipsissewa.'

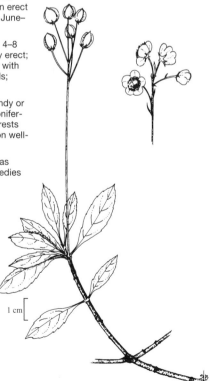

1 cm

TWINFLOWER ♦ *Linnaea borealis*
LINNÉE BORÉALE

Honeysuckle Family (Caprifoliaceae)

Brenda Chambers

General: Evergreen; small, low; stems trailing or creeping, 2 m or more long; branches upward-growing and less than 10 cm tall; branchlets green to reddish-brown, finely hairy, slender and wiry; older stems woody and rarely more than 2 mm in diameter.

Leaves: Opposite; on short, hairy stalks; simple; rounded, oval or egg-shaped, wider above middle with blunt-toothed tip and narrowed base; 1–2 cm long; small, bristle-like hairs on margins and surface; margins slightly rolled under; wider above middle with a few blunt teeth near the tip, narrowed base.

Flowers: Pinkish-white; bell-shaped with 5 lobes, hairy inside; usually in pairs, on long (3–10 cm tall), slender, Y-shaped stalks with 2 tiny bracts at the fork; nodding; June–August.

Fruit: Capsule; tiny, dry and containing a single seed; enclosed by tiny, glandular-hairy bracts; August–September.

Habitat: All moisture regimes, soil textures and stand types; shady areas; moss-covered areas, rotten wood and along forest edges, lakeshores and riversides; common.

Notes: Aboriginal peoples made a mash from twinflower to remedy inflammation of the limbs. A tea was made from the leaves as a cure for insomnia. See caution in Introduction.

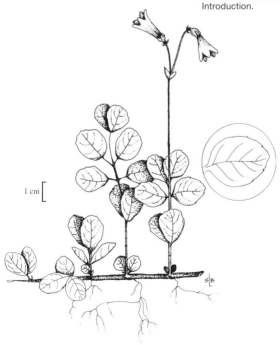

1 cm

Loosestrife Family (Lythraceae)

General: Deciduous; spreading, low to medium-sized shrub; up to 2 m tall; numerous branches; branchlets and buds rusty-brown, covered with many small, brown spots and fine, white, star-shaped hairs; older branches have dark-brownish to greyish bark and are minutely hairy.

Leaves: Opposite; on short, grooved stalks about 1 cm long; simple; oval to egg-shaped with blunt tip and tapered to rounded base; up to 5 cm long and 3 cm wide; upper surface green to greyish-green with a few star-shaped hairs, underside densely covered with silvery, star-shaped hairs and numerous brown dots or scales; thick; margins toothless.

Brenda Chambers

Flowers: Greenish-yellow; tiny, 3–5 mm wide; all male or female; in dense, elongated clusters from leaf nodes; open before leaves in late April–early May.

Fruit: Red to yellowish; oval, 3–6 mm long; cherry-like (drupe), juicy with a smooth pit; bitter; ripens late June–July.

Habitat: Open rocky forests; sandy to gravelly or rocky sites; shorelines and riverbanks.

Notes: The juicy berry pulp feels soapy, and the berries reportedly have a very bitter taste. Aboriginal peoples used these berries to make 'Indian ice-cream,' which was considered a delicacy. Aboriginal peoples also used parts of the buffalo berry plant to treat disorders ranging from indigestion to acne. See caution in Introduction.

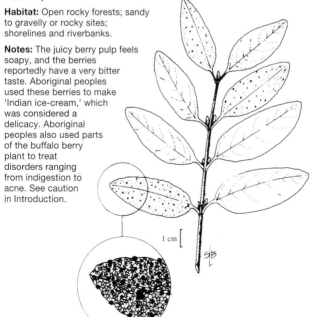

1 cm

RED OSIER DOGWOOD ♦ *Cornus stolonifera*
CORNOUILLER STOLONIFÈRE

Dogwood Family (Cornaceae)

Karen Legasy

General: Deciduous; erect, upward-growing or loosely spreading; 1-3 m tall; branchlets greenish and finely hairy, young branches bright red or purplish and hairless; buds hairy; twigs have white, cork-like oval markings.

Leaves: Opposite; on stalks 0.6–2.5 cm long; simple; egg- to lance-shaped, tapering to sharp point at tip and narrowed or rounded at base; 5–15 cm long, 2.5–9 cm wide; upper surface dark green, hairless to slightly hairy, underside paler with fine, soft hairs; margins toothless; 5–7 pairs of prominent veins curve toward leaf tip.

Flowers: Creamy-white; small; in slightly rounded or flat-topped terminal clusters about 4 cm across; late June.

Fruit: Round, cherry-like (drupe), juicy; about 5 mm wide; white or bluish-tinged; in clusters; oval to rounded pit with a rounded base; August–September.

Habitat: Wet organic and dry to moist upland sites; rich conifer and mixedwood stands; along edges of rivers, marshes and lakes; disturbed ground and roadsides; common.

Notes: The berries have historically been considered edible. See caution in Introduction. • Aboriginal peoples smoked the bark in pipes. The bark was also used to make a red dye, and the branches were used to make baskets. • Red osier dogwood has a very high wildlife value. Moose, white-tailed deer and beaver browse red osier dogwood, and wood ducks, ruffed grouse, chipmunks and other small mammals eat the berries.

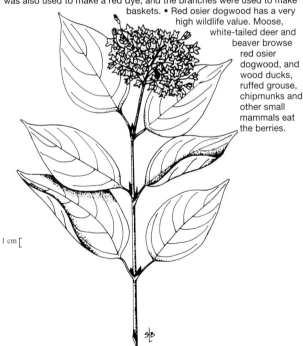

1 cm

Honeysuckle Family (Caprifoliaceae)

General: Deciduous; erect; stems soft or barely woody, essentially hairless, with a large, white pith; up to 3 m tall; branchlets yellowish-grey, older stems greyish-brown, thick and warty.

Brenda Chambers

Leaves: Opposite; on stalks 2.5–5 cm long; compound; 5–11 (usually 7) leaflets, egg-shaped to oval with pointed tip and tapered to rounded base, 5–15 cm long and 2.5–5.5 cm wide, stalkless or on short stalks; upper surface bright green and hairless, underside paler, hairless or with hairs along veins; margins sharply toothed.

Flowers: White; 5 petals; small (about 3 mm wide) and numerous; in long-stalked, compound, flat-topped to slightly rounded terminal clusters 10–18 cm wide; very fragrant; July.

Fruit: Purplish-black, round, berry-like, juicy; 3–5 roughened pits; up to 6 mm wide; in compound clusters; August–September.

Habitat: Low, moist areas; swamps; roadsides and forest edges; common.

Notes: People have often been poisoned by eating the unripe or uncooked berries or by using the hollowed-out stems as peashooters. Aboriginal peoples used the inner bark of Canada elderberry in a toothache remedy. See caution in Introduction. • White-tailed deer, moose, snowshoe hare and small mammals browse elderberry. Moose, small mammals, ruffed grouse and birds eat the fruit. • See notes on red-berried elder (*Sambucus racemosa* ssp. *pubens*) for distinguishing features.

1 cm

1 cm

RED-BERRIED ELDER ◆ *Sambucus racemosa*
SUREAU BLANC ssp. *pubens*

Honeysuckle Family (Caprifoliaceae)

Brenda Chambers

General: Deciduous; erect; branches and stems soft to barely woody; up to 4 m tall; branchlets yellowish-brown and hairy, older branches greyish-brown, thick, warty and with a large, orange to brown pith.

Leaves: Opposite; on stalks 2.5–5 cm long; compound; 5 (sometimes 7) leaflets egg- to lance-shaped with pointed tip and narrowed to rounded and often unequal base, 5–13 cm long and 2.5–5.5 cm wide; stalked; upper surface green, underside paler and soft-hairy to hairless; margins sharply toothed.

Flowers: Whitish; 5 petals; small (3–6 mm wide), numerous; in elongated, rounded or pyramid-shaped clusters 5–13 cm long; May–June.

Fruit: Purple-black, rounded and berry-like; 5–6 mm wide; in pyramidal clusters 4–10 cm long; July–August.

Habitat: Moist to fresh, medium- to coarse-loamy sites; rich conifer and hardwood mixedwoods; open forests and clearings; thickets; roadsides and the edges of forest stands.

Notes: The berries, bark, leaves and roots are considered poisonous. The flowers, crushed leaves and branchlets have a very disagreeable odour. Red-berried elder can be distinguished from Canada elderberry (*Sambucus canadensis*) in that its leaflets are often uneven at the base and its flower clusters are rounded to pyramid-shaped whereas those of Canada elderberry are more flat. • Red-berried elder has a very high wildlife value. Moose occasionally browse the bark, leaves and twigs, and small mammals eat the fruit.

1 cm

Honeysuckle Family (Caprifoliaceae)

General: Deciduous; trailing or climbing and twining vine; often climbing to about 3 m tall; woody; branchlets green to purplish with long, glandular-tipped hairs and purplish-brown spots; older branches brown to grey with shredding bark.

Leaves: Opposite; mostly short-stalked; simple; widely oval to egg-shaped with blunt to pointed tip and rounded to tapered base; 5–13 cm long, 2.5–9 cm wide; upper surface deep green with flattened hairs, underside has downy hairs; margins toothless but fringed with shiny, silky

Karen Legasy

hairs; uppermost 1–2 pairs of leaves fused at base to form broad, saucer-like discs around stem; veiny.

Flowers: Orange to yellow, turning reddish; narrowly tubular with 5 slightly spreading lobes; 2–2.5 cm long; in whorled terminal clusters above saucer-shaped, fused leaves; late June–early August.

Fruit: Orangish-red berries; many-seeded; in stalked clusters from centre of terminal, saucer-shaped leaves; ripen August–September.

Habitat: All moisture regimes, clayey to sandy upland sites; rich conifer and hardwood mixedwoods; frequent in openings, thickets and along shores, less frequent in the forest.

Notes: You can recognize hairy honeysuckle in the field by its opposite, stalkless or short-stalked, hairy leaves with fringed margins, its 1–2 pairs of saucer-shaped leaves at the top and its trailing, woody habit. • The species name *hirsuta* means 'stiffly hairy.'

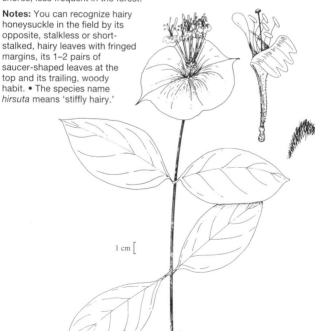

1 cm [

FLY HONEYSUCKLE ♦ *Lonicera canadensis*
CHÈVREFEUILLE DU CANADA

Honeysuckle Family (Caprifoliaceae)

Brenda Chambers

General: Deciduous; erect to straggling or loosely branched; up to 1.5 m tall; branchlets green to purplish, hairless; older branches grey to brownish with bark shredding in thread-like pieces.

Leaves: Opposite; on short stalks fringed with hairs; simple; egg-shaped to oblong with blunt to pointed tip and rounded to slightly heart-shaped base; 3–9 cm long, 1.5–3 cm wide; upper surface bright green and hairless, underside paler; margins toothless, fringed with hairs; thin.

Flowers: Pale yellow to yellowish-green; funnel-shaped with 5 short lobes; 12–18 mm long; in pairs, on long, slender stalks from leaf axils; May–June.

Fruit: Red, egg-shaped berries about 6 mm wide, with 3–4 seeds; spreading in pairs; long-stalked; ripen late June–July.

Habitat: All moisture regimes, soil textures and stand types; well-drained forests and riverbanks; most common in rich hardwood and conifer mixedwoods; frequent.

Notes: To help identify fly honeysuckle in the field, look for its mainly hairless mature leaves with their fringed stalks and margins. • Aboriginal peoples used the twigs and bark in a remedy for urinary disorders. See caution in Introduction.

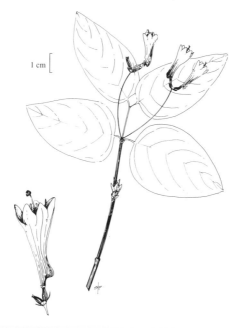

1 cm

Honeysuckle Family (Caprifoliaceae)

General: Deciduous; upright with upward-growing, erect branches; 1–3 m tall; branchlets green to purplish, minutely hairy or hairless, older branches greyish-brown with shredding bark, squarish or slightly 4-angled; pith solid and white.

Leaves: Opposite; on short stalks; simple; inversely egg-shaped to oval with sharply pointed tip and tapered base; 5–15 cm long, 2.5–7.5 cm wide; upper surface dark green, mainly hairless, underside paler and hairy; margins toothless with a fringe of white hairs.

Karen Legasy

Flowers: Yellow, often reddish-tinged; with 5 short and barely spreading lobes; glandular-hairy; in pairs on long, thick stalks from leaf axils; pair of large (1–2 cm), leaf-like bracts at base of flower pair green to purplish, rounded with pointed tips, glandular-hairy; June–July.

Fruit: Purplish-black berries about 8 mm across; shiny; in pairs; covered by large purplish leaves or bracts at first, but these bend back as berries mature; ripen July–September.

Habitat: Wet organic to fresh clayey to sandy upland sites, black spruce and rich conifer and hardwood mixedwood stands; open bogs, shoreline thickets and well-drained white spruce stands; common.

Notes: The berries are considered poisonous. You can recognize bracted honeysuckle by its squarish stem and the sharply pointed tips of its leaves. • Aboriginal peoples made a purple dye from the berry juice.

1 cm

Honeysuckle Family (Caprifoliaceae)

Derek Johnson

General: Deciduous; low, erect or upward-growing with stiff branches; usually less than 50 cm tall; branchlets purplish-red with long, soft, scattered hairs; bark on older branches reddish-brown to grey and peeling to expose a reddish-brown inner layer.

Leaves: Opposite; stalks less than 3 mm long; simple; oval-oblong, wider above middle with blunt or rounded tip and rounded or tapered base; 2.5–6 cm long, 1–3 cm wide; upper surface dark green with flat hairs, underside paler and hairy, especially along veins; firm; margins toothless with white hairs and often rolled under; crowded near branch ends.

Flowers: Yellowish; funnel-shaped with 5 lobes; about 12 mm long; in pairs on short, hairy stalks; May–June.

Fruit: Blue, round berry; produced from fused ovaries on a pair of flowers; short-stalked; July–August.

Habitat: Wet organic to moist clayey to silty upland sites; black spruce and rich hardwood and conifer mixedwoods; sphagnum bogs, clearings, thickets; wet shorelines; frequent.

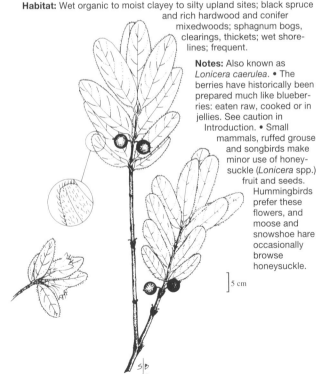

Notes: Also known as *Lonicera caerulea*. • The berries have historically been prepared much like blueberries: eaten raw, cooked or in jellies. See caution in Introduction. • Small mammals, ruffed grouse and songbirds make minor use of honeysuckle (*Lonicera* spp.) fruit and seeds. Hummingbirds prefer these flowers, and moose and snowshoe hare occasionally browse honeysuckle.

5 cm

Honeysuckle Family (Caprifoliaceae)

General: Deciduous; low, upright and spreading; less than 1 m tall; branchlets green to reddish and often have tiny hairs in 2 fine lines; older branches brownish to grey.

Leaves: Opposite; on stalks 3–12 mm long; simple; egg-shaped to oblong, tapering to a long and sometimes curved point at tip, usually rounded at base; 5–13 cm long, 1.5–6 cm wide; upper surface dark green, underside paler; margins sharply toothed and usually fringed with short hairs.

Flowers: Yellow, become orange to brownish-red with age; funnel-shaped with 5 lobes; about 2 cm long; in clusters of 2–7 at branch tips or leaf axils; June to early July.

MNR Photo

Fruit: Slender, oblong capsule with long beak tipped with persistent, thread-like sepals; brown; contains numerous seeds; July–September.

Habitat: Dry to moist areas, all upland soil and stand types; clearings, forests or along forest edges and dry, open shores; common.

Notes: The sharply toothed margins of its leaves distinguish bush honeysuckle from the closely related genus, *Lonicera*. *Lonicera* spp. have leaves with toothless margins. • Aboriginal peoples used the roots in remedies for senility, gonorrhea and urinary disorders. See caution in Introduction. • Songbirds occasionally eat the seeds.

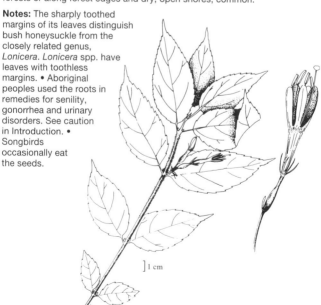

] 1 cm

SNOWBERRY ♦ *Symphoricarpos albus*
SYMPHORINE BLANCHE

Honeysuckle Family (Caprifoliaceae)

BC MOF/Frank Boas

General: Deciduous; small, erect to spreading; usually less than 1 m tall; forms low thickets; branchlets light brown, turn purplish to grey and darker with age, hairless or minutely hairy; slender; bark becomes shredding to fibrous; pith brown, small and hollow in centre.

Leaves: Opposite; on short stalks; simple; oval to egg-shaped with blunt to rounded or sometimes minutely pointed tip and rounded or tapered base; 2–3 cm long, 1–3 cm wide; upper surface dark green and hairless, underside paler and hairless to minutely downy; thin; margins toothless and minutely hairy; leaves on young shoots may be larger with wavy-toothed or lobed margins.

Flowers: Pink to white; bell-shaped, with short lobes, hairy inside; about 6 mm long; in short clusters of 1–5 at branch ends and in axils of upper leaves; August–October.

Fruit: Berry-like; white with tiny dark spot at free end; round; 6–12 mm wide; waxy; spongy; has 2 seeds; solitary or a few together; persist throughout winter.

Habitat: Sandy or rocky open areas; thickets and open forests.

Notes: The berries are poisonous. You can recognize snowberry by its hollow pith, the dark spot at the free end of berries and by its opposite leaves. Snowberry was most likely given its common name for its white berries, which persist over winter.

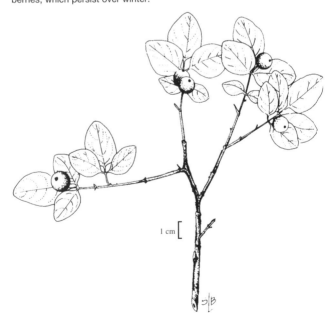

1 cm

Honeysuckle Family (Caprifoliaceae)

General: Deciduous; erect to spreading or straggling; usually less than 2 m tall; branchlets purplish-brown or reddish, hairless and often angled or ridged, older branches grey to brownish; numerous branches.

Leaves: Opposite; on smooth stalks 0.5–4 cm long; simple; usually somewhat maple-leaf-shaped, with 3 shallow, sharply pointed lobes, rounded to heart-shaped or tapered at base; leaves near branch tips may not be lobed; 4–12 cm long, 2.5–12 cm wide; upper surface dark green, hairless, underside paler, with hairs on veins; margins coarsely toothed.

Karen Legasy

Flowers: Whitish; small (4–7 mm across); 5 spreading petals joined at base in short tube; in small, rounded clusters about 2.5 cm wide; usually at ends of short, side branches that have 1 pair of leaves; June–July.

Fruit: Yellow to orange or red; rounded; 6–12 mm long; cherry-like (drupe), juicy, with a large, flat, egg-shaped pit; strong-scented; July–August.

Habitat: Wet organic to clayey to sandy upland sites; conifer and hardwood mixedwood stands; open swampy or boggy areas; shorelines and clearings; common.

Notes: Mooseberry can be distinguished from high-bush cranberry (*Viburnum trilobum*) by its leaves (high-bush cranberry's leaves are deeply lobed while mooseberry's leaves are shallowly lobed), its size (high-bush cranberry is often more than twice the size of mooseberry) and its flowers (high-bush cranberry has much larger and showier flower clusters at the tips of its branches while mooseberry's flower clusters are usually on short side or lateral branches). • The species name *edule* means 'edible' and refers to the berries, which have been eaten raw or used to make jelly. See caution in Introduction. • Mooseberry is a primary food source for beaver, white-tailed deer, snowshoe hare, small mammals, ruffed grouse and other birds, and is a secondary food source for moose and caribou. • See notes on high-bush cranberry (*V. trilobum*).

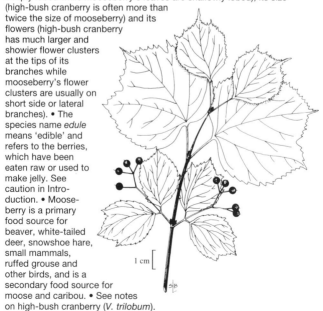

1 cm

HIGH-BUSH CRANBERRY ♦ *Viburnum trilobum*
VIORNE TRILOBÉE

Honeysuckle Family (Caprifoliaceae)

MNR Photo

General: Deciduous; upright and coarse; 1–4 m tall; branchlets grey to brownish-grey.

Leaves: Opposite; on grooved stalks 1–4 cm long; simple; somewhat maple-leaf-shaped, with 3 pointed, deeply cut, spreading lobes; base rounded or slightly heart-shaped; 5–11 cm long and wide; upper surface dark green and smooth, underside paler and hairless or with a few hairs; margins with coarse and rather wavy teeth.

Flowers: White; of 2 kinds, marginal flowers showy, sterile, 15–25 mm wide, central flowers much reduced; in showy, up to 15 cm wide, flat-topped clusters on stalks at branch tips and with 2 pairs of leaves; June–July.

Fruit: Orange to red; rounded, 8–12 mm long, juicy and cherry-like; with 1 flat pit; in loose clusters; August–September.

Habitat: Moist to wet areas; low, cool sites; swamps and bogs; frequent in thickets along shores and in forest openings.

Notes: Also called *Viburnum opulus*. • The species name *trilobum* means 'three-lobed' and refers to the leaves. • The fruit is rich in vitamin C and has historically been considered edible, but it is apparently very sour when raw. High-bush cranberry has been eaten as a cooked fruit and its juices have been used to make cold beverages and jelly. See caution in Introduction. • Red squirrels and other small mammals, songbirds and ruffed grouse eat the berries, and high-bush cranberry provides browse for moose and snowshoe hare. • See notes on mooseberry (*Viburnum edule*).

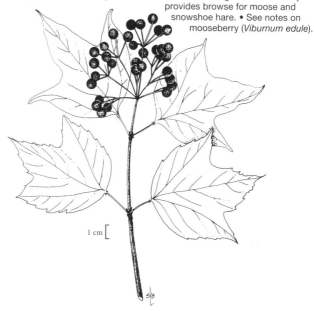

1 cm

Maple Family (Aceraceae)

General: Deciduous; tall shrub or small bushy tree; 3–5 m tall; trunk short, often crooked and divided into a few fairly straight, slender branches growing from the ground upward; branchlets yellowish-green to purplish-grey, covered with short, grey hairs, appear dull and velvety; bark greenish-grey to greyish-brown, thin and flaky; buds covered with grey hairs and have a pair of visible scales.

Leaves: Opposite; reddish-tinged stalks as long as or longer than blade; simple; maple leaf; 3 prominent, pointed lobes, usually 2 smaller lobes near base; 5–12 cm long, 5–10 cm wide; upper surface

Karen Legasy

dark green, hairless, underside paler with fine hairs; margins coarsely toothed.

Flowers: Greenish-yellow; small, about 5 mm wide; in dense, branched, 6–10 cm long, erect terminal clusters on long, slender stalks; appear after leaves in late May to early July.

Fruit: In slender-stalked pairs; reddish-tinged winged nutlets about 2 cm long (including wing); in clusters; July and August.

Brenda Chambers

Habitat: Fresh to moist sites, all upland soil types, hardwood and mixedwood stands; often on rocky slopes and outcrops; in at least partial shade; common in deciduous woods, often forms a conspicuous layer in understorey.

Notes: Mountain maple has a very high wildlife value. It provides browse for beaver, moose and snowshoe hare; red squirrels and other small mammals, songbirds and ruffed grouse eat the seeds.
• Aboriginal peoples treated sore eyes with a lotion made from the pith of mountain maple twigs. See caution in Introduction.

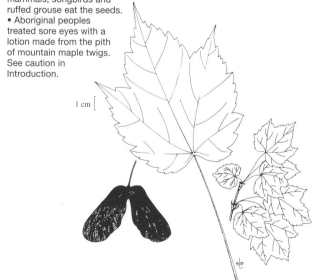

1 cm

HERBS

The herb section is made up of plants that are not woody but do have vascular tissue. There are over 1900 different species of herb in Ontario. Included in this guide are species common to our region.

A chart is included to help you identify unknown plants in the field. The leaf and flower features used in the chart will lead you to page numbers where the unknown plant may be found. Identifying plants is like being a detective—the more distinctive features or 'clues' you find, the more accurate your identification will be. Only the species described in this field guide are listed in the chart. Below is an explanation of how to use the chart.

1. Look at the plant for leaf features such as opposite/alternate or toothed/toothless and make a note of these features.

2. Look for flower features such as colour, shape (e.g., tubular) and the number of petals or sepals (parts). You may find that there are no flowers to help you determine colour, but often there are still sepals around the developing fruits. If the petals or sepals are similar (each part identical) they can be counted to fit into the appropriate category in the chart. This includes flowers such as Asters that have many similar parts (flowers of less than 6 parts go into the Aster-like category). Flowers that have parts that are not identical—such as orchids, peas or clovers—fit into the 'Petals Not Alike' category.

3. A cross-comparison on the chart should narrow the possibilities down to a few pages.

One plant may be found in several different categories on the chart because it might have white or pink flowers, etc. Be patient, and remember the reference guide section for more detailed publications for large specific groups such as goldenrods and asters.

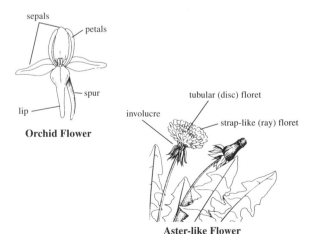

Orchid Flower

Aster-like Flower

Tubular

shown: *Mertensia paniculata*
Northern bluebells

Aster-like

shown: *Taraxacum officinale*
Dandelion

Petals Not Alike

shown: *Platanthera dilatata*
Tall white bog-orchid

Petals Alike (4 parts)

shown: *Oenothera biennis*
Evening primrose

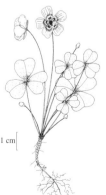

Petals Alike (5 parts)

shown: *Oxalis acetosella* spp. *montana*
Common wood-sorrel

Petals Alike (6 parts)

shown: *Clintonia borealis*
Yellow clintonia

Flowers	*Leaves*			
WHITE	**Opposite**		**Alternate**	
	Toothed	*Toothless*	*Toothed or Dissected*	*Toothless*
Tubular		Melampyrum, p. 202	Campanula, p. 201	Campanula, p. 201
Dense heads or aster-like			Aster, p. 223 Chrysanthemum, p. 216 Erigeron, p. 222	Anaphalis, p. 218 Antennaria, p. 219 Gnaphalium, p. 220
Tiny & crowded			Achillea, p. 217 Polygonum, p. 132	
Petals not alike	Mentha, p. 196 Lycopus, p. 195	Melampyrum, p. 202		
Petals alike 3 parts				
Petals alike 4 parts		Galium, pp. 204–07 Cornus, p. 184		Epilobium, p. 177 Maianthemum, p. 121
Petals alike 5 parts	Mitella, p. 146 Anemone, pp. 138–39	Geocaulon, p. 134 Cerastium, p. 135 Stellaria, p. 136	Campanula, p. 201 Achillea, p. 217 Polygonum, p. 132	Campanula, p. 201 Aralia, p. 179
Petals alike 6 parts				Maianthemum, p. 122
YELLOW				
Tubular				
Dense heads or aster-like			Solidago, pp. 229–32 Bidens, p. 233 Senecio, p. 228 Sonchus, p. 209	
Tiny & crowded				
Petals not alike		Melampyrum, p. 202		
Petals alike 3 parts				
Petals alike 4 parts			Oenothera, p. 173	
Petals alike 5 parts		Hypericum, p. 171	Caltha, p. 143	
Petals alike 6 parts				

Leaves

| Basal | Compound | |
	3 leaflets	>3 leaflets
Petasites, p. 221 Erigeron, p. 222 Antennaria, p. 219		
Plantago, p. 208 Petasites, p. 221	Melilotus, p. 158	Heracleum, p. 181 Sium, p. 182 Actaea, p. 144 Aralia, p. 179–80
Amerorchis, p. 108 Platanthera, pp. 110–112 Viola, pp. 166–68 Goodyera, p. 116 Spiranthes, p. 115		Lathyrus, p. 156
	Trillium, p. 124	
		Thalictrum, p. 145
Orthilia, p. 187 Mitella, p. 146 Pyrola, pp. 188–90, p. 192 Drosera, pp. 130–31 Monotropa, p. 193 Parnassia, p. 147 Moneses, p. 186	Menyanthes, p. 183 Fragaria, pp. 148–49 Anemone, pp. 138–39 Coptis, p. 137 Oxalis, p. 163	Heracleum, p. 181 Sium, p. 182 Aralia, pp. 179–80
Hieracium, p. 212 Taraxacum, p. 210 Sonchus, p. 209 Senecio, p. 228	Trifolium, p. 159	
	Trifolium, p. 159	
Platanthera, p. 113 Corallorhiza, pp. 117–118 Cypripedium, p. 105	Trifolium, p. 159	Corydalis, p. 170 Lathyrus, p. 156 Lotus, p. 157
		Thalictrum, p. 145
Monotropa, p. 193	Ranunculus, pp. 140–41	Geum, p. 152 Ranunculus, p. 142
Clintonia, p. 120		

Flowers | *Leaves*

ORANGE	Opposite		Alternate		
	Toothed	*Toothless*	*Toothed or Dissected*	*Toothless*	
Tubular					
Dense heads or aster-like					
Tiny & crowded					
Petals not alike			Impatiens, p. 169		
Petals alike 3 parts					
Petals alike 4 parts					
Petals alike 5 parts					
Petals alike 6 parts		Lilium, p. 125			
PINK OR RED					
Tubular		Apocynum, p. 199			
Dense heads or aster-like			Erigeron, p. 222		
Tiny & crowded	Eupatorium, p. 214	Rumex, p. 133			
Petals not alike					
Petals alike 3 parts					
Petals alike 4 parts		Epilobium, p. 176	Epilobium, p. 175	Epilobium, p. 174	
Petals alike 5 parts		Apocynum, p. 199 Geocaulon, p. 134	Achillea, p. 217		
Petals alike 6 parts				Streptopus, p. 123	

Leaves

	Basal	Compound	
		3 leaflets	*>3 leaflets*
	Hieracium, p. 211		
			Corydalis, p. 170
		Trifolium, pp. 160–62	
	Rumex, p. 133	Trifolium, pp. 160–62	
	Calypso, p. 107	Trifolium, pp. 160–62	Lathyrus, p. 155
	Platanthera, p. 114		Corydalis, p. 170
	Amerorchis, p. 108		
	Corallorhiza, p. 119		
	Cypripedium, p. 106		
		Trillium, p. 124	
	Pyrola, p. 191	Anemone, p. 139	Potentilla, p. 150
	Sarracenia, p. 129		
	Drosera, p. 130		
	Moneses, p. 186		

Flowers | *Leaves*

VIOLET/ PURPLE OR BLUE	Opposite		Alternate		
	Toothed	*Toothless*	*Toothed or Dissected*	*Toothless*	
Tubular			Campanula, p. 201	Campanula, p. 201 Mertensia, p. 200	
Dense heads or aster-like			Aster, pp. 223, 225–27 Lactuca, p. 213 Cirsium, p. 215 Erigeron, p. 222	Aster, p. 224	
Tiny & crowded	Eupatorium, p. 214				
Petals not alike	Mentha, p. 196 Scutellaria, p. 197	Listera, p. 109 Prunella, p. 198	Viola, p. 164		
Petals alike 3 parts					
Petals alike 4 parts		Halenia, p. 203		Epilobium, p. 174	
Petals alike 5 parts	Geranium, p. 172		Campanula, p. 201	Campanula, p. 201 Mertensia, p. 200	
Petals alike 6 parts					
GREEN OR BROWN					
Tubular					
Dense heads or aster-like					
Tiny & crowded		Rumex, p. 133			
Petals not alike					
Petals alike 3 parts					
Petals alike 4 parts		Galium, pp. 204–07 Halenia, p. 203			
Petals alike 5 parts			Geocaulon, p. 134		
Petals alike 6 parts					

Leaves

Basal	Compound	
	3 leaflets	*>3 leaflets*
Mertensia, p. 200		
Cirsium, p. 215 Aster, pp. 226–27		
Viola, pp. 164–65 Calypso, p. 107 Corallorhiza, p. 118		Lathyrus, p. 155 Vicia, pp. 153–54
Iris, p. 127		
		Thalictrum, p. 145
		Potentilla, p. 150 Geum, p. 151
Sisyrinchium, p. 126		
Aralia, p. 179 Typha, p. 128		Aralia, p. 179–80
Platanthera, pp. 110–11, 113 Corallorhiza, p. 118 Listera, p. 109		
Pyrola, pp. 188–90 Aralia, p. 180 Orthilia, p. 187		Aralia, pp. 179–80

Orchid Family (Orchidaceae)

General: Perennial; 10–70 cm tall; stem unbranched, with leaves.

Leaves: Alternate; clasping stem; simple; egg- to lance-shaped with pointed tip; up to 20 cm long, 5–10 cm wide; bright green with parallel veins and slightly downy surface; margins toothless.

Flowers: Yellow; 1–2, terminal; inflated, sac-like lip petal is wider toward base, usually purple-veined; about 5 cm long; 2 purple-brown, wide-spreading petals lance-shaped to linear, flat or spirally twisted and slightly longer than lip; 2 greenish-yellow, lance-shaped, petal-like sepals, 1 above and 1 below lip; April–August.

MNR Photo

Fruit: Capsules; oval, ridged; numerous dust-like seeds.

Habitat: Swamps, wet and rich woods; scarce.

Notes: Remedies for headache, insomnia and pain have been made from the roots. See caution in Introduction.

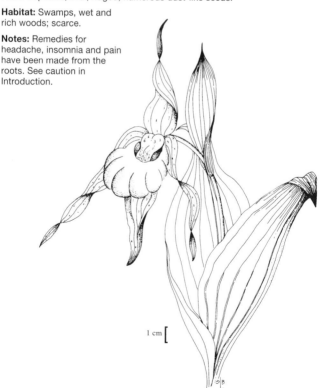

1 cm

Orchid Family (Orchidaceae)

General: Perennial; flower stem 10–55 cm tall, erect, hairy, leafless; single flower (rarely 2) at top.

Leaves: Basal; stalkless, simple, 2, oblong, taper to point at tip, thick and large, up to 20 cm long and 7.5 cm wide; upper surface dark green, underside silvery; sparsely hairy; margins toothless; veins prominent and parallel.

Flowers: Pink with reddish veins, occasionally white; lip pouch-like, inflated, egg-shaped, narrower end near base, about 6.3 cm long, veiny, upper part of interior surface has long, white hairs; sepals petal-like, greenish-purple, lance-shaped and 3.5–5 cm long; petals narrower and longer than sepals; April–July.

Fruit: Capsule; brown; 4.5 cm long; erect.

Brenda Chambers

Habitat: Dry to fresh, rocky to medium-loamy sites; conifer mixedwoods, jack pine and black spruce stands; occasional.

Notes: If you are allergic to pink lady's slipper, contact with it may severely irritate your skin, and ingesting it may cause internal irritation. • Pink lady's slipper is also commonly called 'moccasin flower.' The genus name *Cypripedium* is Latin for 'Venus's slipper.' • **Pink lady's slipper takes 10 years from germination to reach the flowering stage and should not be picked.** • Aboriginal peoples used the roots in a sedative, and the roots were also used in an epilepsy medicine. See caution in Introduction.

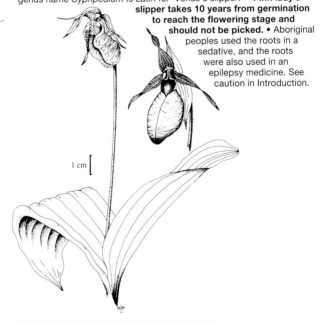

1 cm

Orchid Family (Orchidaceae)

General: Perennial; 5–20 cm tall; from a rounded or oval, solid bulb; stem yellowish-purple to brownish-purple, delicate and covered with small, membranous, sheathing scales.

Leaves: Single; on a slender, 3-angled stalk; oval to rounded and egg-shaped with blunt to rounded and pointed tip and rounded or slightly heart-shaped base; 2–6 cm long, 2–5 cm wide; bluish-green and veiny; margins wavy.

Flowers: Pink; lip white, blotched with purple and has yellow hairs; lip is a sac, resembles a sugar scoop, 1.5–2 cm long; single; 2 petals and 3 petal-like sepals with 3 longitudinal purple lines are erect or spreading above lip; May–June.

Fruit: Capsule; erect; about 1.25 cm long; many-nerved.

Habitat: Calcareous cedar and fir thickets; apparently rare except around Hearst, where it was locally frequent in the drier spruce forest.

MNR Photo

Notes: Calypso is often commonly called 'fairy slipper.' • The solid bulbs are attached by delicate roots easily broken by the lightest touch or pull. The plant usually dies when the flower is picked. • Some aboriginal peoples peeled the bulb-like tubers and ate them raw. See caution in Introduction.

1 cm

SMALL ROUND-LEAVED ORCHID ♦ *Amerorchis*
ORCHIS À FEUILLE RONDE *rotundifolia*

Orchid Family (Orchidaceae)

Brenda Chambers

General: Perennial; 20–30 cm tall; stem slender; short underground stems (rhizomes) and thickened roots.

Leaves: Basal, single; sheathing; simple; oval or rounded, blunt tip, sheathing base; 4–11 cm long; 1–2 sheathing scales below the leaf.

Flowers: White to pale purple; lip white spotted with purple, 6–8 mm long with 3 lobes, 2 lateral lobes short and oval, terminal lobe triangular and notched at tip; spur short; petal-like sepals and lateral petals oblong, 5–8 mm long; petals and upper sepal form hood; spike or cluster of 2–9 flowers on slender stalk 10–25 cm tall; June–July.

Fruit: Capsule; erect, oblong; beakless.

Habitat: Damp coniferous forests, bogs and fens; rare.

Notes: You can recognize small round-leaved orchis by the purple dots on the lips of its flowers. • This plant was formerly known as *Orchis rotundifolia*.

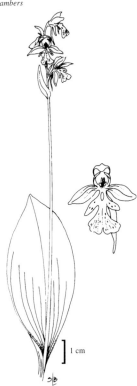

1 cm

Orchid Family (Orchidaceae)

General: Perennial; 6–15 cm tall; very slender, single flowering stem; hairless or slightly hairy above the leaves.

Leaves: Opposite; stalkless and clasping; simple, single pair near middle of stem; widely heart- to egg-shaped; 1–3 cm long, 0.8–4 cm wide.

Flowers: Purplish-brown to pale green; lip narrow, twice as long as lateral petals and divided into 2 slender lobes; 5–16 small flowers in elongated terminal cluster.

Fruit: Capsule; brown; egg-shaped; small; July–August.

BC MOF/Frank Boas

Habitat: Wet organic to moist, fine-loamy sites; black spruce and mixed conifer stands; rare in our region.

Notes: The species name *cordata* means 'heart-shaped' and refers to the leaves.

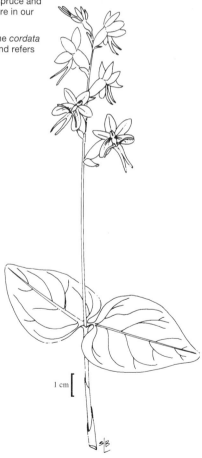

1 cm

BLUNT-LEAF ORCHID ♦ *Platanthera obtusata*
HABENAIRE À FEUILLES OBTUSE

Orchid Family (Orchidaceae)

MNR Photo

General: Perennial; 5–40 cm tall; leafless flowering stem (scape) much taller than leaf; from elongated, fleshy roots.

Leaves: Basal; solitary; inversely egg-shaped with rounded or blunt tip and tapering to stalked base; 2.5–12 cm long, 1–5.5 cm wide.

Flowers: Green to greenish-white; upper petal-like sepal rounded and arching as a hood; lateral petals narrow, arching and upward-growing; lip lance-shaped with blunt tip, 6–10 mm long, 2 mm wide, fleshy and downward-pointing; spur tapered, 4–8 mm long; July–September.

Fruit: Capsules; erect; 8 mm long.

Habitat: Moist upland to wet organic sites; conifer mixedwoods and black spruce stands; scarce.

Notes: Mosquitoes and small moths pollinate blunt-leaf orchid. • Commonly called blunt-leaf orchid because of the blunt tip on its leaf. This plant is also known as *Lysiella obtusata* and *Habenaria obtusata*.

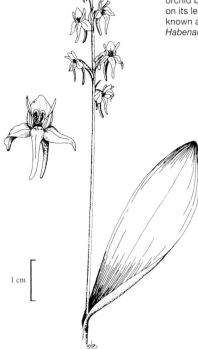

1 cm

Orchid Family (Orchidaceae)

General: Perennial; 20–40 cm tall; fleshy roots; single flowering stem with 1–5 scale-like, narrow, lance-shaped leaves (bracts); hairless.

Leaves: Basal, usually 2 and opposite; stalkless and clasping stem; simple; round with blunt tips; 5–25 cm long and wide; upper surface glossy, underside silvery; usually flattened on ground.

Flowers: Greenish-white, fragrant; with 6 petal-like parts; lip linear-oblong with blunt tip, hanging, somewhat recurved, 10–24 mm long, up to 5 mm wide; spur cylindrical and thickened toward tip; 5–25 in loose, elongated terminal cluster; on stalks up to 1 cm long; July–August.

Fruit: Capsules; brown; erect; 1.5–2 cm long, 4–6 mm thick.

Habitat: Dry to moist hardwood and mixedwood forests, mossy coniferous forests with a thick litter layer, swamps and bogs; shade tolerant; rare to our region.

Notes: The species name *orbiculata* means 'round' and refers to the leaves.

Brenda Chambers

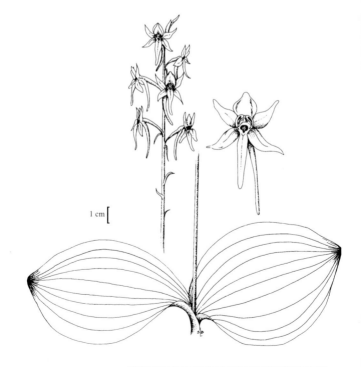

1 cm

TALL WHITE BOG-ORCHID ♦ *Platanthera dilatata*
HABENAIRE DILATÉE

Orchid Family (Orchidaceae)

General: Perennial; height variable, 10–120 cm tall; stems slender, erect, hairless and leafy.

Leaves: Alternate; sheathing; simple; lance-shaped with pointed or blunt tip; 25–30 cm long, 6 cm wide.

Flowers: Creamy white; small, 5–30 in loose to dense terminal clusters up to 40 cm long; lip narrowly lance-shaped with 3 blunt lobes at base, blunt at tip, 5–10 mm long and 2–6 mm wide; spur cylindrical and about as long as lip; flowers have a sweet-spicy, clove-like aroma; June–September.

Fruit: Capsules.

Habitat: Bogs, swamps, fens, open sedge marshes, wet meadows and woods; rare to our region.

Notes: Tall white bog-orchid is also known as *Limnorchis dilatata* or *Habenaria dilatata*.

BC MOF / Frank Boas

] 1 cm

Orchid Family (Orchidaceae)

General: Perennial; 10–40 cm tall; from a thick, underground branch or root; stems hairless and thick.

Leaves: Alternate; sheathing; simple; narrowly oblong to lance-shaped, mostly with pointed tips; 2–10 cm long, 0.5–3 cm wide; soft and flat.

Flowers: Green to yellowish-green; petal-like parts egg-shaped; lip lance-shaped with blunt tip, 3–9 mm long, usually 1–2 mm wide below

MNR Photo

middle, stiff and fleshy, margins hairless; spur somewhat club-shaped, 2–8 mm long, almost equal to or shorter than lip; in narrow, cylindrical spikes 1.5–9 cm long; May–August.

Fruit: Capsules.

Habitat: Bogs, low wet forests, wet open marshes and meadows; roadsides; frequent.

Notes: This plant is also known as *Limnorchis hyperborea* or *Habenaria hyperborea*.

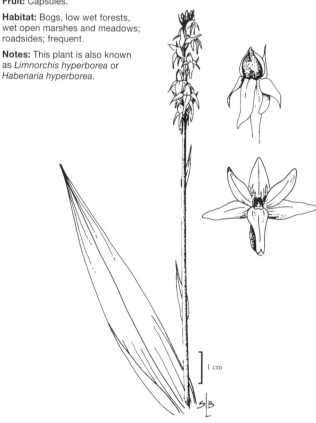

1 cm

S|B

SMALL PURPLE-FRINGED ORCHID ♦ *Platanthera*
HABENAIRE PAPILLON   *psycodes*

Orchid Family (Orchidaceae)

Brenda Chambers

General: Perennial; 20–90 cm tall; stems slender; leafy.

Leaves: Oval, elliptic or lance-shaped, upper ones smaller; 5–20 cm long, 2–7 cm wide.

Flowers: Lilac, rarely white; petals oblong or narrowly spoon-shaped, toothed or toothless near tip; lip 3-parted, parts fan-shaped and fringed, 8–13 mm long and just as wide or slightly wider; spur slender and club-shaped; fragrant; July–August.

Fruit: Capsules.

Habitat: Meadows, swamps, wet woods and open sides of thickets; wet open shores; scarce but occurs in large colonies.

Notes: Small purple-fringed orchid is also known as *Blephariglottis psycodes* and *Habenaria psycodes*. *Psycodes* means 'butterfly-like' and refers to the flower's appearance.

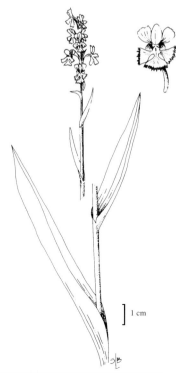

] 1 cm

Orchid Family (Orchidaceae)

General: Perennial; 3–50 cm tall; roots thickish, fleshy, short.

Leaves: Basal; simple; linear to lance-shaped with pointed tips; up to 20 cm long, 5–10 mm wide; leaves gradually reduced upward on stem.

Flowers: Creamy white; 6–12 mm long; 2 petals and 3 petal-like sepals overlap to form an upward-arching hood over a downturned lip; spirally arranged in dense terminal spike; mid-July–August.

Fruit: Capsules; dry, many-seeded.

Habitat: Moist and usually open areas such as meadows, sphagnum bogs, shorelines and ditches; scarce.

Notes: The flowers have a strong, almond-like fragrance.

Brenda Chambers

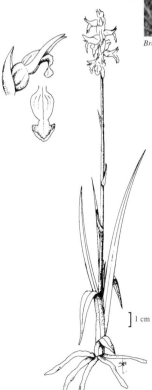

1 cm

Orchid Family (Orchidaceae)

General: Perennial; 10–25 cm tall; slightly creeping underground stems (rhizomes); glandular-hairy; leafless flowering stem (scape) has several small scales.

Leaves: Basal rosette; egg-shaped, taper into sheathing stalk; 1–3 cm long, 0.5–2 cm wide; 5-nerved with scattered, horizontal dark veins and white blotches.

Flowers: Greenish-white; lip inflated and sac-like, tip recurved; petals and sepals 4 mm long; in 1-sided, elongated or spike-like terminal cluster (raceme) 2.5–6 cm long; July–August.

Fruit: Capsules.

Habitat: All moisture regimes, soil textures and stand types (except transition tolerant hardwoods); scarce.

Notes: You can recognize dwarf rattlesnake-plantain by its usually 1-sided flower cluster.

MNR Photo

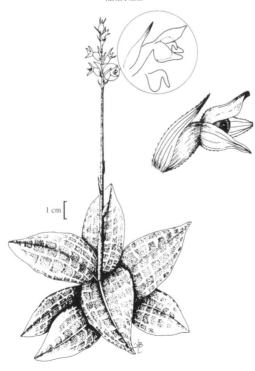

1 cm

Orchid Family (Orchidaceae)

General: Perennial; 8–30 cm tall; from a whitish, intricately branched, coral-like underground stem (rhizome); stem slender and yellowish.

Leaves: Alternate; stem has 2–5 thin, semi-transparent, scale-like sheaths near base.

Flowers: Greenish-yellow to slightly brown-tinged; small, petal-like sepals narrowly oblong to tongue-shaped, bluntish, greenish-yellow and 4.5–6 mm long; lateral petals similar but often have red dots; lip almost as long as lateral petals, notched at tip, whitish and rarely spotted with red or purplish dots; 2–10 in elongated terminal cluster up to 8 cm long; on very short stalks that grow upward at first but eventually bend downward; June–July.

Fruit: Capsule; greenish; about 1 cm long; drooping; July–August.

Habitat: Dry to moist forests, shady areas, bogs and swampy areas; thickets along shores; frequent.

Notes: Early coral-root, at 8–30 cm tall, is just over half the size of large coral-root (*Corallorhiza maculata*), which is 15–50 cm tall. The sheaths on early coral-root's stem are near the base while those on large coral-root extend to above the middle. Large coral-root produces more flowers (10–30) than early coral-root (2–10). See notes on large coral-root.

MNR Photo

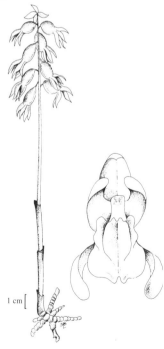

1 cm

Orchid Family (Orchidaceae)

General: Perennial; 15–50 cm tall; from a branched, coral-like underground stem (rhizome); stem slender, purplish or pale yellow to pale green.

Leaves: Alternate; stem has several scale-like, tubular sheaths that are thin, semi-transparent and about 7.5 cm long.

Flowers: Brownish-purple; 3 short, petal-like sepals at top, 2 longer petals at side, lip white and spotted with crimson; about 2 cm long; on short stalks; in elongated terminal clusters of 10–30 flowers; July–September.

Fruit: Capsule; egg-shaped; up to 2.5 cm long; nodding.

Karen Legasy

Habitat: Deciduous to coniferous forests, shady areas; common.

Notes: Large coral-root is saprophytic: it derives its nutrients from decaying organic matter. • It was named for its coral-like roots. See notes on early coral-root (*Corallorhiza trifida*).

] 1 cm

Orchid Family (Orchidaceae)

General: Perennial; 15–50 cm tall; flowering stem stout and purplish; from a branched, coral-like underground stem (rhizome).

Leaves: Alternate; stem's scale-like, tubular sheaths (scales) are thin, semi-transparent and close to base.

Flowers: Purplish-red; lance- to egg-shaped, petals and sepals translucent, purple-veined and form a broad, arching hood; lip tongue-shaped, reddish-purple, striped, about as long as lateral petals; 0.8–2 cm long; drooping; 7–25 in loose terminal clusters; May–August.

Fruit: Capsules; elliptical; strongly bent downward; 1.5–2 cm long.

Habitat: Often in calcareous shaded woods; scarce.

Notes: Striped coral-root is saprophytic: it derives its nutrients from decaying organic matter. It was named for its purple-striped flowers and coral-like roots.

Brenda Chambers

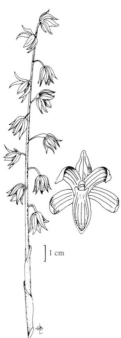

] 1 cm

BLUE BEAD LILY ♦ *Clintonia borealis*
CLINTONIE BORÉALE

Lily Family (Liliaceae)

MNR Photo

General: Perennial; up to 40 cm tall; usually in patches.

Leaves: Basal; simple; 2–4, but usually 3; oblong or tongue-shaped with short, pointed tip and clasping base; up to 30 cm long, 4–9 cm wide; dark green, thick and leathery; margins toothless; upright-growing; veins distinctive and parallel.

Flowers: Greenish-yellow; bell-shaped; 6 'petals' (3 petals and 3 petal-like sepals); in loose clusters of 2–8 flowers on tip of single, leafless stalk; summer.

Fruit: Bead-like berries; blue; dark and shiny; oval to rounded with several seeds; in clusters; ripen August.

Habitat: All moisture regimes, soil and stand types.

Notes: The berries are poisonous. The young leaves were considered edible in salads or as boiled greens and reportedly taste like cucumber. See caution in Introduction. • Aboriginal peoples used the leaves of blue bead lily as a plaster for bruises and sores. • Blue bead lily may be confused with three-leaved smilacina (*Maianthemum trifolium*), but blue bead lily's leaves are basal while three-leaved smilacina's leaves grow alternately along the stem. Also, when three-leaved smilacina's leaves are held up to the light, they are slightly transparent and the parallel veins are clearly visible. • Blue bead lily is also commonly called 'yellow clintonia.'

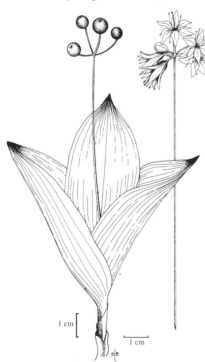

1 cm

1 cm

ᴬᴵ 5/8

Lily Family (Liliaceae)

General: Perennial; 5–25 cm tall; spreads by slender, branching underground stems (rhizomes); often forms extensive patches of single leaves; flowering stem erect and often has a bend or zigzag in it.

Leaves: Alternate; stalkless or occasionally with short stalk; simple, 1–3, usually 2, on flowering stem; egg-shaped with sharply to bluntly pointed tip and heart-shaped base; 2–10 cm long, 1.5–5.5 cm wide; dark green and hairless or sometimes finely hairy beneath; margins toothless.

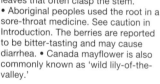

Karen Legasy

Flowers: White; 4 'petals' (2 petals and 2 petal-like sepals); in elongated terminal clusters 1.5–5 cm long; individual flowers small, about 5 mm wide; flower stalks usually longer than flower clusters; May–June.

Fruit: Speckled, pale-red, round berry; hard and green at first; ripens July.

Habitat: All moisture regimes, soil textures and stand types; abundant.

Notes: Canada mayflower may be confused with three-leaved smilacina (*Maianthemum trifolium*). Canada mayflower has 2 petals and 2 petal-like sepals; three-leaved smilacina has 3 petals, 3 petal-like sepals and more elongated leaves that often clasp the stem.

Brenda Chambers

• Aboriginal peoples used the root in a sore-throat medicine. See caution in Introduction. The berries are reported to be bitter-tasting and may cause diarrhea. • Canada mayflower is also commonly known as 'wild lily-of-the-valley.'

1 cm

THREE-LEAVED SMILACINA ♦ *Maianthemum trifolium*
SMILACINE TRIFOLIÉE

Lily Family (Liliaceae)

Brenda Chambers

General: Perennial; up to 20 cm tall; slender; erect; grows in patches.

Leaves: Alternate; stalkless; simple; lance-shaped to oval, taper to pointed tip, sheath or clasp stem at base; 5–12.5 cm long, 1–5 cm wide; hairless; upward-growing; margins toothless; 2–4, usually 3.

Flowers: White; 6 'petals' (3 petals and 3 petal-like sepals); 8 mm wide; grow along slender stem above leaves; June.

Fruit: Dark-red, round berry; ripens July.

Habitat: Wet organic to moist, medium-loamy upland sites; black spruce and conifer mixedwoods; open bogs; common.

Notes: The berries have historically been considered edible, but they may cause diarrhea. • Three-leaved smilacina may be confused with Canada mayflower (*Maianthemum canadense*). The leaves of Canada mayflower are shorter and have a heart-shaped, stalkless base that does not clasp the stem while the leaves of three-leaved smilacina clasp the stem. The flowers of Canada mayflower have 2 petals and 2 petal-like sepals while the flowers of three-leaved smilacina have 3 petals and 3 petal-like sepals. See notes on blue bead lily (*Clintonia borealis*).

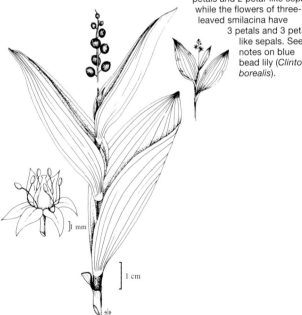

Lily Family (Liliaceae)

General: Perennial; less than 30 cm tall; single or forked stem sparingly hairy, especially at nodes.

Leaves: Alternate; stalkless; simple; lance-shaped to oval, tapering to a long, pointed tip and rounded base; 5–9 cm long, 2–3.5 cm wide; margins toothless to minutely toothed and fringed with fine hairs; slightly clasping to not clasping stem; veins parallel with fine hairs beneath.

Flowers: Rose-coloured to whitish;

Karen Legasy

bell-shaped; about 1 cm long; lobes spreading near tips; 6 'petals' (3 petals and 3 petal-like sepals); solitary on stalks with a bend or twist in middle, 1–3 cm long; flower stalks are opposite leaves and flowers hang below leaves.

Fruit: Red berry with numerous seeds; rounded to oblong; about 1 cm long; ripens in July.

Habitat: Common in all moisture regimes, soil textures and stand types, most common in hardwood and conifer mixedwoods and transition tolerant hardwood stands.

Notes: The roots were historically used in a cough remedy. See caution in Introduction. The berries may cause diarrhea if eaten in quantity.
• White mandarin (*Streptopus amplexifolius*) is a similar-looking species, but it has 1 (sometimes 2) greenish-white flowers per distinctly kinked stalk, its leaves have a heart-shaped, strongly clasping base and the leaf margins don't have a fringe of fine hairs. White mandarin is occasional in old white spruce forests and in woods along shorelines.

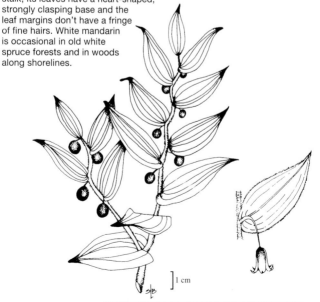

]1 cm

NODDING TRILLIUM ♦ *Trillium cernuum*
TRILLE PENCHÉ

Lily Family (Liliaceae)

Karen Legasy

General: Perennial; 15–60 cm tall; from brown underground stem (rhizome) up to 3 cm thick; 1 or several slender, unbranched stems.

Leaves: In a whorl of 3 at top of stem; on short stalks; simple; diamond-shaped to rounded with pointed tip, narrowed at base; 4–15 cm long and wide; margins toothless.

Flowers: White, rarely pink; 3 petals with tips bent slightly backward, 3 sepals; about 3.8 cm wide; nodding; on curved stalk 0.5–2.5 cm long; solitary; May–early June.

Fruit: Red to purplish berry; egg-shaped; late June–July.

Habitat: Moist, fine-loamy to clayey, herb-rich conifer and hardwood mixedwoods; occasional along streambanks and in damp thickets.

Notes: The species name *cernuum* comes from the Latin word *cernuus*, which means 'drooping' or 'nodding' and refers to the flowers.

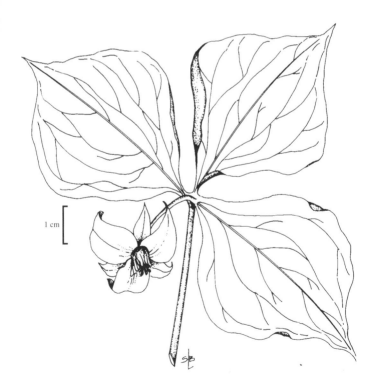

1 cm

Lily Family (Liliaceae)

General: Perennial; 20–105 cm tall; from a small, scaly bulb surrounded by a dense cluster of creamy bulblets; stem erect, hairless.

Leaves: Whorled, 2–6 whorls, each whorl has 3–8 leaves; stalkless; simple; lance-shaped, pointed at both ends or some-times rounded at base; 2.5–10 cm long; shiny, thin; margins finely rough.

Flowers: Orange with oblong to rounded, purplish-brown spots; 6 'petals' (3 petals and 3 petal-like sepals) hairless and taper to narrow base; June–July.

Fruit: Capsules; inversely egg-shaped to oval or oblong but tapering at base; 2.5–5 cm long; seeds have narrow wings.

Habitat: Dry, open forests and shores; sandy soils and thickets; occasional.

Notes: Aboriginal peoples gathered the bulbs for food. See caution in Introduction.

NWO FEC Photo

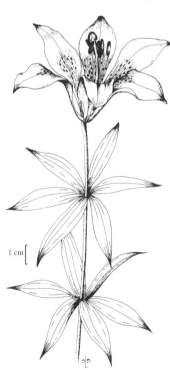

1 cm

Iris Family (Iridaceae)

Karen Legasy

General: Perennial; 10–60 cm tall; erect, tufted, usually pale green and does not often dry blackish; stem unbranched (rarely slightly forked), pale, distinctly flattened and winged along edges.

Leaves: Basal; grass-like with pointed tips; 10–50 cm long, over 6 mm wide; margins finely toothed; half the stem's height or longer.

Flowers: Violet-blue, centre yellow; 6 'petals' (3 petals and 3 petal-like sepals), each tipped with a slender point; on short stalks at stem tips and usually exceeded by a pointed bract; May–July.

Fruit: Capsules; widely oval to rounded; whitish-green to straw-coloured or pale brown; 3–6 mm high.

Habitat: Frequent in ditches and wet clearings; occasional on open shores.

Notes: This plant gets its name from the way the flowers appear like 'blue eyes' on grass-like stems.

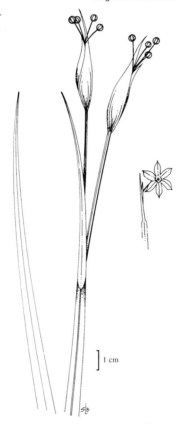

1 cm

Iris Family (Iridaceae)

General: Perennial; 60–90 cm tall; thick, fleshy, horizontal underground stem (rhizome) covered with fibrous roots and either deeply buried or near surface; stem erect and unbranched or with 1–2 branches above and taller than leaves.

Leaves: Basal leaves stalkless, simple, sword-like, 20–80 cm long, 0.5–3 cm wide; alternate stem leaves prolonged but shorter than basal leaves; basal leaves pale green to greyish, fresh leaves often purplish at base; firm; upward-growing.

Flowers: Blue-violet with darker veins and yellow, green and white colouring toward base or middle of flower; 3 petal-like sepals spread horizontally with 3 petal-like styles arching over them, 3 narrower and erect petals; 6.3–10 cm wide; May–August.

Fruit: Capsule; oblong, 3-sided; 1.5–6 cm long; thick and firm; inner surface looks varnished; seeds D-shaped, brown and 5–8 mm long; opens late and often stays over winter.

Brenda Chambers

Habitat: Wet areas; swamps, marshes, wet fields, ditches; shorelines; common.

Notes: The rootstock is extremely poisonous. • Aboriginal peoples used the roots in poultices for sores, inflammation, burns and any other type of pain. See caution in Introduction. They believed snakes would shun the scent of blue flag, so they carried a piece of the root and handled it from time to time to protect themselves from poisonous snakes. Aboriginal peoples also used blue flag's leaves to make various shades of green dye and to weave mats and baskets.

1 cm

Cat-tail Family (Typhaceae)

Karen Legasy

General: Perennial; 1–2.7 m high; from coarse, creeping underground stems (rhizomes); stems filled with pith.

Leaves: Alternate; sheathing; simple; long, flat and narrow (grass-like); up to 2.5 cm wide and taller than stem; greyish-green, somewhat spongy.

Flowers: Tiny and numerous; male and female on adjacent terminal spikes each up to 15 cm long; female spike lowermost, 1.2–3.5 cm thick, greenish, dark brown at maturity; male above female, cream-coloured, bright yellow at maturity, deteriorates after pollen release leaving a bare stalk; May–July.

Fruit: Dry, hard, single-seeded (achene); elliptical; about 1 mm long; designed to float with numerous long, slender hairs at base.

Habitat: Common in marshes; occasionally colonizes wet ditches and clearings.

Notes: The leaves can be used to weave baskets, rugs and other items. The roots contain carbohydrates, and have historically been eaten raw or baked. See caution in Introduction.
• Cat-tails are a primary food source and habitat for muskrat.

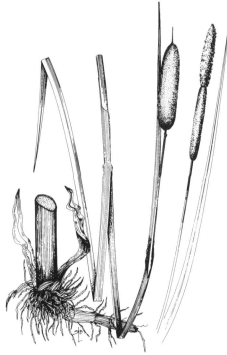

Pitcher Plant Family (Sarraceniaceae)

General: Perennial; 20–60 cm tall; flowering stem leafless, slender, hairless.

Leaves: Basal rosette; base narrows into a stalk; simple; pitcher-shaped with erect, broad, flap-like hood, hood's inner surface covered in dense, stiff, downward-pointing hairs; 10–30 cm long; purple-veined or sometimes green or yellowish all over; spreading to upward-growing; curved and winged.

Flowers: Purplish-red or occasionally yellowish; rounded (globe-like); 5 petals arch over yellowish, umbrella-like style; 5–7 cm wide; solitary; nodding; May–August.

Karen Legasy

Fruit: Capsules; granular surface, 5 sections, contain numerous seeds.

Habitat: Open sphagnum bogs; frequent.

Notes: Pitcher plants are carnivorous. They attract and trap insects in their leaves with the stiff hairs in their hoods and then use the hairs to force the insects further down through the smooth-surfaced, narrow neck and into the cavity below. The plants then release secretions to prevent the insect from escaping and to dissolve it. • Aboriginal peoples used the hollow, inflated leaves as drinking cups when they were out in the forest, and used the roots to make an infusion for curing smallpox. See caution in Introduction.

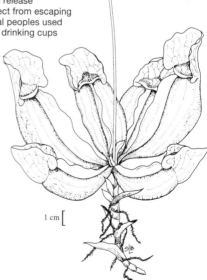

1 cm

Sundew Family (Droseraceae)

MNR Photo

General: Perennial; small, 5–25 cm tall; flower stalk erect, slender, hairless and rises from rosette of leaves.

Leaves: Basal rosette; leaf blades at least as wide as long, 4–10 mm long, abruptly narrow to a flat, hairy stalk 1.3–5 cm long; upper surface covered with reddish, glandular hairs that release sticky fluid.

Flowers: White to red or pink-tinged; 5 petals; about 6 mm wide; 3–15 flowers along 1 side of stem; June–August.

Fruit: Capsules; seeds elongated and tapered at both ends.

Habitat: Wet organic black spruce stands; nutrient-poor soils, wet sand, sphagnum bogs and wet fields; silty and boggy shores; frequent.

Notes: Sundew plants eat insects, which are attracted to the glistening, sticky fluid on the glandular leaf hairs. When an insect lands on one hair, the other hairs sense it and bend over the insect, making it adhere to the sticky fluid so the plant can eventually absorb the insect's nutrients. The hair glands then release an acid and enzymes that dissolve all the soft parts of the insect, and other leaf glands absorb the released nutrients. The same insects used for food often pollinate the plant.

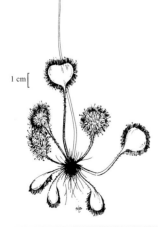

1 cm

Sundew Family (Droseraceae)

General: Perennial; 6–13 cm tall; leafless flowering stem (scape) often lower than leaves but sometimes exceeds them; hairless.

Leaves: Basal rosette; on hairless stalks 3–7 cm long; simple; linear, flat with blunt or rounded tip; 1–6 cm long, 1.5–3 mm wide; densely covered with glandular hairs.

Flowers: White; solitary or few; 6–8 mm wide at top of leafless flowering stem (scape); June–August.

Fruit: 3-parted capsule; seeds oblong, black, 0.5–0.8 mm long, hairless and shiny.

Habitat: Fens; wet, limy shores; rare.

Notes: Slender-leaved sundew's long, slender or linear leaves distinguish it from round-leaved sundew (*Drosera rotundifolia*), which has nearly circular leaves. See notes on round-leaved sundew.

Brenda Chambers

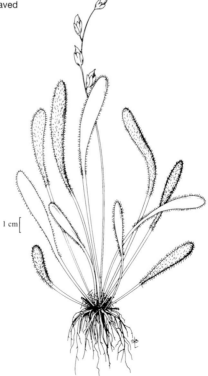

1 cm

FRINGED BINDWEED ♦ *Polygonum cilinode*
RENOUÉE À NOEUDS CILIÉS

Buckwheat Family (Polygonaceae)

General: Perennial; stem 30–300 cm long, reddish, twining, laying on ground or nearly erect, freely branching and climbing, sparingly hairy.

Leaves: Alternate; stalked; simple; widely triangular-egg-shaped or sometimes arrowhead-shaped with pointed tip and deeply heart-shaped base; 5–12 cm long, 2.5–10 cm wide; margins wavy; finely hairy; stipules are abruptly bent and bristly at base.

Flowers: White or pink-tinged; small; in terminal or leaf-axil branched clusters; June–September.

Karen Legasy

Fruit: Dry, hard, single-seeded (achene); 3-angled; oblongish and pyramid-shaped or inversely egg-shaped; 3–4 mm long; hairless and shiny; black.

Habitat: Rocky areas, dry thickets; forest edges; cutovers and other disturbed sites; roadsides; frequent.

Notes: Songbirds occasionally eat fringed bindweed seeds.

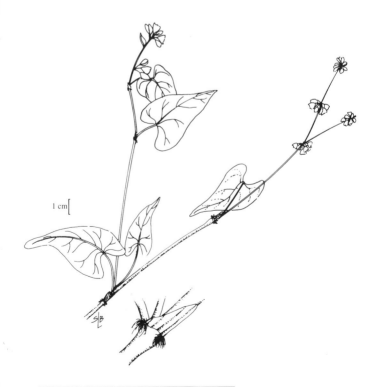

1 cm

Buckwheat Family (Polygonaceae)

General: Perennial or annual; 15–50 cm tall; hairless; stem slender, erect or almost so, unbranched or branched; underground stem (rhizome) woody and horizontal or creeping.

Leaves: Basal leaves on long stalks; stem leaves on short stalks or stalkless; simple; narrowly arrow-shaped with blunt or pointed tip and 2 lobes at base; 2.5–10 cm long; covered with minute, nipple-shaped projections (papillae).

Flowers: Reddish to yellowish; small; 3 petals and 3 petal-like sepals; on stalks in erect, loose and narrow clusters (racemes); June–September.

Fruit: Dry, hard, single-seeded (achene); nutlike; shiny, yellowish-brown; 3-angled.

Habitat: Disturbed areas; roadsides; fields, gardens, lawns and waste places, frequent in neglected sandy fields, common in open, dry forests and clearings, locally abundant in sandy jack pine forests.

Notes: The crushed leaves and stems may irritate skin and cause an allergic reaction, and the pollen may trigger an allergic reaction which takes the form of respiratory problems. The leaves are rich in vitamin C and apparently have a sour taste like that of rhubarb.
• The leaves have been found to contain oxalic acid, which can interfere with the body's calcium metabolism. See caution in Introduction.

Ray Demey

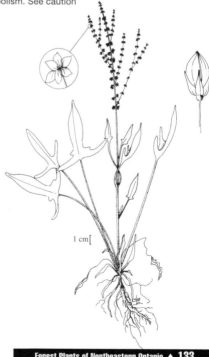

1 cm

Sandalwood Family (Santalaceae)

MNR Photo

General: Perennial; 10–25 cm tall; from slender, reddish and creeping underground stems (rhizomes); stem erect, usually unbranched; grow as individuals or clumped.

Leaves: Alternate; on short stalks; simple; oval with blunt or rounded tips, narrowed at base; 1–2.5 cm long and 0.5–1 cm wide; thin; pale lead-coloured to purplish; margins toothless.

Flowers: Greenish to purplish; 5 petal-like sepals, small, about 2 mm long; in clusters of 2–4 from leaf axils; June–July.

Fruit: Rounded, fleshy or pulpy and berry-like (drupe); fluorescent-orange to scarlet; 6–10 mm diameter; solitary or rarely 2; ripens August–September.

1 cm

Habitat: Wet organic and moist upland sites; occasional.

Notes: This plant is also known as *Commandra livida*. • Northern commandra is a parasite on the roots of other plants. • Some people have considered the berries edible, but they are apparently not very tasty. See caution in Introduction.

Pink Family (Caryophyllaceae)

General: Perennial; 10–65 cm tall; horizontally spreading, ascending or erect; hairy.

Leaves: Opposite; stalkless; simple; basal and lower leaves spoon-shaped to oblong with blunt tip, upper leaves oblong with blunt to pointed tip; 0.5–4 cm long, 1.5–15 mm wide; hairy; margins toothless.

Flowers: White; 5 deeply notched petals; about 6 mm wide; in terminal clusters of 3–60; May–September.

Karen Legasy

Fruit: Capsules; small, cylindrical, curved, 7–11 mm long; seeds brown, 0.5–0.7 mm in diameter.

Habitat: Fields; roadsides; cultivated ground, waste places; common.

Notes: Mouse-ear chickweed was formerly known as *Cerastium vulgatum*. • The common name 'mouse-ear' comes from the fuzzy little leaves. • Historically, the leaves were boiled and eaten as greens. See caution in Introduction. • This plant is often a troublesome weed in gardens and lawns. See notes on chickweed (*Stellaria borealis*).

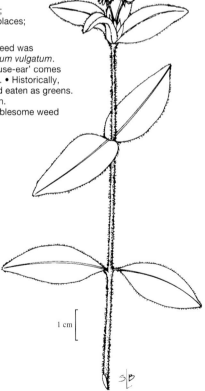

1 cm

CHICKWEED ♦ *Stellaria borealis*
STELLAIRE CALYCANTHE

Pink Family (Caryophyllaceae)

Linda Kershaw

General: Perennial; stems 3–50 cm long, hairless or slightly rough, unbranched or loosely branched, reclining, upward-growing or erect, often matted; underground stems (rhizomes) slender.

Leaves: Opposite; stalkless; simple; narrowly egg-shaped or elliptic to lance-shaped with pointed or slightly pointed tip; 0.8–4 cm long, 2–8 mm wide; hairless except for a few minute hairs on margin near base; margins often rough-hairy.

Flowers: White to greenish; small; solitary in leaf axils or in open terminal clusters; 5 petal-like sepals widely lance-shaped to oblong with pointed or blunt tip, 2–5.5 mm long; petals absent or shorter than sepals.

Fruit: Capsules; cone-shaped to inversely egg-shaped; pale brown; thin-walled.

Habitat: Wet areas; meadows, thickets, moist forest openings, wet ditches; streambanks; frequent.

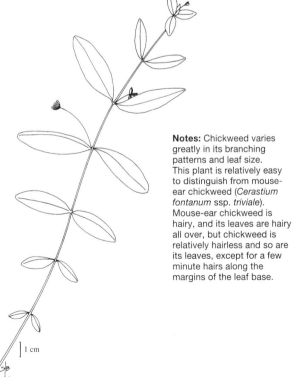

Notes: Chickweed varies greatly in its branching patterns and leaf size. This plant is relatively easy to distinguish from mouse-ear chickweed (*Cerastium fontanum* ssp. *triviale*). Mouse-ear chickweed is hairy, and its leaves are hairy all over, but chickweed is relatively hairless and so are its leaves, except for a few minute hairs along the margins of the leaf base.

1 cm

Buttercup Family (Ranunculaceae)

General: Perennial; 7–15 cm tall; underground stem (rhizome) small, slender, creeping, distinctively bright yellow or gold.

Leaves: Basal; on long, slender leafstalks; compound, 3 leaflets; kidney-shaped; 2.5–5 cm wide; upper surface shiny, dark green, underside paler; leaflets stalkless with rounded teeth on margins.

Flowers: White; star-shaped; 5–7 petals; usually solitary at tip of long, slender, leafless stalks; spring to early summer.

Fruit: Slender capsules, splitting along 1 side, beaked, 7–12 mm long; 3–7; in a spreading cluster; July–August.

Brenda Chambers

Habitat: All moisture regimes, soil and stand types; common.

Notes: Aboriginal peoples made a yellow dye from the roots. The roots were also used in a mouthwash for cankers, sore throat, sore gums and teething. See caution in Introduction. • You can recognize goldthread by its golden, thread-like roots.

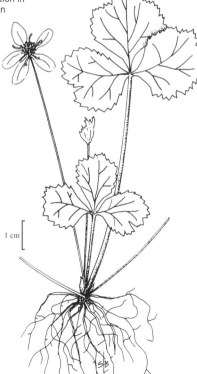

1 cm

CANADA ANEMONE ♦ *Anemone canadensis*
ANÉMONE DU CANADA

Buttercup Family (Ranunculaceae)

MNR Photo

General: Perennial; 20–70 cm tall; from an underground stem (rhizome); hairy; branches from centre of leaf whorls or crowns.

Leaves: Basal leaves have long stalks; stem leaves stalkless; compound, in 3–5 sections with deeply cut lobes; leaves wider than long; basal leaves 5–15 cm wide; veins prominent, covered with soft hairs on underside; margins toothed toward top of lobes.

Flowers: White; 5 unequal, widely oblong, petal-like sepals 1–2.5 cm long; individuals on stalks rising from centre of leaf whorls.

Fruit: In a round (globe-like) head; dry, hard, single-seeded (achene), flat, almost circular, hairy, with a stout style at tip.

Habitat: Fields; occasionally along gravelly shores, damp areas with shrubs or thickets and along slopes; more common in dry, open areas and along roadsides; forms large colonies.

Notes: Anemones contain a toxic compound which may irritate skin.
• Aboriginal peoples washed sores and wounds in a remedy made from anemone roots and leaves. Some aboriginal peoples chewed the roots before singing to help clear their throats. See caution in Introduction.

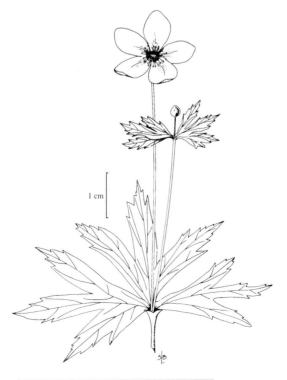

1 cm

Buttercup Family (Ranunculaceae)

General: Perennial; 5–30 cm tall; from a whitish, crisp, toothed, horizontal, 1–4 mm thick underground stem (rhizome); stem slightly hairy; delicate.

Leaves: Basal, single; on a long stalk; 3 stem leaves similar but smaller; compound; 3 leaflets often deeply cut so there appears to be 5, narrowly triangular to egg-shaped or oblong, narrower end toward base, 1–5 cm long; margins irregularly and coarsely toothed.

Flowers: Whitish to purplish or pinkish-tinged; 4–9 (usually 5) petal-like sepals 0.6–2.5 cm long; solitary; May–June.

Fruit: Dry, hard, single-seeded (achene); hairy; in round (globe-like) clusters; develop late June–July.

Habitat: All moisture regimes, soil and stand types; common.

Notes: Wood anemone contains a toxic compound which may irritate skin. • Anemones have been called 'wind flowers' because their slender stalks tremble easily in a breeze.

MNR Photo

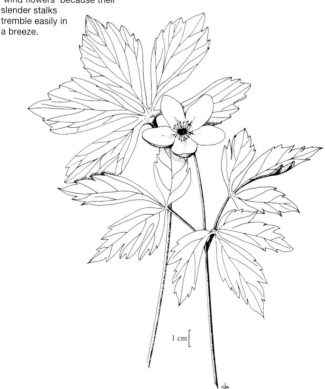

1 cm

TALL BUTTERCUP ◆ *Ranunculus acris*
RENONCULE ÂCRE

Buttercup Family (Ranunculaceae)

General: Perennial; 60–90 cm tall; 1 or several stems from slender roots; erect; hairy; branched above; stem hollow.

Leaves: Basal leaves on long stalks, simple, palm-shaped, 2.5–10 cm wide, divided into 3–7 (usually 5) stalkless, deeply cut sections (lobes) with pointed tips; stem leaves alternate, on short stalks, simple, smaller and scattered.

Flowers: Yellow; glossy; 5 petals and 5 small, greenish sepals; about 2.5 cm wide; on hairy stalks; in loose clusters; May–September.

Karen Legasy

Fruit: In round (globe-like) heads; dry, hard, single-seeded (achenes), hairless, flattish, margined, 2.5–3.5 mm long with a curved beak.

Habitat: Dry to moist soils; neglected pastures, disturbed areas; roadsides; common, but occurs less frequently in forest clearings.

Notes: Tall buttercup's leaves were historically used in a headache remedy. See caution in Introduction. The roots contain an antibiotic principle of protoanemonine which apparently acts against a broad range of bacteria. • The species name *acris* refers to the acrid stem and leaf juice.

1 cm

Buttercup Family (Ranunculaceae)

General: Perennial; stem 0.2–1.2 m long, upward-growing, curved downward or trailing, branched, soft, hollow, hairy; roots thick and fibrous.

Leaves: On stalks; compound; 3 widely oblong to egg-shaped leaflets with pointed tips, wedge-shaped, deeply cut and lobed; 5–7.5 cm long.

Flowers: Yellow; 2–24; petals widely and inversely egg-shaped or rounded, 3.5–6 mm long, 2.5–5 mm wide; sepals hairy, bent backward and 3–6 mm long; June–August.

Fruit: Dry, hard, single-seeded (achene); sharp, pointed beak at tip; thin; margins narrow.

Habitat: Thickets with alluvium (clay, silt, sand, gravel or similar detrital material deposited by running water), damp openings in forests, ditches; occasional.

Notes: Woodchucks and woodland jumping mice eat buttercups.

Karen Legasy

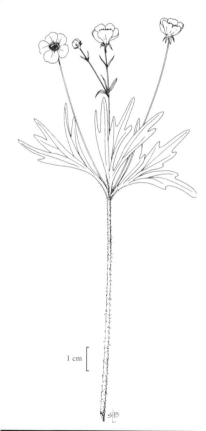

1 cm

KIDNEYLEAF BUTTERCUP ♦ *Ranunculus abortivus*
RENONCULE ABORTIVE

Buttercup Family (Ranunculaceae)

Brenda Chambers

General: Perennial; 15–60 cm tall; roots slender and fibrous; stems hairless or sparingly hairy, green, erect and branched.

Leaves: Alternate; basal leaves on long stalks, usually simple, kidney-shaped to round with blunt tip and heart-shaped base, 1.3–3.8 cm wide, bright green, thick, with rounded teeth or sometimes lobed; stem leaves stalkless, 3- to 5-lobed and mostly toothed.

Flowers: Yellow; petals oblong, 2–3 mm long, shorter than the 5 petal-like sepals, 1.5–4 mm long; few- to many-flowered; April–August.

Fruit: In a round to ovoid head, dry, hard, single-seeded (achene); rounded, tipped with minute, curved beak; 1.2–1.5 mm long; shiny.

Habitat: Damp forests, moist areas, alder thickets; streambanks; occasional.

Notes: With their small petals, the flowers of kidneyleaf buttercup do not look much like buttercups.
• Kidneyleaf buttercup was historically used to treat syphilis and to help increase perspiration. See caution in Introduction.

1 cm

Buttercup Family (Ranunculaceae)

General: Perennial; stem 15–80 cm tall, erect or reclining, hairless, grooved, branching, thick, hollow and succulent.

Leaves: Alternate; on stalks, upper leaves become stalkless; simple; rounded to heart- or kidney-shaped; 5–17.5 cm wide; glossy, dark green; margins with pointed to rounded teeth or nearly toothless.

Flowers: Bright yellow; 5–9 petal-like sepals, widely oval to narrowly egg-shaped; on stalks from leaf axils at top of stem, showy; 2.5–4 cm wide; April–June.

Brenda Chambers

Fruit: Arranged in a small head; 6–12, prominently beaked and shiny 'pods' (follicles), split open along 1 side, contain numerous small, black seeds; 1–1.5 cm long.

Habitat: Wet organic to moist, fine-loamy to clayey upland sites; black spruce stands and conifer mixedwoods, swamps, wet areas in meadows, open woods, ditches; marshy creeks; common.

Notes: Marsh marigold leaves contain a toxin that makes them **poisonous when raw.** It is said that the toxin can be destroyed with cooking, but that has not been verified. See caution in Introduction.
• The flowers resemble large buttercups.

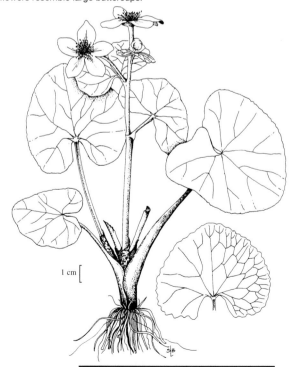

1 cm

RED BANEBERRY ♦ *Actaea rubra*
ACTÉE ROUGE

Buttercup Family (Ranunculaceae)

General: Perennial; 30–80 cm tall; erect and bushy; hairy to hairless.

Leaves: Alternate; stalked; compound, divided 2–3 times into groups of 3; leaflets egg-shaped, about 6 cm long, commonly hairy on veins beneath, sharply toothed with irregular and lobed margins.

Flowers: White; small, with 4–10 narrow petals; about 7–10 mm wide; in dense, terminal, egg-shaped or cylindrical clusters on long stalks; May–June.

Fruit: Round, red (sometimes white) berries; shiny; on thin stalks; in clusters; ripen July–August.

Habitat: Moist to fresh, clayey to coarse-loamy upland sites; hardwood and mixedwood stands; occasional.

Notes: White baneberry (*Actaea pachypoda*) is a similar species, but its berries ripen to white instead of red and its flower stalks are thick while red baneberry's are thin. • **The berries of red and white baneberry are considered poisonous.** All parts of the plant are said to contain a toxic oil. • After giving birth, aboriginal women drank a tea made from the roots of red baneberry, to 'clear up their systems.' See caution in Introduction.

Karen Legasy (primary)
Bill Crins (inset)

1 cm

Buttercup Family (Ranunculaceae)

General: Perennial; 60–200 cm tall; stem thick and erect, hairless to hairy, purplish, branched above.

Leaves: Alternate; on stalks, upper stem leaves stalkless or almost stalkless; compound; leaflets oblong to egg-shaped, shaped like a duck's foot, with 3 pointed lobes at tip; up to 15 cm or more long; surface firm, dark green; margins toothless and rolled downward; prominently veined and finely hairy.

Flowers: Greenish to purplish; petal-like sepals lance-shaped to narrowly egg-shaped with slender tip; small, 3–5 mm long; in branching clusters; on drooping stalks; June–August.

Karen Legasy

Fruit: Small, dry, hard, single-seeded (achene); egg-shaped; hairless to hairy; has 6–8 ridges.

Habitat: Moist to wet areas; fields, swamps and damp thickets.

Notes: Aboriginal peoples made a tea from the roots to help reduce fever. See caution in Introduction. Some aboriginal peoples believed this plant had the powers of a love potion, and would put meadow rue seeds into the food of quarrelling couples, believing it would help to mend their differences.

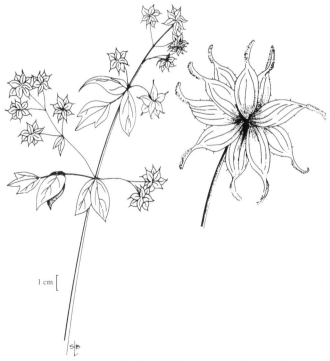

1 cm

NAKED MITREWORT ♦ *Mitella nuda*
MITRELLE NUE

Saxifrage Family (Saxifragaceae)

Karen Legasy

General: Perennial; 5–20 cm tall; small; delicate; flowering stem solitary, erect and usually leafless.

Leaves: Basal; on long stalks; simple; rounded to kidney-shaped with heart-shaped base; 1–3 cm long; distinctive, bristly, stiff, whisker-like hairs on upper surface; margins slightly lobed or deeply toothed.

Flowers: Yellowish to greenish; saucer-shaped; 5 hair-like petals with long fringes; on separate stalks along flower stem in a long, loose cluster; appear May–June.

Fruit: Capsules; short and flat; contain black, smooth, shiny seeds.

Habitat: Wet organic and moist to fresh, clayey to sandy sites; rich black spruce and conifer and hardwood mixedwood stands; common.

Notes: You can frequently see just the leaves with their scattered, whisker-like hairs. The common name 'mitrewort' presumably comes from the seed capsules, which were thought to resemble a bishop's mitre or headdress. • The woodland jumping mouse eats naked mitrewort, and ruffed grouse occasionally eat the leaves.

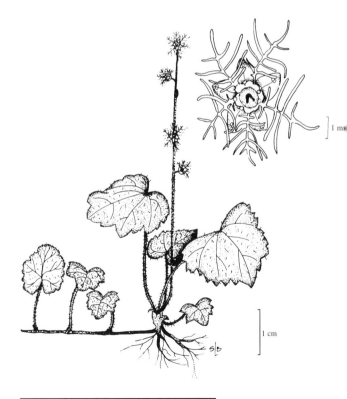

1 mm

1 cm

Saxifrage Family (Saxifragaceae)

General: Perennial; 8–35 cm tall; from short underground stems (rhizomes); hairless; flowering stalk usually has an egg-shaped, clasping leaf below the middle.

Leaves: Basal (mainly); on slender stalks; simple; egg-shaped with blunt tip and usually heart-shaped base; 3–5 cm long, 1.5–4.5 cm wide.

Flowers: White; petals greenish- or yellowish-veined, oval and 8–15 mm long; solitary on flowering stem; July–August.

Fruit: Capsules; egg-shaped; many-seeded.

Habitat: Wet, rocky shores and clearings; ditches; scarce.

Notes: Although called grass-of-Parnassus, this plant is not grass-like.

MNR Photo

1 cm

Rose Family (Rosaceae)

General: Perennial; 7.5–15 cm tall; several trailing stems or runners from thick, short rootstock; often forms large patches.

Leaves: Basal; on hairy stalks; compound, divided into 3 leaflets; leaflets widely oval or egg-shaped with narrower end near base; leaves 5–15 cm long; margins coarsely toothed, tooth at leaflet tip shorter and narrower than teeth on either side of it; veins straight and prominent.

Flowers: White; 5 petals; 1.5–2.5 cm wide; 2–15, in loose clusters that do not overtop leaves at maturity; May–June.

Fruit: Strawberry; red; pulpy and juicy; rounded to egg-shaped, 0.5–2 cm in diameter; small, dry, pit-like seeds (achenes) embedded on fruit surface; ripens July.

Brenda Chambers

Habitat: All moisture regimes, soil textures and stand types; fields, clearings, disturbed areas; roadsides; common.

Notes: The berries are edible and often are tastier than domestic strawberries. Aboriginal peoples used the roots in a cure for stomachache. See caution in Introduction. • The least chipmunk eats only the seeds, and leaves neat little piles of fruit pulp on rocks. Other small mammals, such as the deer mouse, meadow jumping mouse, woodland jumping mouse and American marten, eat the berries, as do the red fox and black bear. • See woodland strawberry (*Fragaria vesca* ssp. *americana*) for notes on distinguishing features.

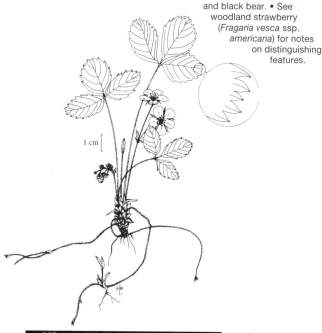

1 cm

Rose Family (Rosaceae)

General: Perennial; 7.5–15 cm tall; from long, trailing stems or runners (stolons) growing from a thick, short rootstock; flowering stems greenish or lightly reddish- or purplish-tinged; hairy, stout and tufted.

Leaves: Basal; on hairy stalks; compound, with 3 leaflets; leaflets egg-shaped with somewhat pointed tip and wedge-shaped base; upper surface dark green with prominent, straight veins, underside silky-hairy; margins coarsely toothed, tooth at tip longer than 2 on either side.

Flowers: White; 5 petals; about 1.0–1.5 cm wide; in loose clusters of 3–15; at maturity flowers usually extend above leaves; May–June.

Fruit: Strawberry; red; pulpy and juicy; egg- to cone-shaped; about 1 cm across; seeds on smooth surface and not in pits; above leaves; ripens July.

MNR Photo

Habitat: Usually on drier sites; along rivers or streambanks; disturbed areas, sandy and rocky forest openings; roadsides; occasional.

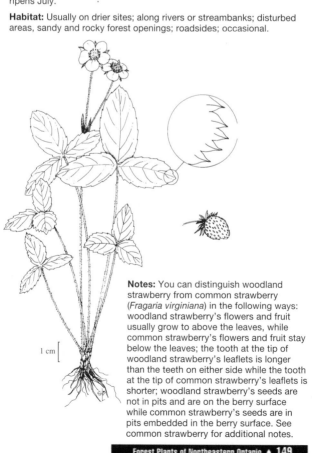

1 cm

Notes: You can distinguish woodland strawberry from common strawberry (*Fragaria virginiana*) in the following ways: woodland strawberry's flowers and fruit usually grow to above the leaves, while common strawberry's flowers and fruit stay below the leaves; the tooth at the tip of woodland strawberry's leaflets is longer than the teeth on either side while the tooth at the tip of common strawberry's leaflets is shorter; woodland strawberry's seeds are not in pits and are on the berry surface while common strawberry's seeds are in pits embedded in the berry surface. See common strawberry for additional notes.

**MARSH CINQUEFOIL ♦ *Potentilla palustris*
POTENTILLE PALUSTRE**

Rose Family (Rosaceae)

General: Perennial; 10–60 cm tall; stout stems grow upward from reclining, woody, rooting base or stem; reclining stems hairless; upper stems hairy.

Leaves: Alternate; on stalks; compound; 5–7 leaflets arranged on both sides of common stalk or axis; leaflets oval to oblong with blunt to slightly pointed tips and narrowed base, 2–10 cm long and 0.7–3.8 cm wide;

Karen Legasy

margins sharply toothed; upper leaves smaller, almost stalkless, in groups of 3–5.

Flowers: Reddish-purple; 5 petals; about 2 cm wide; in loose clusters near top of stem; June–August.

Fruit: Small, dry, hard, single-seeded (achene); hairless; oval to egg-shaped; numerous; borne on an enlarged, hairy, spongy receptacle.

Habitat: Wet areas, swamps, marshes and peat bogs; shorelines; common.

Notes: The woody stems root in water. • The common name 'cinquefoil' means 'five leaves' (there are often 5 leaflets in the compound leaves).

1 cm

Rose Family (Rosaceae)

General: Perennial; 0.3–1.2 m high; erect; stem usually unbranched, hairy.

Leaves: Alternate; basal leaves stalked, up to 30 cm long, 3- to 5-lobed, terminal lobe largest, wedge-shaped; 2–4 lateral lobes are egg-shaped to triangular, irregularly toothed; smaller stem leaves distantly spaced, on short stalks or stalkless, simple or compound, toothed or irregularly lobed.

Flowers: Purplish; about 2 cm wide; nodding; sepals purple, ascending, triangular, 7–10 mm long; petals erect, inversely egg-shaped, notched and abruptly narrowed into a claw; May–August.

Brenda Chambers

Fruit: In an erect, stalked head; dry, hard, single-seeded (achene); hairy; 3–4 mm long with a 6–8 mm long style hooked at tip, spreading in the head.

Habitat: Ditches and wet clearings; occasional.

Notes: See notes on large-leaved avens (*Geum macrophyllum*) for distinguishing features.

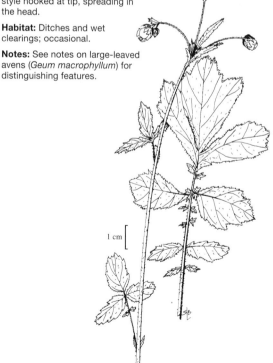

1 cm

LARGE-LEAVED AVENS ♦ *Geum macrophyllum*
BÉNOÎTE À GRANDES FEUILLES

Rose Family (Rosaceae)

General: Perennial; 0.3–1 m high; stem erect, bristly-hairy and branched or unbranched.

Leaves: Basal leaves stalked, 3- to 7-lobed; terminal lobe largest, rounded to kidney-shaped with toothed margins, 5–12 cm wide; 3–6 oval or inversely egg-shaped side leaflets interspersed with smaller ones; stem leaves on short stalks or stalkless, with 2–4 wedge-shaped lobes or leaflets.

Flowers: Bright yellow; saucer-shaped; petals inversely egg-shaped, 3.5–5 mm long, 3–5 mm wide; on short stalks; single or in few-flowered terminal clusters; June–August.

Fruit: In rounded or globe-like clusters; 1.2–1.8 cm in diameter; dry, hard, single-seeded (achene); style slender and hairy.

Habitat: Low areas; rich sites and damp thickets; open shores; wet clearings and roadside ditches; frequent.

Notes: Large-leaved avens' bright-yellow flowers and rounded terminal leaflet distinguish it from water avens (*Geum rivale*), which has purplish flowers and a more wedge-shaped terminal leaflet. Yellow avens (*G. aleppicum*) is a similar, yellow-flowering species; it has a widely egg- to wedge-shaped terminal leaflet.

Karen Legasy
(primary and inset)

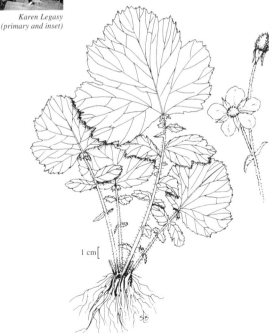

1 cm

Pea Family (Leguminosae)

General: Perennial; climbing or trailing stem 60–120 cm long, slender, weak and tufted; finely hairy or sometimes hairless.

Leaves: Alternate; nearly stalkless; branching, thread-like, twining tendril at tip; compound, 5–10 pairs of leaflets; leaflets linear to oblong with blunt to somewhat pointed and bristled tip; about 2.5 cm long; thin; margins and stipules toothless.

Flowers: Bluish-purple; pea-like; about 1.3 cm long; in elongated, 1-sided clusters of often 30 or more flowers that bend downward; clusters are from leaf axils and equal to or just exceeding the leaves; May–August.

Karen Legasy

Fruit: Pods; brownish; on short stalks; narrow and lance-shaped, flattened; 2–3 cm long, 5–7 mm wide.

Habitat: Roadsides, forest trails; fields; common.

Notes: You can recognize cow vetch by its dense, 1-sided flower clusters on long stalks and by its somewhat flat, brownish seed pods.

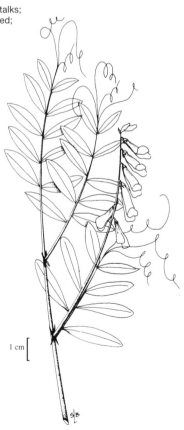

1 cm

Pea Family (Leguminosae)

General: Perennial; stem up to 1 m long, trailing or climbing by leaf tendrils; often tangled; hairless or with some appressed hairs.

Leaves: Alternate; nearly stalkless; branched, thread-like, twining tendril at tip; compound, 4–7 pairs of leaflets; leaflets egg-shaped to oblong with blunt or sometimes shallowly notched, with sharp, abrupt point (mucronate), rounded at base; 1.5–3.5 cm long, 0.6–1.4 cm wide; hairless to hairy; margins toothless; lateral veins prominent and rib-like on underside when dry; stipules sharply toothed.

Flowers: Bluish-purple; pea-like; 1.5–2 cm long; 3–9 in loose elongated clusters shorter than leaves; June–July.

Fruit: Pods; on short stalks; 2.5–3.5 cm long; hairless; 4–7 seeds slightly rounded and 4 mm long.

Habitat: Thickets along shores, forest openings; occasional.

Jim Pojar

Notes: Several *Vicia* species are reported to be toxic to humans and livestock. • Vetches are summer food for caribou. Ruffed grouse occasionally eat the plants.

1 cm

Pea Family (Leguminosae)

General: Perennial; from a slender, creeping underground stem (rhizome); stems 10–120 cm long, slender, angled, usually winged, mainly hairless, climbing.

Leaves: Alternate; on stalks; compound with 2–5 pairs of opposite leaflets; leaflets egg- to lance-shaped with pointed tip and rounded base, 2–8 cm long, 3–20 mm wide, firm; small, paired, leaf-like stipules at leaf bases slightly lance- to arrowhead-shaped.

Flowers: Purple to violet, reddish or pinkish; pea-like; 1–2.5 cm long; in clusters of 2–9 nearly level with or taller than leaves; June–September.

Fruit: Pods; 3.5–6 cm long; slightly hairy or hairless; stalkless.

Habitat: Moist or wet areas; open shores; marshes, damp meadows and thickets along rivers; occasional.

Notes: Wild pea's winged stem and purplish flowers distinguish it from pale vetchling (*Lathyrus ochroleucus*), which has wingless stems and white to yellowish-white flowers.
• Aboriginal peoples used wild pea root to lure beaver and other game to traps.

Brenda Chambers

] 1 cm

PALE VETCHLING ♦ *Lathyrus ochroleucus*
GESSE JAUNÂTRE

Pea Family (Leguminosae)

NWO FEC Photo

General: Perennial; 30–100 cm tall; rootstocks slender; hairless, slightly waxy; stem slender, angled, climbing or trailing.

Leaves: Alternate; on stalks; compound with 3–5 pairs of leaflets and a usually branched, thread-like tendril at tip; leaflets egg-shaped to widely oval with blunt tip and rounded base, 2.5–5 cm long; margins toothless; paired leaf-like stipules at leaf base are 1.5–3 cm long and slightly heart- to egg-shaped.

Flowers: White to yellowish-white; pea-like; 1–1.5 cm long; 5–10 in elongated clusters from leaf axils; June.

Fruit: Pods; hairless; 2.5–5 cm long; open August–September.

Habitat: Fresh to moist upland sites; rich conifer and hardwood mixedwood stands; roadsides and shorelines; disturbed areas, clearings and thickets; frequent.

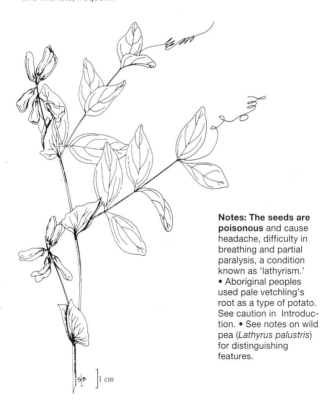

] 1 cm

Notes: The seeds are poisonous and cause headache, difficulty in breathing and partial paralysis, a condition known as 'lathyrism.' • Aboriginal peoples used pale vetchling's root as a type of potato. See caution in Introduction. • See notes on wild pea (*Lathyrus palustris*) for distinguishing features.

Pea Family (Leguminosae)

General: Perennial; stems numerous, slender, on ground or upward-growing, 7.5–60 cm long, with flat hairs or hairless; from a long root.

Leaves: Alternate; compound with 5 leaflets; on short stalks; leaflets egg-shaped or oblong with blunt to pointed tips, 0.6–1.7 cm long; stipules gland-like.

Flowers: Yellow; pea-like; about 1.3 cm long; in flat-topped terminal clusters of 3–12 flowers on stalks; June–September.

Fruit: Pods; slender; with several seeds; about 2.5 cm long.

Habitat: Roadsides; waste places and fields.

Notes: This plant gets its name from the pods' arrangement, which is said to resemble a bird's foot.

Karen Legasy

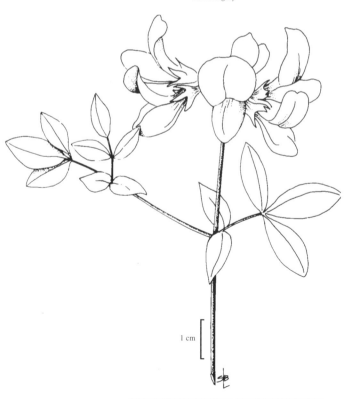

1 cm

WHITE SWEET CLOVER ♦ *Melilotus alba*
MÉLILOT BLANC

Pea Family (Leguminosae)

General: Annual; 90–240 cm tall; erect; branching; hairless or young branches and leaves sometimes finely hairy.

Leaves: Alternate; on stalks; compound; 3 leaflets, oblong, narrowed toward base and squared to rounded at tip, 1–2.5 cm long; margins toothed; leaves distantly spaced.

Flowers: White; pea-like; small, about 6 mm long; many and crowded in slender, elongated clusters up to 20 cm long; May–October.

Fruit: Pod; egg-shaped; turns black when ripe; hairless with raised veins on surface; 1- to 2-seeded.

Habitat: Roadsides; waste places and fields; extends into forest clearings; occasional to frequent.

Karen Legasy

Notes: Yellow sweet clover (*Melilotus officinalis*) is a similar species with yellow flowers, slightly wider leaflets and yellowish-brown pods that are not as strongly veined when ripe. Both species were introduced from Europe as forage crops, and are used as pasture crops to enrich soil with nitrogen.

1 cm

Pea Family (Leguminosae)

General: Annual; up to 45 cm tall; hairless to slightly hairy; erect to upward-growing; stem branched.

Leaves: Alternate; on short stalks only slightly longer than the lance-shaped stipules; compound, 3 leaflets; leaflets stalkless or equally short-stalked, oblong to egg-shaped, widest above middle, with blunt to notched tip and narrowed base, 10–15 mm long; margins finely toothed.

Flowers: Yellow, become brown with age; pea-like; small; in oblong to cylindrical, dense clusters 1–2 cm long, 1–1.5 cm thick and above leaves; June–September.

Fruit: Pods; egg-shaped, usually 1-seeded.

Habitat: Roadsides; fields and waste places; occasional.

Karen Legasy

Notes: You can distinguish hop-clover by its yellow flowers in oblong to cylindrical clusters and by its essentially stalkless leaflets. • Hop-clover is rich in protein and has historically been considered edible as cooked greens or in salads, but the leaves and flowers are apparently difficult to digest when raw. The seeds and flowers were reportedly ground into a flour. See caution in Introduction. • The woodchuck, ruffed grouse, snowshoe hare, meadow vole and American porcupine all eat clover foliage.

1 cm

ALSIKE CLOVER ♦ *Trifolium hybridum* ssp. *elegans*
TRÈFLE HYBRIDE

Pea Family (Leguminosae)

General: Perennial; 30–80 cm tall; mostly hairless; stem arched or bent to erect, hollow, soft and branched.

Leaves: Alternate; on long stalks; compound, 3 leaflets; leaflets on short stalks, oval to egg-shaped with narrow end toward base, 2.5–4 cm long and 2–3 cm wide; margins minutely toothed; pairs of small leaf-like stipules at base of leafstalks are egg- to lance-shaped with pointed tips.

Flowers: Pink to pinkish and whitish, become dull brown with age, pea-like, 8–11 mm long, on slender stalks; clustered in round heads 2–3.5 cm in diameter, on 2–9 cm long stalks from upper leaf axils; May–October.

Fruit: Pods with 2–4 green to black, lens-shaped seeds.

Habitat: Common along roadsides, in fields and waste areas; rare in forest openings and clearings.

MNR Photo

Notes: You can distinguish alsike clover by its long-stalked, pinkish flower clusters and its upward-growing stem. • Historically considered edible in salads or as a cooked green, it is apparently hard to digest when raw. Clover is rich in protein. The seeds and flower heads have been made into a flour that is apparently nutritious. See caution in Introduction.

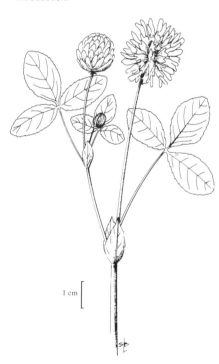

1 cm

Pea Family (Leguminosae)

General: Biennial or short-lived perennial; stems upward-growing, branched, 5–40 cm tall; usually hairy.

Leaves: Alternate; lower leaves on long stalks, upper leaves short-stalked to stalkless; compound with 3 (rarely 4) leaflets; leaflets on short stalks, oval to egg-shaped with narrow end toward base and a blunt or sometimes notched tip, 1–3 cm long and 0.5–1.5 cm wide; lighter, slightly V-shaped marking near middle; small leaf-like stipules at base of leafstalks are oval to egg-shaped, prominently veined.

Karen Legasy

Flowers: Reddish or rose to deep pink, rarely white; pea-like, about 1.3 cm long; in dense, rounded to egg-shaped clusters 1.2–3 cm long, stalkless or rarely on short stalks; May–September.

Fruit: Pods containing 1–2 seeds.

Habitat: Roadsides; fields, clearings and waste areas, lawns; has spread into remote clearings and along roadsides because of its use as fodder for logging horses; common.

Notes: Introduced from Europe, red clover is planted for hay and pasture in crop rotation. Bacteria in clover roots take nitrogen from the air, give it to the plant and increase the soil's fertility. See notes on white clover (*Trifolium repens*).

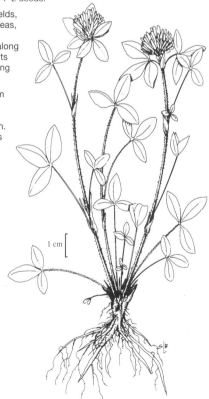

1 cm

WHITE CLOVER ♦ *Trifolium repens*
TRÈFLE RAMPANT

Pea Family (Leguminosae)

Karen Legasy

General: Perennial; stem 10–25 cm long, creeping, branching at base, often rooting where leaves join stem (nodes); hairless or with a few hairs.

Leaves: Alternate; on long stalks; compound, 3 (rarely 4) leaflets; leaflets egg-shaped with narrow end toward base and rounded and slightly notched tip, 0.5–2 cm long; lighter, slightly V-shaped marking near middle, margins toothed; small leaf-like stipules at base of leafstalk are egg- to lance-shaped with pointed tips.

Flowers: White to pinkish, turn brown with age; pea-like; 6–13 mm long; in rounded or globe-like clusters 1.5–3 cm in diameter and on long, leafless stalks from creeping stem; May–October.

Fruit: Pods with 3–4 round to kidney-shaped seeds.

Habitat: Common in fields, waste places, open areas and lawns; occasional along roadsides and in forest clearings.

Notes: You can recognize white clover by its creeping stem, white to pinkish flowers and leaflets with a V-shaped marking near the middle. White clover's creeping stem distinguishes it from alsike clover (*Trifolium hybridum* ssp. *elegans*) and red clover (*T. pratense*), which have upward-growing stems, and white clover's flowers are on long, leafless stalks. White clover is the typical clover of lawns—the one people examine hoping to find a 'lucky' four-leaf clover.

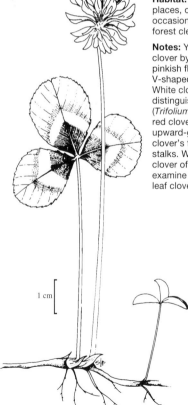

1 cm

Wood-Sorrel Family (Oxalidaceae)

General: Perennial; 7.5–15 cm tall; from pale, scaly underground stem (rhizome); creeping and low-growing; leaves clover-like.

Leaves: Basal; on stalks; compound; 3 stalkless leaflets widely heart-shaped at tip and narrowed base; 1.2–3 cm wide; surface shiny with a few hairs; margins hairy.

Flowers: Whitish to pinkish with deep-pink or red veins; 5 petals oblong and notched; solitary on leafless stem (scape) equal to or taller than leaves; about 2 cm wide; late June–early July.

Fruit: Capsule; cylindrical to awl-shaped; seeds with distinctive, white-crested, horizontal ridges.

Karen Legasy

Habitat: Moist to fresh, coarse-loamy to silty sites; transition tolerant hardwood and rich conifer and hardwood mixedwoods; occasional.

Notes: Some of common wood-sorrel's flowers are produced later in the season on curved stems at the base of the plant. These flowers do not open but produce seeds and capsules. The leaves close at night. • The sour-tasting leaves have historically been used in salads; however, it has been found that consuming large amounts may cause a calcium depletion in the body. The leaves were also used to brew a beverage. See caution in Introduction.

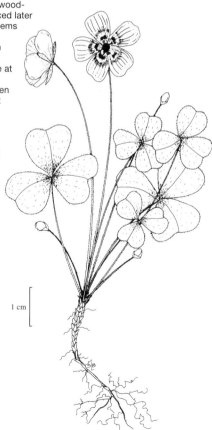

1 cm

HOOKED-SPUR VIOLET ♦ *Viola adunca*
VIOLETTE À ÉPERON CROCHU

Violet Family (Violaceae)

NWO FEC Photo

General: Perennial; up to 10 cm tall; underground stem (rhizome) woody and jagged; usually stemless at first, later develops slender, numerous and spreading stems; hairless to finely hairy.

Leaves: Basal, alternate on stem; leaves near base on long stalks, egg-shaped with slightly heart-shaped base and gradually narrowing to blunt tip; upper stem leaves narrower, on shorter stalks and less rounded at tips; margins finely scalloped; small, leaf-like stipules at axils deeply toothed.

Flowers: Purple to violet-blue; usually above leaves on stalks 3.5–10 cm long; lateral petals bearded; lip with fine, dark lines; spur long and often hooked or curved upward; 5–15 mm long; May–July.

Fruit: Capsules; small; rounded, seeds dark brown.

Habitat: Common in sandy and rocky forest openings; abundant in areas where sandy jack pine forests have been burned or cleared.

Notes: Hooked violet can be distinguished by its numerous spreading stems which have both basal and stem leaves. • The leaves and flowers have historically been used in salads. See caution in Introduction.

1 cm

Violet Family (Violaceae)

General: Perennial; flowering stalks 7.5–12.5 cm tall; rootstock stout and branching; more or less hairy except for earliest leaves.

Leaves: Basal; on slender, wiry stalks often purplish at base; simple; egg- to kidney-shaped with somewhat pointed but blunt tip and heart-shaped base; 3–7 cm wide; pale green, often purplish beneath; margins, veins and stalks are fringed with hairs; margins with 10–26 teeth.

Flowers: Deep violet to pale lilac; petals variable, 3 lowest bearded at base; 0.8–1.3 cm wide; solitary on leafless flowering stems; with a spur; May.

Fruit: Capsules; rounded; purple or sometimes green; 5–8 mm long; seeds dark brown.

Habitat: Damp, open forests; streambanks; shore thickets; occasional.

Notes: You can recognize northern blue violet by the fringe of hairs along its leaf margins.

Brenda Chambers

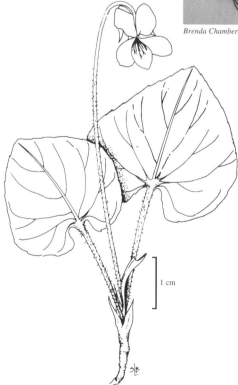

1 cm

SWEET WHITE VIOLET ♦ *Viola blanda*
VIOLETTE AGRÉABLE

Violet Family (Violaceae)

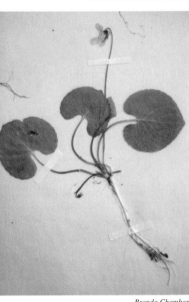

Brenda Chambers

General: Perennial; 7.5–12.5 cm tall; from underground stems and slender runners (stolons); leafstalks and leafless flower stems (scapes) hairless, usually tinged with red; flower stems taller than leaves.

Leaves: Basal; on stalks; simple; rounded with sharp, pointed tip and heart-shaped base, basal sinus narrow with lobes almost overlapping; up to 6.3 cm wide; dark green, hairless except for scattered, minute hairs on surface, shiny; margins toothed.

Flowers: White; 5 hairless petals, upper pair narrow and bent strongly backward, lateral petals and lower petal have brown-purple veins; about 1.3 cm wide; solitary on long, leafless slower stems; fragrant; with a spur; April–May.

Fruit: Capsules; purplish; egg-shaped; 4–6 mm long; seeds dark brown and minutely wrinkled.

Habitat: Rich and mainly deciduous forest areas.

Notes: Sweet white violet is very similar to northern white violet (*Viola macloskeyi* ssp. *pallens*), but you can distinguish sweet white violet by its reddish leafstalks and flower stems and its purplish seed capsules. This plant is also known as *V. incognita*.

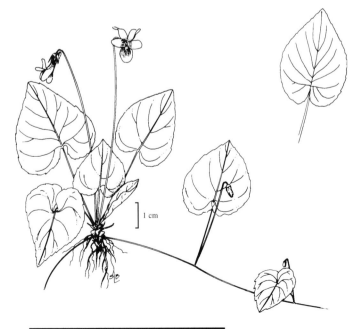

1 cm

Violet Family (Violaceae)

General: Perennial; 2.5–12.5 cm tall; slender, thread-like, rooting runners (stolons); leafstalks and flower stalks often red-dotted in summer and slightly hairy; flower stalks taller than leaves.

Leaves: Basal; on stalks; simple; blades widely egg-shaped to rounded or heart-shaped with blunt or rounded tips, 1–5 cm long and 1–5 cm wide; hairless; margins have low, rounded teeth.

Flowers: White; usually with purple veins on lower and lateral petals; upper petals widely egg-shaped; lateral petals usually have small tuft of hairs; fragrant; 7–10 mm long; with a spur; May.

Fruit: Capsules; green, rounded to cylindrical; seeds become black.

Habitat: Low, wet areas; forests, thickets, open areas; along streams or by springs; common.

MNR Photo

Notes: You can recognize northern white violet by the red dots that appear on its leafstalks and flower stalks during the summer. The flowers and leaves grow on separate basal stalks and the flowers are taller than the leaves. See notes on sweet white violet (*Viola blanda*).

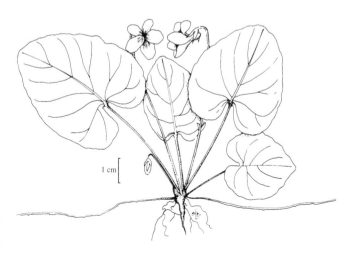

1 cm

KIDNEY-LEAVED VIOLET ♦ *Viola renifolia*
VIOLETTE RÉNIFORME

Violet Family (Violaceae)

Karen Legasy

General: Perennial; 2.5–10 cm tall; from underground stem (rhizome) that becomes scaly and stout with age; small, slender.

Leaves: Basal; on long stalks; simple; blades kidney-shaped to circular with a rounded or blunt tip and heart-shaped base; 1.5–8 cm wide; soft, white hairs on upper surface and underside of young leaves and on leafstalk; upper surface occasionally hairless; margins have broad, flat or rounded teeth.

Flowers: White with brownish-purple stripes or veins on the lower petals; 5 petals; on erect stalks usually shorter than leaves; short, rounded spur; May–June.

Fruit: Purplish capsule containing brown, round seeds; July–August.

Habitat: Wide variety of damp forest habitats; common.

Notes: The leaves and flowers have historically been considered edible. See caution in Introduction. The flowers have been used to scent teas, vinegars and perfumes. The roots were apparently used to induce vomiting. • Kidney-leaved violet can be recognized by its kidney-shaped leaves.

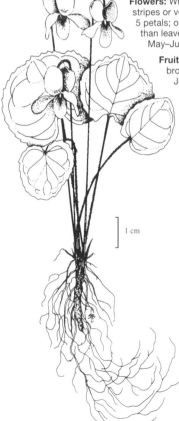

1 cm

Touch-me-not Family (Balsaminaceae)

General: Annual; 60–150 cm tall; hairless; stem semi-transparent, branched, soft and watery.

Leaves: Alternate; on slender stalks 1–10 cm long; simple; egg-shaped; 3–9 cm long; underside pale and with fine, whitish, waxy powder (glaucous); thin; margins coarsely toothed, teeth often end in a sharp point.

Flowers: Orange with crimson or reddish-brown spots; sac cone-shaped, longer than wide with a slender, hooked tip (spur); 3 petals, lower petals lobed; about 2.5 cm long; horizontal, hanging on slender stalks; July–October.

Karen Legasy

Fruit: Capsule; fragile; swollen; bursts at maturity to eject seeds.

Habitat: Wet humus in low forest areas, shore thickets; marsh edges; wet, shaded ditches; common.

Notes: Spotted touch-me-not was formerly known as *Impatiens biflora* and is also commonly known as 'spotted jewelweed.'
• Ruffed grouse eat the seeds.

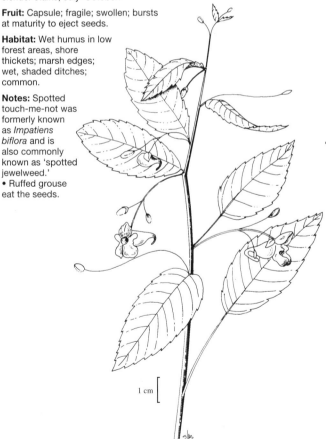

1 cm

PALE CORYDALIS ♦ *Corydalis sempervirens*
CORYDALE TOUJOURS VERTE

Poppy Family (Papaveraceae)

Brenda Chambers

General: Annual or biennial; 30–60 cm tall; erect or upward-growing, freely branching; pale green, covered with fine, whitish, waxy powder (glaucous); hairless; from taproot; soft and watery.

Leaves: Alternate; lower leaves on short stalks, upper leaves nearly stalkless; compound with leaflets in opposite pairs; leaflets again divided into 3-lobed, inversely egg- or wedge-shaped segments, tips blunt or rounded and often abruptly pointed (mucronate), about 1.3 cm long; margins toothed or toothless.

Flowers: Pink with yellow tips; tubular, sac-like with a rounded spur; 1.3 cm long; in loose clusters at branch ends; May–September.

Fruit: Capsules, pod-like, narrowly linear and erect; 3–5 cm long, 1.5–2 mm wide, knobby when mature; seeds black, shiny, with raised 'bumps' (tubercles).

Habitat: Rock outcrops, disturbed soils, burn areas; roadsides; frequent.

Notes: Pale corydalis is also called *Capnoides sempervirens*. • The bitter roots were historically used in a remedy for parasitic intestinal worms and to promote menstrual discharge. See caution in Introduction.

1 cm

St. John's-wort Family (Guttiferae)

General: Perennial; 30–90 cm tall; stems 2-edged, tough, many-branched and usually clustered from flattened base.

Leaves: Opposite; stalkless; simple; oblong or linear with blunt tip; 2.5–5 cm long on main axis, half as long on branches; more or less black-dotted.

Flowers: Yellow; 5 petals with black dots on margins; 2–2.5 cm wide; June–September.

Fruit: Capsules; brown; egg-shaped; pointed; 3-celled and glandular; conspicuous network of raised veins and pits.

Habitat: Dry roadsides; fields, waste places; occasional.

Notes: The glandular dots on this plant's leaves contain a **phototoxin** which can make some people susceptible to sunburn and dermatitis.
• St. John's-wort is said to bloom on June 24th, the Feast of St. John.
• This plant was introduced from Europe and is often a troublesome weed.

Karen Legasy

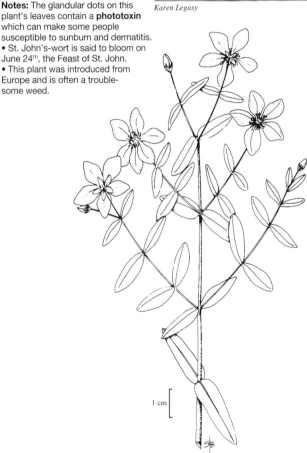

1 cm

Geranium Family (Geraniaceae)

Karen Legasy

General: Annual or biennial; 15–60 cm tall; usually much-branched, may be unbranched; stem hairy and spreading.

Leaves: On slender stalks; deeply cut into 5 wedge-shaped segments further cut into oblong lobes; generally rounded, 2–7 cm wide; hairy along veins.

Flowers: Pinkish to purplish; 2 per stalk; petals notched, 5–7 mm long; July–September.

Fruit: Beaked, about 1.5–2.3 cm long, glandular-hairy, splitting open from below with 5 segments curling upward; seeds thick, cylindrical and clearly veined (reticulate).

Habitat: Disturbed areas, clearings, open woods and roadsides; often locally abundant following fire; frequent.

Notes: Bicknell's cranesbill grows abundantly for a few years after a wildfire or a clearcut followed by slash burning. • The roots were used in a gargle for canker sores in the mouth and throat. The roots were also used in remedies for diarrhea and hemorrhoids. See caution in Introduction. • The eastern chipmunk eats the seeds.

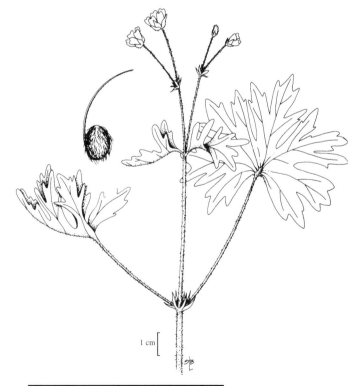

1 cm

Evening-primrose Family (Onagraceae)

General: Biennial; 0.5–1.5 m high; stem erect, usually stout, unbranched and 'wand-like' or branched, more or less hairy, rarely hairless, green to purple-tinged; from stout taproot.

Leaves: Alternate, forming a leafy rosette in the first year; stalkless or lowest short-stalked; simple; lance-shaped to oblong with pointed tip and narrowed base; 10–20 cm long; margins slightly toothed or toothless.

Flowers: Yellow; large; in a leafy terminal spike; 4 sepals form a tube at first but eventually separate and bend back; 4 petals 1.2–2.5 cm long; June–September.

Fruit: Capsules; oblong and narrowed toward top; hairy; erect; about 2.5 cm long.

Habitat: Clearings; roadsides; fields.

Notes: Evening primrose is so-named because its flowers open in the evening. • The roots have historically been considered edible. See caution in Introduction.

Karen Legasy

1 cm

FIREWEED ♦ *Epilobium angustifolium*
ÉPILOBE À FEUILLES ÉTROITES

Evening-primrose Family (Onagraceae)

General: Perennial; 10–200 cm tall; erect; stem usually unbranched with upper part often purplish.

Leaves: Alternate; on very short stalks; simple; narrowly lance-shaped with pointed tips, narrowed at base; 3–20 cm long; upper surface green, underside paler with a network of veins; margins toothless to slightly toothed; numerous.

Flowers: Deep pink, purplish or magenta, rarely white; 4 petals; about 2.5 cm wide; in elongated terminal clusters; numerous; late July–August.

Fruit: Linear capsules; green to red or purplish; 3–7 cm long; split open to release numerous 1–1.3 mm, spindle-shaped seeds with fluffy, white tufts of soft hairs 9–14 mm long.

Habitat: All moisture regimes, soil textures and stand types, disturbed areas, open forests, fields; riverbanks, common along roadsides; locally abundant following fire.

Brenda Chambers

Notes: The silky hairs from fireweed seeds were mixed with cotton or fur to make stockings, and the stem pith was used to make an ale. Aboriginal peoples used the roots and leaves to make a variety of poultices for bruises, swellings and sores. See caution in Introduction.
• Moose occasionally browse fireweed, and small mammals eat its seeds.

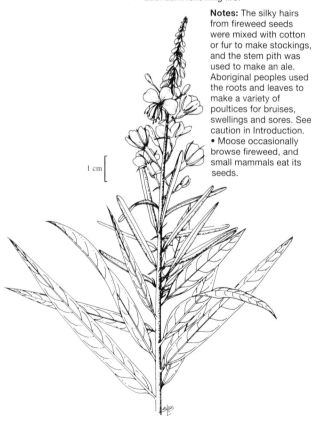

1 cm

Evening-primrose Family (Onagraceae)

General: Perennial; 30–90 cm tall; erect; usually much-branched.

Leaves: Alternate; stalkless to short-stalked; simple; lance- to egg-shaped, bluntish or sometimes pointed tip; usually up to 6 cm long; margins sparingly and minutely toothed.

Flowers: Pink or white; 5–15 mm wide, 4–6 mm long; usually nodding at first; sepals with glandular hairs; July–September.

Fruit: Linear capsules; with glandular hairs; 4–8 cm long, on stalks 6–15 mm long; seeds about 1 mm long, inversely egg-shaped with abrupt, short beak and tuft of tawny, silky hairs 3.5–6.5 mm long.

Habitat: Moist to wet areas.

Notes: Northern willow-herb was formerly known as *Epilobium adenocaulon* and *E. leptocarpum*.

BC MOF / Frank Boas

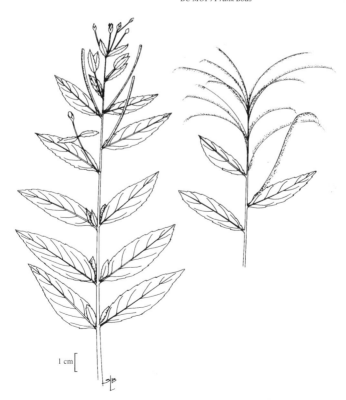

1 cm

MARSH WILLOW-HERB ♦ *Epilobium palustre*
ÉPILOBE PALUSTRE

Evening-primrose Family (Onagraceae)

General: Perennial; 15–45 cm tall; from underground shoots and rooting runners (stolons); erect or reclining with upward-growing tip; slender; usually unbranched; greyish-white above with short hairs.

Leaves: Opposite (mostly); stalkless; oblong to linear with blunt tip and narrowed base; 2.5–6.3 cm long, 0.3–0.7 cm wide; hairless but with minute hairs along veins and margins; margins toothless to obscurely toothed and often rolled downward; erect or upward-growing; distinctly veined.

Flowers: Pink or whitish; petals deeply notched; 4–8 mm long; a few near the top; nodding at first; July–August.

Fruit: Capsules; 3–9 cm long, on stalks 1–3 cm long; seeds narrowly ovoid, 1.5–2 mm long with a 5–7 mm long tuft of soft, white hairs.

Habitat: Bogs and mossy, open areas; roadside ditches in wet forests; apparently rare.

Notes: Marsh willow-herb's common name indicates its preferred growth habitat—soft, wet marsh areas with grasses or cattails.

Linda Kershaw

1 cm

Evening-primrose Family (Onagraceae)

General: Perennial; 30–90 cm tall; from underground shoots and thread-like runners; erect and usually much-branched; densely hairy with whitish, somewhat spreading hairs.

Leaves: Alternate or opposite; stalkless; simple; short, lance-shaped with blunt or bluntish tip; 2–5 cm long, 0.4–0.9 cm wide; covered with greyish velvet; upward-growing; margins mostly toothless; veins evident; tufts of smaller leaves in leaf axils.

Flowers: Pink or whitish; about 0.4 cm wide; in axils of upper leaves; July–September.

Fruit: Linear capsules; covered with fine, greyish-white hairs; 3.5–6 cm long, nearly 2 mm thick; on short stalks.

Habitat: Bogs and swamps; wet, silty shores; open thickets and sedge marshes; common.

Notes: Downy willow-herb may be confused with marsh willow-herb (*Epilobium palustre*). Downy willow-herb is up to twice as large as, and is more densely hairy than, marsh willow-herb. Its flower clusters often have glandular hairs, which are not often found in marsh willow-herb.

Brenda Chambers

1 cm

Evening-primrose Family (Onagraceae)

Karen Legasy

General: Perennial; 10–25 cm tall; from an underground stem or rootstock (rhizome); weak-stemmed and soft.

Leaves: Opposite; on narrowly winged stalks; simple; egg- to heart-shaped, pointed at tip; 1–6.5 cm long; upper surface hairless to short-haired, underside more prominently hairy; margins coarsely toothed; thin.

Flowers: White; small, about 2 mm long; 2 deeply lobed petals; in sparse, elongated terminal clusters; flower stalks 5–6 mm long; July–September.

Fruit: Small, club- or pear-shaped capsules about 2 mm long; covered with soft, hooked hairs.

Habitat: Wet organic to moist, coarse-loamy upland sites; conifer and hardwood mixedwoods and yellow birch stands; occasional.

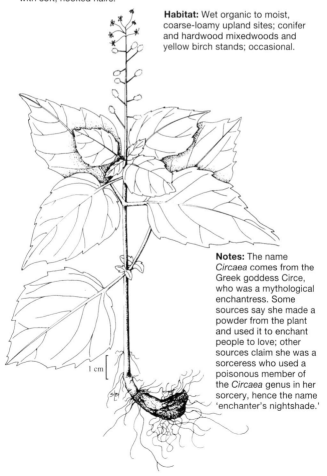

1 cm

Notes: The name *Circaea* comes from the Greek goddess Circe, who was a mythological enchantress. Some sources say she made a powder from the plant and used it to enchant people to love; other sources claim she was a sorceress who used a poisonous member of the *Circaea* genus in her sorcery, hence the name 'enchanter's nightshade.'

Ginseng Family (Araliaceae)

General: Perennial; up to 50 cm tall; stem short (barely reaches soil surface); single leaf taller than flower stalk; from extensive, creeping underground stems (rhizomes).

Leaves: Basal; on a long stalk; single; twice compound; 3 sections, each with 3–5 leaflets; leaflets egg-shaped or oval, tips pointed, 5–12.5 cm long; margins finely toothed.

Flowers: Greenish-white; small;

Karen Legasy

5 petals about 2.5 mm long; numerous; usually in 3 round clusters at top of leafless stalk.

Fruit: Rounded, purplish-black berries 6–8 mm long; in clusters; ripen July–August.

Habitat: All moisture regimes, soil and stand types; shady to open areas; abundant.

Notes: During wars and on hunting excursions, aboriginal peoples subsisted on the nutritious rhizomes, which were also used in remedies for nosebleeds, wounds and sores. The berries were used to make wine, and to add flavour to a beer made from the rhizomes. See caution in Introduction.

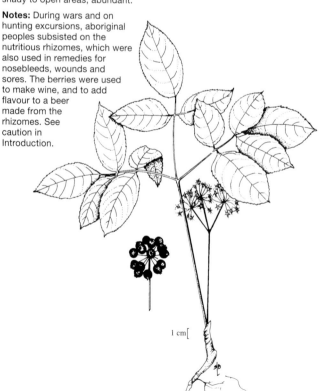

1 cm[

9

BRISTLY SARSAPARILLA ♦ *Aralia hispida*
ARALIE HISPIDE

Ginseng Family (Araliaceae)

General: Perennial; 20–90 cm tall; erect; leafy; stem has sharp, slender spines near base; from stout underground stem (rhizome).

Leaves: Alternate; several on stalks shorter than blades; compound, 3 sections with 3–5 leaflets each; leaflets oblong to egg-shaped with pointed tips; 2.5–5 cm long; hairless or with hairs on underside along veins; margins sharply toothed.

Flowers: Greenish-white; in 2–10 rounded terminal clusters on slender stalks.

Fruit: Dark-purple, round berries; 5-lobed when dry.

Habitat: Sandy or rocky areas; clearings or open forests; frequent.

Notes: Bristly sarsaparilla is also commonly known as 'dwarf-elder' or 'wild elder.' • The roots and bark were historically used in a remedy for kidney and urinary problems. See caution in Introduction.

Brenda Chambers

] 1 cm

Parsley Family (Umbelliferae)

General: Perennial; large, 1.2–2.7 m high; from a thick taproot or cluster of fibrous roots; stout, hairy or woolly; single stem ridged, often 5 cm thick at base, hollow; rank-smelling.

Leaves: Alternate; stalks inflated and winged, with a dilated sheath at base; widely oval, compound; 3 maple-leaf-like leaflets; 7.5–15 cm wide; thin, very hairy on underside; margins lobed and coarsely toothed.

Flowers: White, often purple-tinged; about 1.3 mm wide; petals notched; numerous in flat-topped, umbrella-like, compound terminal clusters 10–20 cm wide, 1–4 smaller clusters from side shoots on main stem; June–August.

Fruit: Widely oval to heart-shaped; flat; about 10 mm long and nearly as wide; finely hairy; 1-seeded.

Habitat: Moist areas; roadsides and streambanks; clearings and open forests, ditches; damp, open shores; frequent.

Karen Legasy

Notes: Caution: Similar-looking plants such as water hemlock are extremely poisonous. • The stem and leafstalks have historically been considered an edible green. Aboriginal peoples ate cow parsnip. The taste is apparently similar to celery but the texture is more rhubarb-like. See caution in Introduction.
• The American black bear eats cow parsnip.

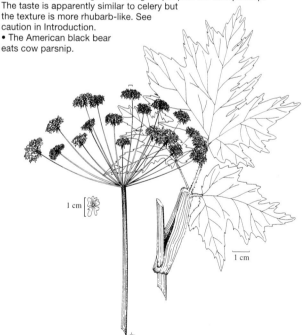

1 cm

1 cm

Parsley Family (Umbelliferae)

General: Perennial; 60–180 cm tall; stem base very short and erect, roots fibrous; stem ridged, stout, hollow, branchless and mostly branched near top.

Leaves: Alternate and basal; on stalks; compound; 5–17 leaflets linear to lance-shaped or lance-oblong, 3–15 cm long; margins sharply toothed; submerged leaves very finely dissected; uppermost leaves smaller.

Flowers: Dull white; tiny; in umbrella-like compound clusters 3–12 cm wide; stalks in clusters prominently ridged; July–September.

Karen Legasy

Fruit: Oval to egg-shaped; tiny, 2.5–3 mm long and nearly as wide; with prominent ribs.

Habitat: Wet areas; wet meadows, swamps, wet, open thickets; shorelines; shallow water; frequent.

Notes: Water parsnip is also known as 'wild carrot.' The carrot-like roots have historically been considered edible, but **it is best not to eat any part of water parsnip because of its resemblance to the poisonous water hemlock.** See caution in Introduction. • Animals and birds are not known to use water parsnip.

Karen Legasy

] 1 cm

Buckbean Family (Menyanthaceae)

General: Perennial; up to 30 cm tall; from thick, spongy, scaly and submerged rootstocks scarred by bases of former leafstalks; flowering stems upward-growing to erect.

Leaves: Alternate; crowded near base of flowering stem; stalks 10–30 cm long and sheathing at base; compound, divided into 3 leaflets; leaflets oblong or inversely egg-shaped with blunt tip and narrowed, stalkless base, 3–8 cm long; margins toothless.

Flowers: White, usually with a purplish or pinkish tinge; short, funnel-shaped with 5 spreading lobes; lobes covered with long, white hairs on inner surface; 1–1.3 cm long; stalks 5–15 mm long; few to many in dense terminal clusters; May–July.

Bill Crins

Fruit: Capsules; egg-shaped with blunt tip, irregularly rupturing at maturity; about 1 cm long; seeds flattened, egg-shaped, smooth, shiny and brown.

Habitat: Fens; shallow marsh water; wet, mucky shores; occasional.

Notes: Buckbean flowers have a foul odour. • The roots were historically used in a tonic which, when taken in small doses, was said to add vigour to the stomach and strengthen digestion, but when taken in large doses apparently caused vomiting. See caution in Introduction. The entire plant is said to be bitter.

1 cm

BUNCHBERRY ♦ *Cornus canadensis*
QUATRE-TEMPS

Dogwood Family (Cornaceae)

Karen Legasy

General: Perennial; 10–20 cm tall; stem erect; often growing in large patches; from creeping underground stems (rhizomes).

Leaves: Opposite, but appearing whorled; essentially stalkless; simple; egg-shaped to oblong, taper to point at tip and base; 2–9 cm long; 4–6 at top of stem; margins toothless; 7–9 prominent major veins parallel to leaf margin; normally 1–2 pairs of small leaves on stem below main leaves.

Flowers: In a tight cluster surrounded by 4 white, 1–2 cm long, petal-like bracts (the inflorescence resembles a flower); greenish or purplish, tiny; June–July.

Fruit: Bright-scarlet, round berries; single-seeded, pulpy; in clusters; ripen July–August.

Habitat: All moisture regimes, soil textures and stand types.

Notes: The berries are apparently not very palatable, although they have been considered edible. The plant was used in a cold remedy, and its roots were used in a colic remedy. See caution in Introduction.
• Songbirds such as the veery and Philadelphia vireo eat bunchberries, as do ruffed and spruce grouse and the rock vole.

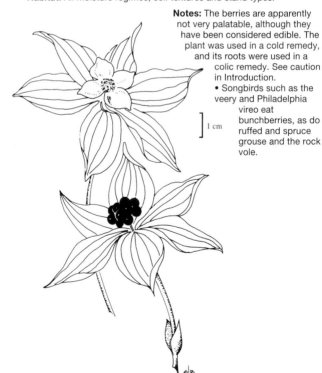

1 cm

Primrose Family (Primulaceae)

General: Perennial; less than 25 cm tall; erect; stem single, unbranched; from slender underground stems (rhizomes).

Leaves: 5–10 in single terminal whorl; stalkless; simple; lance-shaped, tapering to slender point at tip and base; 4.5–10 cm long; hairless, shiny; margins toothless; veins prominent; tiny, scale-like leaf or leaves on stem below whorl.

MNR Photo

Flowers: White; star-shaped; 10–12 mm across; 1–3 with 7 petals; stalks long, slender, growing from centre of leaf whorl; May–June.

Fruit: Round capsule with tiny, black seeds; July.

Habitat: All moisture regimes, soil and stand types; abundant.

Notes: Aboriginal peoples included starflower root in a smoke-making mixture used for attracting deer to hunters.

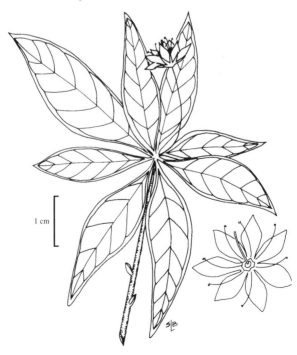

1 cm

s|B

ONE-FLOWERED WINTERGREEN ♦ *Moneses uniflora*
MONÉSÈS UNIFLORE

Wintergreen Family (Pyrolaceae)

Karen Legasy

General: Perennial; 3–13 cm tall; from slender underground stem (rhizome); stem has 1–3 pairs or whorls of leaves near its base, leafless above except for 1–2 small, scale-like leaves (bracts).

Leaves: In a basal rosette or whorls of 3 near stem base; on short stalks; simple; round to inversely egg-shaped, tip blunt to rounded, base narrowed to rounded or slightly heart-shaped; 1–3 cm long; margins toothed or nearly toothless; thin; veiny.

Flowers: Waxy, white to rarely pinkish; 5 petals; solitary, terminal, nodding; fragrant; 1–2 cm wide; July–August.

Fruit: Capsules; round (globe-like); 6–8 mm across; brown; erect; August.

Habitat: All moisture regimes and soil types; conifer and hardwood mixedwood stands; occasional.

Notes: One-flowered wintergreen was historically used in a tea to remedy such ailments as diarrhea, cancer, smallpox and sore throat; the tea was also believed to bring power and good luck. See caution in Introduction.

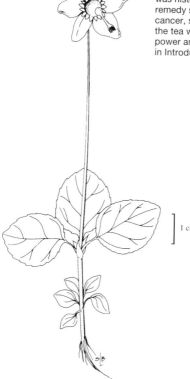

1 cm

Wintergreen Family (Pyrolaceae)

General: Perennial; 5–25 cm tall; from slender, creeping underground stem (rhizome); flowering stem often woody and leafy toward base and has scattered, scale-like leaves (bracts).

Leaves: Alternate, on lower part of stem but not in a basal rosette; on stalks; simple; blades egg-shaped to oval or nearly round, usually pointed at tip and rounded to narrowed at base, 1.5–3 cm long; margins wavy to finely toothed; mainly thin.

Flowers: Whitish to greenish; bell-shaped with 5 petals; about 6 mm wide; nodding on short stalks; style straight, 3–4 mm and protruding; 6–20 flowers in 1-sided, elongated, erect to drooping terminal cluster; July–August.

Fruit: Capsules; round, style persisting; 3–5 mm wide.

Habitat: All moisture regimes, soil and stand types.

Notes: One-sided pyrola was formerly known as *Pyrola secunda*. Its 1-sided flower cluster helps to distinguish this pyrola from others.

Brenda Chambers

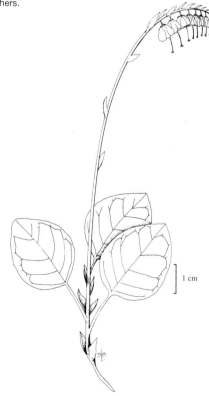

1 cm

GREENISH-FLOWERED PYROLA ♦ *Pyrola chlorantha*
PYROLE À FEUILLES VERDÂTRES

Wintergreen Family (Pyrolaceae)

Brenda Chambers

General: Perennial; 7–30 cm tall; from creeping underground stem (rhizome); single flowering stem leafless or rarely has 1–2 small, scale-like bracts.

Leaves: In a basal rosette; stalks longer than blades; simple; blades rounded or widely oval, usually blunt or rounded at both ends, base occasionally narrowed, 1–3 cm long, 1.5–3.5 cm wide; leathery, dull; margins have small, obscure and rounded teeth; numerous.

Flowers: Greenish-white (white with green veins); 5 petals, 5–7 mm long; style downward-bent with upturned tip and protruding; 2–13 in loose, cylindrical, elongated terminal cluster; on short stalks, nodding; July–August.

Fruit: Capsules; nodding; 5.5–9 mm long; style persisting and 4–7 mm long.

Habitat: Wet organic to dry, sandy upland sites; black spruce and conifer and hardwood mixedwood stands; scarce.

Notes: You can distinguish greenish-flowered pyrola by its greenish-white flowers with protruding styles and its long-stalked, dull, leathery leaves. This plant is also called *Pyrola virens*. • The leaves contain acids and have historically been used to treat skin sores. See caution in Introduction. • The genus name *Pyrola* is said to be derived from the Latin word *pyrus* ('pear').

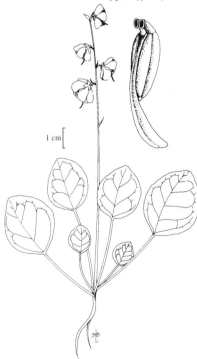

1 cm

Wintergreen Family (Pyrolaceae)

General: Perennial; 12–30 cm tall; from a creeping underground stem (rhizome); single flowering stem leafless except for 1–2 small, scale-like bracts.

Leaves: Basal rosette; on stalks; simple; blade widely oval to oblong or egg-shaped with narrow end toward base and extending slightly down leafstalk, rounded or bluntly pointed at tip, 2–8 cm long, normally longer than leafstalk; thin; dark green, dull; margins wavy or with small, rounded teeth.

Flowers: Greenish-white or creamy; 5 spreading petals are egg-shaped with narrow end toward base; nodding, on short stalks; about 16 mm wide; style long, protruding and bent; 3–21 flowers in loose, cylindrical, elongated terminal cluster; July–August.

Fruit: Capsule; 5 chambers or sections, style persisting; August.

Habitat: Wet organic to fresh, sandy upland sites; black spruce and hardwood mixedwoods; frequent.

Notes: You can recognize shinleaf by its creamy-coloured flowers and its dull, thin leaf blades that are usually longer than their stalks and extend slightly down them.
• Aboriginal peoples used the roots in a remedy for weakness and back ailments. See caution in Introduction.

Brenda Chambers

1 cm

LESSER PYROLA ◆ *Pyrola minor*
PYROLE MINEURE

Wintergreen Family (Pyrolaceae)

Ray Demey

General: Perennial; 5–26 cm tall; from slender underground stem (rhizomes); single flowering stem leafless or with 1–2 scale-like bracts.

Leaves: In a basal rosette or slightly scattered; on stalks; simple; blades widely oval to rounded with blunt to slightly pointed tip and slightly heart-shaped or narrowed to rounded base, 1–4.5 cm long, shorter than or equal to leafstalk; thin, dull, dark green; margins have small, rounded teeth.

Flowers: White to pinkish; petals 3–5 mm long; styles short, straight and do not protrude; 6–17 in loose, cylindrical or elongated terminal clusters 1.3–7 cm long; nodding; June–August.

Fruit: Capsules; rounded; styles short and persisting.

Habitat: Moist coniferous, mossy or mixedwood forests; humus; frequent.

Notes: Lesser pyrola is the only pyrola that does not have a style protruding from its flowers. • The leaves have historically been used in a salve or poultice for sores and wounds. See caution in Introduction.

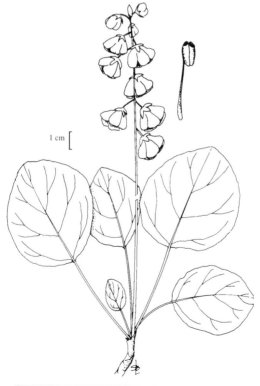

1 cm

Wintergreen Family (Pyrolaceae)

General: Perennial; 10–30 cm tall; from extensively creeping underground stem (rhizome); flowering stem leafless except for 1–3 small, scale-like bracts.

Leaves: In a basal rosette; narrowly margined stalks longer than blades; simple; blades kidney- to heart-shaped or rounded with blunt tip, equal to or greater in width than length, 2–6.5 cm long; shiny, leathery; margins wavy or with rounded teeth.

Flowers: Pink to pale purple; 5 petals; individuals nodding, on short stalks, style protruding; 4–22 in loose, cylindrical, elongated terminal clusters 3–20 cm long; July–August.

Fruit: Capsule; rounded with persisting style; nodding; August.

Habitat: Wet organic to fresh, sandy upland sites; conifer to hardwood mixedwoods and transition tolerant hardwood stands; occasional.

Karen Legasy

Notes: You can distinguish pink pyrola by its purplish to pinkish flowers (the flowers of other pyrolas are whitish), and by its shiny, leathery leaves that are usually shorter than their stalks. • Aboriginal peoples used the leaves in remedies for a variety of ailments. See caution in Introduction.

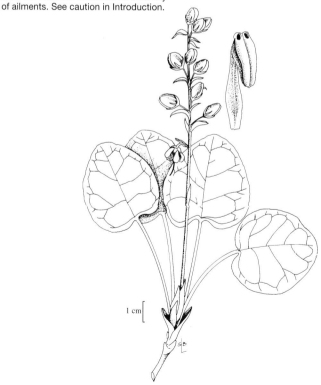

1 cm

ROUND-LEAVED PYROLA ♦ *Pyrola americana*
PYROLE À FEUILLES RONDES

Wintergreen Family (Pyrolaceae)

MNR Photo

General: Perennial; 10–30 cm tall; from creeping underground stem (rhizome); single flowering stem leafless except for 1–7 brownish, scale-like bracts.

Leaves: In a basal rosette; on stalks; simple; blades rounded, 1.8–5 cm long; thick, leathery and shiny; margins wavy or with small, rounded teeth; leafstalk winged.

Flowers: Creamy to white; individuals on stalks, nodding, with protruding, downward-arching styles; petals 5–7 mm long and 4–6 mm wide, thick, firm and only scarcely veiny; 3–13 in loose, cylindrical, elongated terminal clusters; fragrant; July–August.

Fruit: Capsules; nodding; style persisting.

Habitat: Moist areas; sphagnum bogs and gravelly to sandy thickets.

Notes: You can recognize round-leaved pyrola by its rounded leaves and its winged leafstalk with the leaf base running slightly down it. • Round-leaved pyrola was historically used to wash tumours and cancerous sores. The leaves were also used on wounds and bruises to help reduce pain. See caution in Introduction.

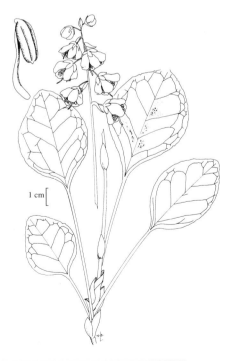

1 cm

Indian-pipe Family (Monotropaceae)

General: Perennial, 10–40 cm tall; from fleshy roots; hairy or downy; brownish-orange to yellowish, sometimes red, turns black when dried; fleshy; unbranched.

Leaves: Alternate; simple, scale-like; small, up to 1.5 cm long; thick; more crowded toward stem base; same colour as stem.

Flowers: Brownish-orange to yellowish, same colour as stem; 4 petals on side flowers, 5 petals on terminal flower; drooping when young, erect at maturity; about 1.3 cm long; many in dense terminal cluster; June–November.

MNR Photo

Fruit: Capsule; egg-shaped to rounded; turns brown and splits open when dry; erect.

Habitat: Humus of coniferous forest soils; uncommon.

Notes: Also known as *Monotropa hypopitys*. • Pinesap gets its nourishment from fungi associated with the roots of neighbouring trees. It is also saprophytic—it obtains nutrition from decayed organic matter.

1 cm

INDIAN PIPE ♦ *Monotropa uniflora*
MONOTROPE UNIFLORE

Indian-pipe Family (Monotropaceae)

Brenda Chambers

General: Hairless; waxy; white or rarely pinkish, turns black when dry; 5–30 cm tall; roots brittle, in matted mass; stems unbranched.

Leaves: Alternate; lance-shaped to oval; scale-like; often overlap; up to 10 mm long.

Flowers: White; solitary; terminal; urn- or bell-shaped; nodding at first, become erect as fruiting capsule matures; 4–5 petals; late July–September.

Fruit: Capsule; erect; brown; splits open when mature; often stays on stem through winter.

Habitat: Fresh to moist, medium- to coarse-loamy sites; transition tolerant hardwood stands; occasional in all other stand types.

Notes: Indian pipe gets its nourishment through fungal connections from its roots to those of nearby trees. • The root was historically used as a remedy for epileptic seizures. Aboriginal peoples used the plant in a remedy to soothe and heal sore eyes. See caution in Introduction. • Indian pipe is also referred to as 'corpse plant' because of its colour, and 'ice plant' because if it is rubbed, it appears to melt like ice.

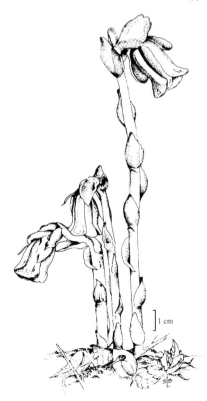

]1 cm

Mint Family (Labiatae)

General: Perennial; 10–40 cm tall; from runners (stolons) and short, fleshy tuber just below soil; stem squared.

Leaves: Opposite; stalkless or nearly so; simple; lance-shaped to slightly oblong, tapered at both ends; 2–11 cm long, 0.5–3.5 cm wide; light green; margins coarsely toothed.

Flowers: White; tiny, about 3 mm long; in dense clusters in leaf axils; calyx lobes broad-triangular.

Fruit: Nutlets; smooth with thicker margins, squared top and narrowed base.

Brenda Chambers

Habitat: Low ground; silty shores; marshes and wet areas; frequent.

Notes: Northern bugle-weed belongs to the mint family and resembles field mint (*Mentha arvensis*), but it does not have a mint fragrance. Cut-leaved water horehound (*Lycopus americanus*) is a similiar species that has deeply and sharply lobed leaf margins.

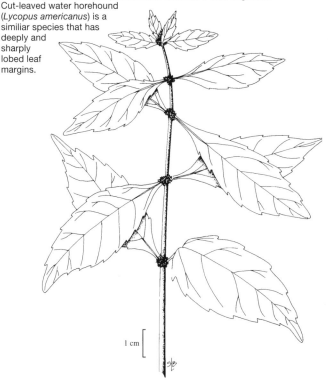

1 cm

Mint Family (Labiatae)

General: Perennial; 15–80 cm tall; stem square, erect, unbranched or branched, slender; downward-pointing hairs on angles, hairy or hairless on sides; aromatic, with a distinctive mint scent.

Leaves: Opposite; on stalks; simple; blades egg- to lance-shaped or oblong, tips of lower leaves pointed to blunt, base rounded; 3–7 cm long but smaller near top; margins toothed.

Flowers: Pale lilac to purplish, pinkish and sometimes white; bell-shaped; tiny, about 6 mm long and 3 mm wide; in dense, round clusters at leaf axils; July–September.

Karen Legasy

Fruit: Nutlet; egg-shaped; smooth.

Habitat: Moist to wet areas; shorelines; wet forest openings and damp deciduous forests; common.

Notes: You can recognize the mints by their strong minty aroma. Field mint may be confused with northern bugle-weed (*Lycopus uniflora*), but northern bugle-weed does not smell like a mint. • The leaves have historically been used to flavour beverages, jellies and sauces. Aboriginal peoples used the leaves or top of the plant in a fever remedy. See caution in Introduction.

Karen Legasy

1 cm

Mint Family (Labiatae)

General: Perennial; 30–50 cm tall; finely hairy to hairless; stems erect, square and usually branched.

Leaves: Opposite; on short stalks or upper leaves stalkless; simple; oblong to lance-shaped with pointed tip and slightly heart-shaped to rounded base; 3–5 cm long, upper leaves much smaller; thin; margins toothed, sometimes toothless on upper leaves.

Flowers: Blue; tubular, slender, slightly wider at tip, gradually tapering to slender base; 2 lips; about 1.5–2.5 cm long; 2 sepals at flower base form short tube; upper bract-like sepal with a conspicuous bump; in pairs from leaf axils; July–August.

Fruit: Nutlets; rounded to flattish, covered with minute bumps.

Habitat: Moist to wet areas; swamps, marshes, clearings, ditches and wet shorelines; frequent.

Karen Legasy

Notes: Marsh skullcap is a member of the mint family, but it does not have a mint fragrance. • Skullcaps were historically used in remedies for nervous disorders, hysteria, convulsions and cases of severe hiccupping. See caution in Introduction.

1 cm

HEAL-ALL ♦ *Prunella vulgaris*
PRUNELLE VULGAIRE

Mint Family (Labiatae)

General: Perennial; 15–30 cm tall; stems square, hairy or almost hairless, slender, trailing to upward-growing or erect, usually unbranched but sometimes branched, from running under-ground stems (rhizomes).

Leaves: Opposite; stalked; simple; egg-shaped to oblong with blunt to slightly pointed tip and usually narrowed base; 2–5 cm long; margins slightly toothed or toothless.

Flowers: Purple; 2-lipped, upper lip arched, lower lip 3-lobed, drooping; 1.3 cm long; greenish, hairy, small, leaf-like bract under each flower; in dense, terminal, cylindrical spikes 2–5 cm long; May–September.

Karen Legasy

Fruit: Nutlets; egg-shaped; smooth.

Habitat: Roadsides and shorelines; fields, clearings, waste areas and lawns; common.

Notes: Heal-all is named for its historical use in healing. It was used to stop internal and surface bleeding, heal wounds and cure hemorrhoids. It was also used as a remedy for sore throat and mouth ulcers. See caution in Introduction.

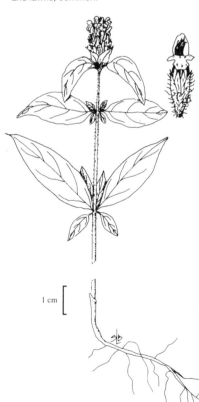

1 cm

Dogbane Family (Apocynaceae)

General: Perennial; 10–70 cm tall; from horizontal underground stems (rhizomes); numerous, wide-spreading branches, mostly hairless; stems and leaves release a milky juice when broken.

Leaves: Opposite; on short, slender stalks; usually spreading or drooping; simple; egg-shaped to oval with short, abrupt point at tip and rounded to narrowed base; 2–7 cm long, 2.5–6.3 cm wide; upper surface hairless, underside paler and usually covered with downy hairs; margins toothless.

Brenda Chambers

Flowers: Pinkish, fragrant; bell-shaped with 5 spreading lobes; small, about 8 mm wide; upwardly spreading to drooping, on stalks; in showy terminal clusters or sometimes from leaf axils; June–July.

Fruit: Pods; long and slender, cylindrical, 8–12 cm long; in pairs; open along 1 side; numerous elongated seeds with tufts of long, cottony hair.

Habitat: Sandy to coarse-loamy, well-drained soils, dry to fresh areas; edges of dry forest areas or roadsides; disturbed sites, fields and clearings; occasionally locally abundant.

Notes: Spreading dogbane can be recognized in the field by its release of a milky juice when the stems or leaves are broken. The juice may irritate sensitive skin. • Aboriginal peoples used the roots in remedies for headache, nervousness, heart palpitations, kidney problems and as an oral contraceptive. See caution in Introduction.

1 cm

Borage Family (Boraginaceae)

Karen Legasy

General: Perennial; 20–80 cm tall; stem erect, unbranched or loosely branched above, branches slender; usually hairy, feels rough; dark green.

Leaves: Alternate; simple; basal leaves on long stalks, egg-shaped and rounded to heart-shaped at base, 5–20 cm long; stem leaves on winged stalks near base and almost stalkless near top, egg- to lance-shaped with pointed tip and tapered base; margins toothless; thin; coarsely hairy, rough to touch; prominently veined.

Flowers: Blue, pinkish in bud; bell- or funnel-shaped with 5 lobes; 1–1.5 cm long; drooping; in loosely branched, open clusters; June–July.

Fruit: Nutlets; small and rounded; July–September.

Habitat: Moist to fresh, clayey to medium-loamy and wet organic sites; rich hardwood and conifer mixedwood stands; streambanks, shores, roadsides and forest edges; moist fields and thickets; common.

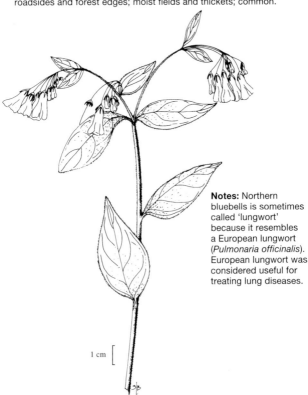

1 cm

Notes: Northern bluebells is sometimes called 'lungwort' because it resembles a European lungwort (*Pulmonaria officinalis*). European lungwort was considered useful for treating lung diseases.

Bluebell Family (Campanulaceae)

General: Perennial; 30–60 cm tall; stems slender, reclining or spreading; 3-angled with stiff, downward-pointing hairs on stem angles, leafy.

Leaves: Alternate; stalkless; simple; narrowly linear to linear-lance-shaped and gradually tapering with a pointed tip; 2–8 cm long, up to 8 mm wide; short, stiff hairs bent downward on margins and midribs; margins toothless or minutely toothed.

Flowers: Bluish; bell-shaped; 4–12 mm long, lobed to about one-third of its length; on thread-likestalks in a loose, widely branching, few-flowered cluster; June–August.

Fruit: Capsules; slightly rounded; 5–10 cm long; on slender stalks; open near base.

Habitat: Wet fields, marshes and alder thickets; frequent.

Notes: *Campanula* means bell-shaped. • This plant was formerly known as *Campanula uliginosa*.

Brenda Chambers

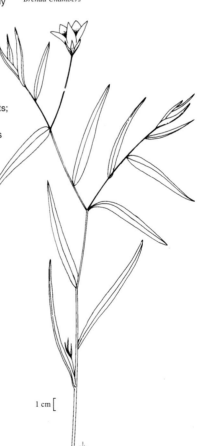

1 cm

COW WHEAT ♦ *Melampyrum lineare*
MÉLAMPYRE LINÉAIRE

Figwort Family (Scrophulariaceae)

Karen Legasy

General: Annual; 5–50 cm tall; stem slender, slightly squared, unbranched to branched.

Leaves: Opposite; on short stalks; simple; lance- to linear-lance-shaped with pointed tips, upper leaves sometimes squared at base; 2–6 cm long; margins of lower leaves toothless, upper leaves toothless or with 1 or more bristle-like teeth near base.

Flowers: Whitish with yellow tips and throat; tubular; 2-lipped; about 6–12 cm long; on short stalks; from leaf axils, often in leafy clusters; June–July.

Fruit: Capsule; 3–5 mm wide; 1–4 white seeds ripen to blackish with white to brown tips; July–August.

Habitat: Dry to fresh, rocky to coarse-loamy sites; conifer and conifer mixedwood stands; partial shade; common.

Notes: The genus name *Melampyrum* combines Greek words for 'wheat' and 'black' and apparently was chosen because cow wheat's seeds are often black and resemble wheat. Some people find that the flowers resemble a snake's head.

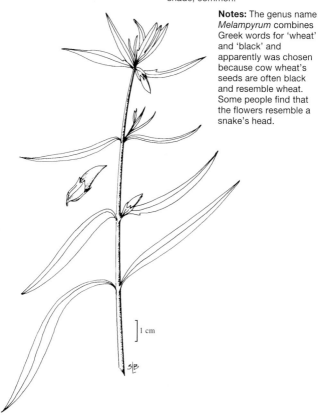

1 cm

Gentian Family (Gentianaceae)

General: Annual or biennial; 10–50 cm tall; stem erect, unbranched or branched.

Leaves: Opposite; basal leaves inversely egg-shaped or spoon-shaped with blunt tip and narrowed base, on stalks; stem leaves stalkless, egg- to lance-shaped with pointed tips, 2.5–5 cm long; 3–5 prominent nerves.

Flowers: Greenish, purplish or white; 4 pointed lobes and 4 downward-pointing spurs; 0.8–1.5 cm long; in terminal clusters and in leaf axils; July–August.

Fruit: Capsules; narrowly oblong; about 1.5 cm long.

Habitat: Damp or moist, cool forests or thickets; occasional.

Notes: The species name *deflexa* means 'bent abruptly downward' and refers to the spurs on the flowers.

Brenda Chambers

1 cm

FRAGRANT BEDSTRAW ♦ *Galium triflorum*
GAILLET À TROIS FEUILLES

Madder Family (Rubiaceae)

NWO FEC Photo

General: Perennial; 20–80 cm long; stems square, hairless, weak, often trailing or leaning on other plants; plant sometimes feels rough.

Leaves: Usually in whorls of 6; stalkless; simple; narrowly oblong with short bristle-point at tip; 2–8.5 cm long; often has coarse hairs on underside; margins toothless but rough with stiff hairs; single vein.

Flowers: Greenish-white; small; 4 petals; in loose clusters on long, spreading stalks, angled from leaf axils or terminal; in groups of 3; appear in June.

Fruit: 2 small (2–3 mm), joined balls densely covered with hooked bristles; appear in August.

Habitat: Wet organic to dry to moist upland sites; black spruce and rich conifer and hardwood mixedwoods; thickets along shores; prefers some shade; common.

Notes: Fragrant bedstraw has a strong vanilla fragrance and contains a substance which apparently prevents blood from clotting. • The dried and roasted fruit has historically been used as a coffee substitute. See caution in Introduction.

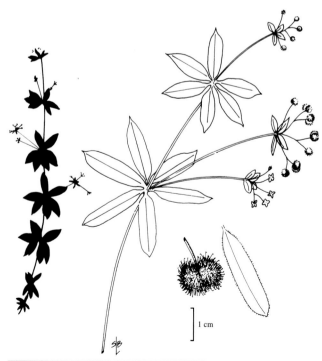

1 cm

Madder Family (Rubiaceae)

General: Perennial; 50–180 cm long; stem much-branched and leaning on bushes or sometimes erect and climbing, rough with downward-pointing, stiff hairs.

Leaves: In whorls of 6 (4–5 on branchlets); stalkless; simple; narrowly oval to lance-shaped with sharp, firm, pointed tip (cuspidate) and narrowed base; 1–2 cm long, 2–4 mm wide; midrib and margins rough with stiff hairs.

Flowers: White; 4–6 (usually 4) petals; 2–3 mm wide; numerous in clusters, terminal or from leaf axils; on slender, spreading stalks; June–August.

Brenda Chambers

Fruit: Smooth nutlets, in pairs; shiny; about 2 mm long.

Habitat: Moist soils; damp thickets; low-lying areas, ditches; occasional.

Notes: Rough bedstraw is distinctly rough and can stick to clothing.
• This plant was historically used in a remedy for kidney ailments.
See caution in Introduction.

1 cm

LABRADOR MARSH BEDSTRAW ♦ *Galium labradoricum*
GAILLET DU LABRADOR

Madder Family (Rubiaceae)

Karen Legasy

General: Perennial; 5–40 cm long; stems slender, hairless, 4-angled, erect or upward-growing.

Leaves: Whorled, in 4s; simple; spoon- or lance-shaped with widest part toward tip, base narrowed; 0.5–1.5 cm long; margins rough with stiff hairs; loosely spreading or bent downward.

Flowers: White; 4-lobed; about 2 mm wide; few; solitary or in small clusters (usually in 3s); June–August.

Fruit: Nutlets in pairs; round in cross-section, 1–1.5 mm in diameter, smooth.

Habitat: Wet organic to moist clayey sites; black spruce and rich conifer mixedwoods; fens, mossy woods, thickets, sedge marshes; frequent.

Notes: Marsh bedstraw's distinguishing feature is its spoon-shaped leaves, which are widest above the middle and in whorls of 4.

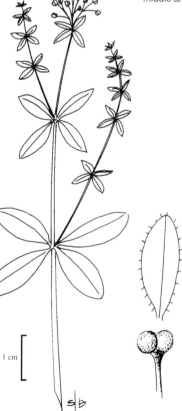

1 cm

Madder Family (Rubiaceae)

General: Perennial; 20–60 cm tall; erect; hairless; stems straight, unbranched or branched, leafy, square.

Leaves: In whorls of 4; lance-shaped to linear with blunt to pointed tips; 2.5–6 cm long, 2–6 mm wide; 3 nerves or veins; margins sometimes fringed with hairs.

Flowers: White; small, 3 mm wide, 4-lobed; in dense, showy terminal clusters; May–August.

Fruit: Nutlets; in pairs, usually densely hairy, sometimes almost hairless when mature; about 2 mm wide.

Habitat: Gravelly or rocky areas; shorelines; clearings, ditches; occasional.

Notes: Aboriginal peoples used northern bedstraw's roots to make a red dye. • Northern bedstraw is usually hairless; this distinguishes it from rough bedstraw (*Galium asprellum*) which feels rough because of its stiff, backward-pointing hairs.

Robert Norton

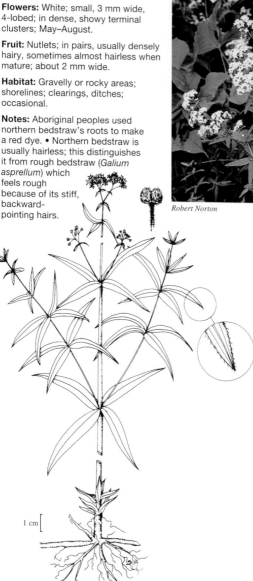

1 cm

COMMON PLANTAIN ♦ *Plantago major*
PLANTAIN MAJEUR

Plantain Family (Plantaginaceae)

General: Perennial; 15–45 cm tall; underground stem (rhizome) short, thick and erect; hairless to slightly hairy.

Leaves: Basal; on long stalks; simple; egg-shaped; 5–30 cm long; minute hairs; firm and usually slightly rough when dry; margins toothless; lengthwise ribs prominent and almost parallel; upward-growing or laying on ground.

Flowers: Greenish; small, 2 mm long; in narrow, elongated terminal spike 5–25 cm long; June–October.

Fruit: Capsule; 2–4 mm long; brown or purplish, top comes off like a lid; 6–15 seeds, 1 mm long.

Karen Legasy

Habitat: Roadsides, waste areas, lawns; open shores; forest clearings; common.

Notes: This introduced species is a weed in lawns. • The mature leaves were considered too stringy to eat, but the young leaves have historically been eaten in salads and as cooked greens. See caution in Introduction. • The woodchuck and meadow vole eat common plantain, and ruffed grouse eat the foliage.

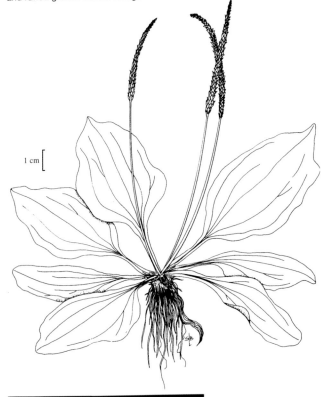

1 cm

Composite Family (Compositae)

General: Perennial; 0.4–1.2 m high; extensively creeping underground stems (rhizomes); deep roots; hairless; stem leafy near base, nearly leafless toward top.

Leaves: Alternate; basal and lower stem leaves on short stalks, sharply incised or lobed to appear compound (pinnatifid), 6–40 cm long, 2–15 cm wide; margins prickly; upper leaves clasping, smaller and not as lobed.

Karen Legasy

Flowerheads: Yellow; dandelion-like; 3–5 cm wide; florets all strap-like; sepal-like bracts (involucre) 15–22 mm long, with coarse, spreading, gland-tipped hairs and small tufts of matted hairs; several in loose, rounded or flat-topped clusters; on long stalks with coarse glandular hairs; July–October.

Fruit: Dry, hard, single-seeded (achene); 2.5–3.5 mm long; oblong; compressed; with 5–10 wrinkled longitudinal ribs; tuft of soft, white hairs on tip.

Habitat: Low areas; roadsides, shorelines; fields, thickets, forest openings and waste places; common and may be locally abundant.

Notes: The young leaves have historically been eaten raw in salads and as a cooked vegetable. See caution in Introduction.
• This plant is not a true thistle (*Cirsium* spp.). When corn sow-thistle's stem is broken, it releases a milky fluid whereas the stems of true thistles do not.

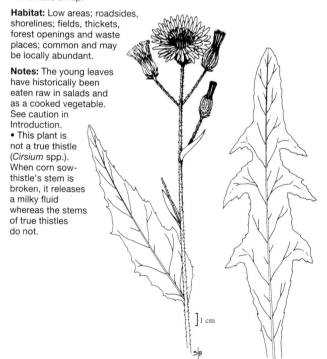

1 cm

DANDELION ♦ *Taraxacum officinale*
PISSENLIT OFFICIAL

Composite Family (Compositae)

Karen Legasy

General: Perennial; 5–45 cm tall; taproots thick, deep and often about 25 cm long; stem has a milky juice.

Leaves: Basal; on stalks; simple; oblong to spoon-shaped with pointed to blunt tips, narrowing to slender and slightly winged stalks at base; 5–40 cm long; often slightly hairy; margins with irregular, downward-pointing teeth or lobes.

Flowerheads: Yellow; florets all strap-like; small sepal-like bracts (involucre) at base narrow, pointed, outer ones bend backward; 2–5 cm long; solitary at tips of slender, leafless stalks; April–September.

Fruit: Small (3–4 mm long), not splitting open, dry, hard, single-seeded (achenes), with long beak and tuft of white bristles on top; mature heads silky or downy and globe-like when ripe.

Habitat: Fields, waste places, disturbed sites; roadsides; open areas and dry to wet sites; abundant.

Notes: Dandelions are related to lettuce and their young leaves have historically been used in salads. The roots were used as a coffee substitute. The flowers are used to make dandelion wine and the entire plant has been used to brew beer. See caution in Introduction. • The irregular teeth of the leaves are said to resemble lion's teeth, thus the name *dent de lion* or dandelion. • This is an alien species from Europe. • The woodchuck eats dandelions, and deer mice use the silky down of the fruiting heads to line their nests.

1 cm

Composite Family (Compositae)

General: Perennial; 20–70 cm tall; slender stem leafless or rarely has 1–2 stalkless leaves; hairy and glandular; with long underground stems (rhizomes) and runners (stolons).

Leaves: In a basal rosette; simple; oblong to spoon-shaped with blunt tip and narrowed base; 4–20 cm long, 1–3.5 cm wide; coarsely hairy; margins toothless or sometimes slightly toothed.

Flowerheads: Orange; florets all strap-like (ray); small, green sepal-like bracts at base are covered with blackish glandular hairs; about 2 cm wide; in rounded terminal clusters; June–August.

Karen Legasy

Fruit: Dry, hard, single-seeded (achene), oblong, with dirty-white, hair-like bristles at tip.

Habitat: Sandy roadsides; fields and clearings, disturbed areas, dry soils, rocky shores; common.

Notes: Orange hawkweed is also called 'devil's paintbrush.' • This weedy species was introduced from Europe. • See notes on yellow hawkweed (*Hieracium caespitosum*) for ways to distinguish the 2 plants.

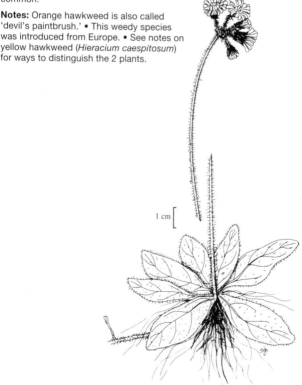

1 cm

YELLOW HAWKWEED ♦ *Hieracium caespitosum*
ÉPERVIÈRE DES PRÉS

Composite Family (Compositae)

Karen Legasy

General: Perennial; 30–60 cm tall; stem leafless or has 1–2 leaves below middle; covered with long hairs, hairs on stem blackish.

Leaves: In a basal rosette; on winged stalks or stalkless; simple; narrowly oblong with blunt tip and tapered base; 6–25 cm long, 10–20 mm wide; both sides hairy; margins toothless or with a few distantly spaced, minute, glandular-tipped teeth.

Flowerheads: Yellow; about 1.3 cm wide; florets all strap-like; small, green sepal-like bracts (involucre) at base covered with gland-tipped, black hairs; in loose, irregular and slightly flat-topped clusters; May–August.

Fruit: Dry, hard, single-seeded (achene), oblong.

Habitat: Fields, clearings, disturbed areas; roadsides; occasional.

Notes: Yellow hawkweed is very similar to orange hawkweed (*Hieracium aurantiacum*); you can differentiate them by their flower colours when they are in bloom, and by the shapes of their leaves when they are not. Yellow hawkweed's leaves are narrowly oblong, while orange hawkweed's are more spoon-shaped.

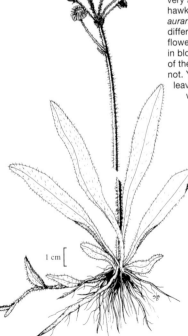

1 cm

Composite Family (Compositae)

General: Annual, biennial or perennial; tall; stems leafy; foliage releases milky juice when crushed.

Leaves: Alternate; dandelion-like; usually deeply lobed, sometimes without lobes; variable.

Flowerheads: Yellow, white, pink or blue; florets all strap-like (ray), 5-toothed at tip; sepal-like bracts (involucre) arranged in a cone or cylinder; in spreading clusters, rarely solitary; summer and fall.

Ray Demey

Fruit: Small, dry, hard, single-seeded (achene); oval, oblong or linear; flat; 3–5 ribs on each side; tipped with a thread-like beak (or beakless) and a cluster of soft hairs which fall separately.

Habitat: Moist thickets and woods; shorelines; occasional to frequent depending on species.

Notes: The genus name *Lactuca* comes from the Latin word *lac*, which means 'milk' and refers to the milky juice the plants release when the foliage is crushed. • Due to the large amount of variation in this genus, it is often difficult to identify wild lettuce to the species level in the field.

1 cm

JOE-PYE WEED ♦ *Eupatorium maculatum*
EUPATOIRE MACULÉE

Composite Family (Compositae)

General: Perennial; 60–180 cm tall; from a horizontal underground stem (rhizome); stem purple or purple-spotted, usually has longitudinal lines.

Leaves: In whorls of 3–5; on stalks to almost stalkless; simple; egg- to lance-shaped, taper at tip and base; 6–20 cm long, 2–9 cm wide; upper leaves smaller; upper surface slightly rough, underside minutely hairy to hairless and rough; thick; margins coarsely toothed.

Karen Legasy

Flowerheads: Pinkish to purplish; cylindrical, thick and fluffy; about 8 mm wide; florets all tubular; cluster of sepal-like bracts (involucre) 6–9 mm high, hairy, often purplish; in flat-topped clusters 10–14 cm wide; July–September.

Fruit: Dry, hard, single-seeded (achene), 3–4 mm long, glandular dotted; tipped with a cluster of fluffy, brownish hairs.

Habitat: Moist soils; thickets, wet clearings; shorelines; common.

Notes: The roots were historically used in a remedy for urinary and kidney problems. See caution in Introduction. • The species name *maculatum* means 'spotted.'

1 cm

Composite Family (Compositae)

General: Biennial; 0.5–2 m tall; small, forking and slightly turnip-shaped root; stem woolly or hairy when young, becomes hairless, slender and leafy, hollow.

Leaves: Alternate; basal leaves on long stalks, egg-shaped to elliptic and deeply lobed, 10–20 cm long; simple; stem leaves stalkless, thin, smaller than basal leaves, unlobed, toothed or deeply cut (cleft) almost to midrib to form lance-shaped to oblong lobes; spines usually tipped with slender prickles; densely white or woolly beneath when young, sometimes hairless on both sides when mature.

Karen Legasy

Flowerheads: Purple to rose-purple; about 3.5 cm wide; florets all tubular; small sepal-like bracts (involucre) at base cottony and sticky; lacking prickles; several to many, on long stalks, in loose or crowded inflorescence; July–September.

Fruit: Small, dry, hard, single-seeded (achene), oblong, flattish, not ribbed.

Habitat: Moist, silty to clayey upland sites; hardwood mixedwoods; swamps, lowland forests, wet clearings and ditches, thickets; streambanks; frequent.

Notes: Aboriginal peoples used thistle roots in a remedy for back pain. See caution in Introduction.

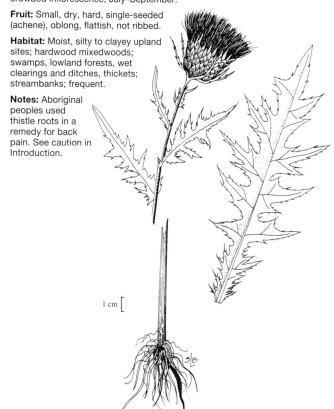

1 cm

OX-EYE DAISY ♦ *Chrysanthemum leucanthemum*
MARGUERITE

Composite Family (Compositae)

General: Perennial; 30–100 cm tall; stems hairless to finely hairy, erect, slender, lacking branches or forked near the top.

Leaves: Alternate; basal leaves on long, slender stalks, spoon- or egg-shaped with narrower end near base, 4–15 cm long; simple; stem leaves usually stalkless and partly clasping stem, oblong, smaller than basal leaves; margins coarsely and regularly toothed or lobed.

Flowerheads: White with yellow disc in centre; 2.5–5 cm wide; solitary; 20–30 outer strap-like (ray) florets; tubular florets yellow, forming central disc; sepal-like bracts (involucre) overlapping (imbricate), with dark-brown margins; June–August.

Fruit: Small, dry, hard, single-seeded (achene), black with about 10 white ribs.

Habitat: Roadsides; waste places, fields, meadows, clearings; common and abundant in abandoned fields.

Karen Legasy

Notes: Ox-eye daisy is also known as *Leucanthemum vulgare*, and is a weed species introduced from Europe. • It gets its common name 'daisy' from the yellow centre disc of the flower, which resembles the sun or 'day's eye.'

1 cm[

Composite Family (Compositae)

General: Perennial; 30–70 cm tall; rootstocks horizontal, spreading; stem erect, branched near top; covered with woolly or cobweb-like hairs to nearly hairless.

Leaves: Alternate; stem leaves stalkless, 2–10 cm long, up to 1 cm wide; basal leaves longer and usually stalked; fern-like, lance-shaped to narrowly oblong and twice- or thrice-cut into narrow segments (bi- to tripinnate).

Flowerheads: White; 4–6 mm wide; 4–6 strap-like (ray) florets surrounding 10–30 tiny tubular (disc) flowers; sepal-like bracts (involucre) 4–5 mm high, overlapping, dry, membranous margins; in slightly rounded to flat-topped clusters; June–September.

Karen Legasy

Fruit: Dry, hard, hairless, single-seeded (achene).

Habitat: Dry to moderately dry soils; roadsides; fields, disturbed and open areas; shade intolerant; common.

Notes: Some people have an allergic skin reaction when they come into contact with yarrow. • Yarrow was historically used for ailments such as colds, fevers, stomach cramps, bleeding from the lungs and diabetes. The leaves were used to stop bleeding and reduce swelling, but they were also said to cause nosebleed when put into the nostrils. See caution in Introduction. • Some people believed that washing one's head with yarrow could prevent baldness. • Ruffed grouse occasionally eat yarrow leaves.

1 cm [

Composite Family (Compositae)

Karen Legasy

General: Perennial; 10–90 cm tall; stem erect, white-woolly and leafy; branched near top to form flower cluster; from spreading underground stems (rhizomes).

Leaves: Alternate; stalkless; simple; narrowly lance-shaped; 7.5–13 cm long, up to 1.5 cm wide; slightly hairy above, densely woolly beneath; whitish-green; midvein visible; margins toothless.

Flowerheads: Pearly-white with yellowish centres; round (globe-like), about 6 mm wide; florets tubular (disc), all of 1 sex or nearly so; sepal-like bracts (involucre) overlapping, 5–7 mm high, scarious, pearly-white; in dense, broad terminal clusters; July–September.

Fruit: Dry, hard, single-seeded (achene) with tuft of white, hair-like bristles; fall separately from the petals.

Habitat: Exposed mineral soils, dry, sandy soils, rocky areas; roadsides, clearings, cutovers, open areas; shade intolerant; often forms extensive colonies on dry roadsides; common.

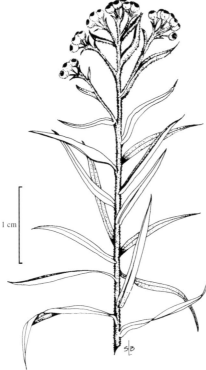

Notes: The flowers are often dried and used in flower arrangements.
• Pearly everlasting was historically used as a substitute for tobacco. The flowers were used in a remedy for paralysis and as a charm to keep evil spirits away. They were also used to help heal burns. See caution in Introduction.

1 cm

Composite Family (Compositae)

General: Perennial; 15–40 cm tall; loosely spreading by runners or rooting branches (stolons) which develop terminal rosettes of leaves.

Leaves: Alternate; simple; basal leaves in rosette, wedge- to spoon-shaped with widest part toward tip, tip rounded or with an abrupt, sharp point, base tapered, 1.5–6.5 cm long, 0.5–1.3 cm wide, upper surface green, hairless to thinly woolly, underside white-woolly; margins toothless, usually single prominent vein on underside; 3–8 stem leaves stalkless, linear, smaller toward stem top.

BC MOF / Frank Boas

Flowerheads: Whitish; either male or female; rounded; sepal-like bracts (involucre) 7–10 mm high, overlapping, tips sharply pointed, dry and membranous; female heads about 1 cm wide; male heads smaller, 2–8 in flat-topped clusters; April–May.

Fruit: Dry, hard, single-seeded (achene), rough, many fine, white hairs at tip.

Habitat: Sterile soil, dry to moist areas; fields, openings, rocky open shores; occasional.

Notes: Many people pick and dry field pussytoes for ornamental bouquets.

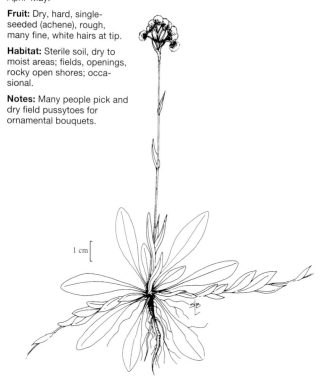

1 cm

CLAMMY EVERLASTING ♦ *Gnaphalium viscosum*
GNAPHALE VISQUEUSE

Composite Family (Compositae)

Bill Crins

General: Annual or biennial; 60–90 cm tall; stem very leafy, glandular, sticky, branched at top; fragrant.

Leaves: Alternate; stalkless, lower edges extending down stem (decurrent); simple; lance–shaped or widely linear with slightly pointed tip or lowest leaves shorter and slightly spoon-shaped; 2.5–7.5 cm long, 0.4–0.6 cm wide; upper surface hairless or loosely covered with white wool, underside densely white-woolly; margins toothless.

Flowerheads: Whitish; in several compact, rounded clusters of 2–6 heads each; small sepal-like bracts (involucre) at base yellowish-white or brownish, egg-shaped with pointed tips, outer bracts woolly at base; July–September.

Fruit: Dry, hard, single-seeded (achene); hairless but tipped with a tuft of long, hair-like bristles.

Habitat: Open areas; moist or dry sites; rare.

Notes: Clammy everlasting was formerly known as *Gnaphalium decurrens* or *G. macounii*. This plant may be confused with pearly everlasting (*Anaphalis margaritacea*) since both species are generally white-woolly, but pearly everlasting's flower heads have yellowish centres while those of clammy everlasting are white.

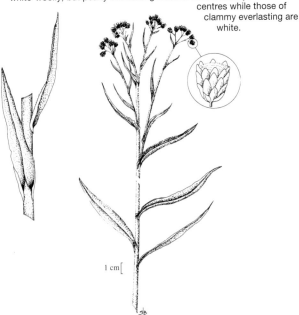

1 cm

Composite Family (Compositae)

General: Perennial; .
10–30 cm tall;
from extensively creeping, thick, cord-like underground stems (rhizomes); flowering stems appear before leaves emerge.

Leaves: Basal; on long, slender stalks; simple, circular to kidney-shaped with 5–7 lobes cut over halfway to base; 5–25 cm wide; upper surface green, hairless, underside white-woolly; margins coarsely toothed; flowering stem has alternate, scale-like bracts with parallel veins.

Karen Legasy

Flowerheads: Creamy white; mainly male or female, with both strap-like (ray) and tubular (disc) florets; in a terminal cluster; fragrant; May.

Fruit: Dry, hard, single-seeded (achene); 1.5–2.5 mm long; with a tuft of long, white hairs, form soft, fluffy seed heads; late May–early June.

Habitat: Wet organic to fresh to wet upland sites; conifer and rich conifer and hardwood mixedwood stands; common.

Notes: Sweet coltsfoot was formerly known as *Petasites palmatus*. *Palmatus* means 'palmate' or 'shaped like a palm' and refers to the leaves.

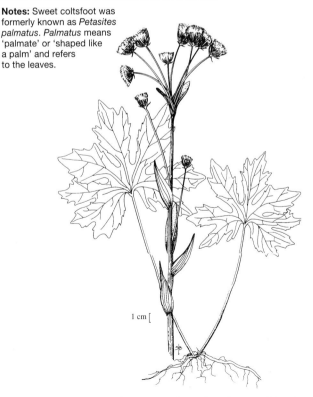

1 cm [

ROUGH DAISY FLEABANE ♦ *Erigeron strigosus*
ÉRIGÉRON HISPIDE

Composite Family (Compositae)

Karen Legasy

General: Annual; up to 70 cm tall; stem has minute, ash-coloured, appressed, stiff hairs.

Leaves: Alternate; lower leaves spoon-shaped to oblong, taper to slender stalk, margins usually toothed; stem leaves usually stalkless, simple, linear to oblong, minutely hairy to hairless, margins usually toothless.

Flowerheads: White or purplish with a yellow disc in centre; 50–100 strap-like (ray) florets up to 6 mm long; rays shorter than to slightly larger than width of central disc; tubular (disc) florets yellow, 1.5–2.5 mm long; several to many in open, flat-topped cluster; May–August.

Fruit: Small, dry, hard, single-seeded (achene); numerous; tipped with 10–15 fragile hairs and some short bristles.

Habitat: Dry, open areas; fields and pastures; roadsides; common.

Notes: You can recognize rough daisy fleabane by its short, strap-like florets (rays).

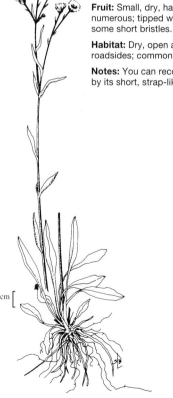

1 cm

Composite Family (Compositae)

General: Perennial; 20–120 cm tall; rootstocks woody and branched; stems upward-growing to erect and sparsely to densely hairy, slender, purplish or green, with wide-spreading to upwardly arched branches from near or below the middle.

Leaves: Alternate; stalkless; simple; stem leaves broadly lance-shaped to oblong lance-shaped, tip gradually tapered and pointed, base tapered; primary leaves 5–15 cm long, 5–30 mm wide; basal leaves small, spoon- or lance-shaped, widest toward tip, upper surface has short hairs pointing in 1 direction, underside usually hairless; margins toothed.

Flowerheads: White to pale-purple with pale-yellow to purplish or brownish disc or centre, less than 1.3 cm wide; 8–15 strap-like (ray) florets, 4.5–7.5 mm long, 0.7–2 mm wide; sepal-like bracts (involucre) overlapping, 5–7.5 mm high, hairless to sparsely hairy; usually crowded on 1 side of straggly side branches; August–October.

Fruit: Small, dry, hard, single-seeded (achene), compressed and cone-shaped with wider part toward tip; minutely hairy and tuft of sparse, long flat hairs, 0–1 rib per side.

Habitat: Dry to moist soil; dry open shores, deciduous forests and clearings; frequent in thickets along dry shores.

Notes: The flower discs range from pale yellow to purplish or brownish on the same plant, and even a single flower may have these colours at the same time.

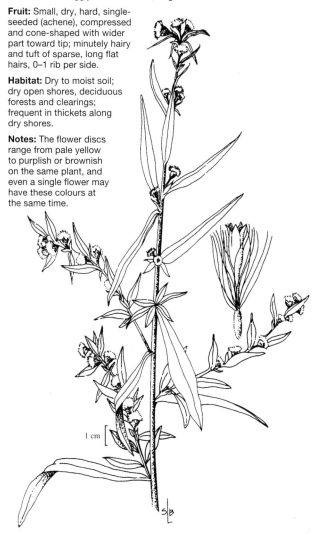

1 cm

BOG ASTER ♦ *Aster nemoralis*
ASTER DES BOIS

Composite Family (Compositae)

Karen Legasy

General: Perennial; 20–70 cm tall; from an elongated, creeping underground stem (rhizome); stems sparsely hairy, single, erect, slender, unbranched or branched near top at flower cluster.

Leaves: Alternate; stalkless; simple; oblong to lance-shaped, both ends pointed; 1–6 cm long and 2–12 mm wide; hairy, stiff; margins toothless or toothed and often curled downward; numerous and crowded on upper stem.

Flowerheads: Purplish to rose-pink, with yellow disc at centre (eventually becoming purple); daisy-like; 2.5–4 cm wide; 15–25 strap-like (ray) florets 11–18 mm long and 1.2–2.6 mm wide; sepal-like bracts (involucre) overlapping, 5–7.5 mm high, purplish to greenish, hairless to sticky-hairy; solitary or few in clusters; August–September.

Fruit: Small, dry, hard, single-seeded (achene), glandular hairy; tuft of cottony, bristle-like hairs at tip.

Habitat: Acidic sphagnum bogs; edges of open bogs and boggy ditches.

Notes: You can distinguish bog aster from other asters by its unbranched or few-branched stem, its small, stiff and crowded leaves with downward-curled margins and its solitary or few flowers. • Aboriginal peoples used bog aster in an earache remedy. See caution in Introduction.

2.5 cm

Composite Family (Compositae)

General: Perennial; 40–170 cm tall; from a thick, woody, branched underground stem (rhizome); stems erect, hairless to (usually) covered with spreading, bristle-like hairs, purplish to reddish.

Leaves: Alternate; stalkless, clasping; simple; narrowly to widely lance-shaped with pointed tips; up to 20 cm long and 1–4 cm wide; upper surface hairless to rough with sharp, stiff hairs, underside hairless or with hairs along midrib; margins toothless to sharply toothed.

Flowerheads: Blue-violet to purplish with yellow disc at centre (eventually turns purple); daisy-like; 2.5–4 cm wide; 30–50 strap-like (ray) florets 7–15 mm long and 0.9–1.3 mm wide; sepal-like bracts (involucre) overlapping, 6–10 mm high, hairless to sparsely hairy; usually numerous in loose to dense and slightly flat-topped cluster; July–September.

Karen Legasy

Fruit: Small, dry, hard, single-seeded (achene), with tuft of cottony, bristle-like hairs at tip; seeds fluffy, white.

Habitat: Moist areas, swamps, fields, thickets; shorelines; frequent.

Notes: Purple-stemmed aster is a highly variable species. Its distinguishing features are its large, clasping leaves and purplish, bristly stem. • The woodchuck, snowshoe hare and white-tailed deer eat asters.

1 cm

CILIOLATE ASTER ♦ *Aster ciliolatus*
ASTER CILIOLÉ

Composite Family (Compositae)

Karen Legasy

General: Perennial; 20–100 cm tall; from long, creeping underground stems (rhizomes); stem erect and hairless or with slightly hairy lines, sparingly leaved; may appear as a group of basal leaves without flowering stem.

Leaves: Alternate; simple; lower leaves on long, winged, slender stalks fringed with fine hairs; narrowly egg-shaped, slightly heart-shaped or rounded at base, taper to pointed tip, firm, hairless to sparsely hairy, margins sharply toothed; upper stem leaves stalkless, lance-shaped and sparsely hairy, margins toothless.

Flowerheads: Bluish, rarely pink, with yellow disc at centre (turns purple); daisy-like; 15–25 strap-like (ray) florets 7–11 mm long and 1.2–2 mm wide; sepal-like bracts (involucre) overlapping, 4–6 mm high, hairy on margins near tips, glandless; usually few in open, elongated clusters; August.

Fruit: Dry, hard, single-seeded (achene), hairless, with tuft of white, hair-like bristles; seed heads fluffy white.

Habitat: All moisture regimes, soil and stand types; open forests to fields and along roadsides; common.

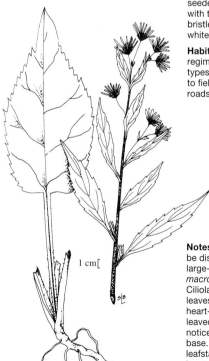

1 cm

Notes: Ciliolate aster can be distinguished from large-leaved aster (*Aster macrophyllus*) by its leaves. Ciliolate aster's basal leaves are only slightly heart-shaped, while large-leaved aster's have a more noticeably heart-shaped base. Also, the winged leafstalks of ciliolate aster have a fringe of fine hairs along the edge; those of large-leaved aster do not.

Composite Family (Compositae)

General: Perennial; flowering stems zigzag, up to 1 m high, reddish; rootstocks long and thick; basal leaves large, distinctive.

Leaves: Alternate; 1–4 basal leaves on stalks, heart-shaped with pointed tip, large, up to 20 cm long and 15 cm wide; upper surface usually hairy and rough; thick; margins broadly toothed; stem leaves smaller, narrower, oblong, uppermost stalkless.

Karen Legasy

Flowerheads: Pale blue to purplish or lilac with yellowish disc at centre (turning reddish-brown); daisy-like; 9–20 strap-like (ray) florets 8–15 mm long, 1.5–2 mm wide; tubular (disc) florets 6–7.5 mm long; sepal-like bracts (involucre) overlapping, 7–10 mm high, often purple-tinged, hairy glandular; in loose, open, flat-topped clusters with sticky hairs; late summer.

Fruit: Narrow or linear dry, hard, single-seeded (achene) with fluffy tuft of white hairs at tip; September.

Habitat: Dry to moist and all upland soil types; hardwood to mixedwood stands, open areas; forest edges, roadsides; disturbed ground; abundant.

Notes: Aboriginal peoples ate the young, tender leaves and brewed a tea from the young roots to bathe the head as a remedy for headaches. See caution in Introduction. • Songbirds and small mammals eat the seeds.

1 cm

GOLDEN RAGWORT ♦ *Senecio aureus*
SÉNEÇON DORÉ

Composite Family (Compositae)

General: Perennial; 30–60 cm tall; underground stems (rhizomes) and basal offshoots horizontally creeping; hairless or nearly so throughout; stems slender, solitary or tufted.

Leaves: Alternate; thin, not fleshy; basal leaves on long, slender stalks, simple, heart- to egg- or kidney-shaped with blunt, rounded tip, 1.3–15 cm long, margins round-toothed; lower stem leaves lance-shaped to oblong with narrow, pointed lobes or large terminal lobe and smaller lower lobes, 2.5–9 cm long; upper stem leaves alternate, stalkless, small, clasping.

Flowerheads: Golden-yellow; daisy-like; 2 cm wide; 8–12 yellow strap-like (ray) florets and a yellow central disc of numerous tubular florets; sepal-like bracts (involucre) overlapping, 5–8 mm high, often purple-tipped; in flat-topped clusters; May–July.

Karen Legasy

Fruit: Dry, hard, single-seeded (achene); hairless; with tuft of soft, white hairs at tip.

Habitat: Swamps, moist woods, forest openings and wet meadows; frequent.

Notes: Golden ragwort has historically been used to promote menstrual discharge and urination. See caution in Introduction. Extended use may cause a variety of symptoms including loss of appetite, vomiting, weakness and bloody diarrhea. **In serious cases it may result in liver damage and death.**

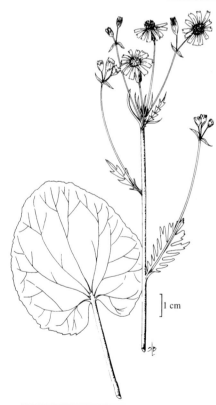

] 1 cm

Composite Family (Compositae)

General: Perennial; 30–150 cm tall; from long, creeping underground stems (rhizomes); stems slender, hairless at base to hairy toward top, unbranched to clustered and branched.

Leaves: Alternate; stalkless or lowest ones on stalks; simple; lance-shaped; about 6–13 cm long and 0.5–1.8 cm wide; slightly to roughly hairy; margins sharply toothed to toothless; numerous and crowded on stem; 3 parallel veins (triple-nerved).

Flowerheads: Yellow; about 4–5 mm; 6–12 strap-like (ray florets, about 2 mm long, 0.2–3 mm wide; 2–7 tubular (disc) florets, about 2.5 mm long; sepal-like bracts (involucre) overlapping, 2–3 mm high, yellowish; numerous on upper side of flowering branches that often are curved; in a somewhat triangular cluster; August–September.

Karen Legasy

Fruit: Small, dry, hard, single-seeded (achene); slightly hairy; with a tuft of hair-like, white bristles at tip.

Habitat: Dry to moist areas; roadsides; fields, clearings, disturbed areas and thickets; streambanks; occasional.

Notes: A yellow dye was made from the flowers. Goldenrod was historically used as a tea substitute. See caution in Introduction.
• The woodchuck, ruffed grouse, spruce grouse, American porcupine, meadow vole and white-tailed deer all occasionally eat goldenrod.

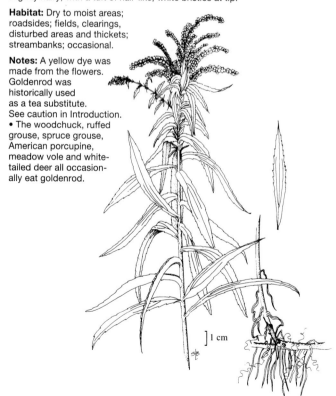

] 1 cm

ROUGH-STEMMED GOLDENROD ♦ *Solidago rugosa*
VERGE D'OR RUGUEUSE

Composite Family (Compositae)

Bill Crins

General: Perennial; 30–180 cm tall; from long, creeping underground stems (rhizomes); stems solitary or in small clumps, tall, leafy, rough, hairy and have diverging or arching branches with flower heads on upper side.

Leaves: Alternate; stalkless; simple; oval or lance-shaped with pointed tip, rarely blunt, base narrowed or pointed; 3.8–12.5 cm long, 13–40 mm wide; hairy, wrinkled and rough; margins sharply toothed.

Flowerheads: Yellow; 6–11 strap-like (ray) florets, 2.5–2.8 mm long, 0.4–0.7 mm wide; 4–8 tubular (disc) flowers, 3–3.3 mm long; sepal-like bracts (involucre) overlapping, 2–4 mm high; in 1-sided clusters on spreading or arching branches of usually large, compound flower head; July–October.

Fruit: Dry, hard, single-seeded (achenes); with minute, sharp, stiff hairs; tuft of soft, white, hair-like bristles at tip.

Habitat: Thickets and fields; roadside ditches, forest edges and open shores; frequent.

Notes: Rough-stemmed goldenrod varies greatly in size, flowerhead shape and hairiness.

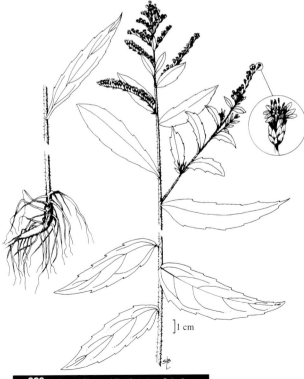

]1 cm

BOG GOLDENROD ♦ *Solidago uliginosa*
VERGE D'OR DES MARAIS

Composite Family (Compositae)

General: Perennial; 30–120 cm tall; stems solitary or few, hairless; flower cluster branches hairy.

Leaves: Alternate; simple; oblong and lance-shaped with pointed tip and narrowed, sheathing base; lower and basal leaves stalked, 10–35 cm long, 0.5–6 cm wide, margins toothed; upper stem leaves stalkless, 2–5 cm long, 0.5–1 cm wide, margins toothless; thick, hairless and not strongly veined.

Flowerheads: Yellow; 1–8 strap-like (ray) florets, 3.2–3.7 mm; 6–8 tubular (disc) florets, 4.5–5 mm long; 46 mm long; sepal-like bracts (involucre) 3–5 mm high, overlapping, outer ones egg-shaped, inner ones linear to lance-shaped, with marginal hairs at tips; in clusters varying from elongated, narrow, 1-sided and few-headed to elongated, wide with branches strongly upward-growing, not 1-sided; many; August–September.

Brenda Chambers

Fruit: Dry, hard, single-seeded (achene); hairless; with tuft of soft, white hairs at tip.

Habitat: Marshy and boggy sites around lakes; sandy shores and openings; damp, open thickets; common.

Notes: Bog goldenrod's appearance is highly variable but you can recognize it by its sheathing basal and lower stem leaves.

HAIRY GOLDENROD ♦ *Solidago hispida*
VERGE D'OR HISPIDE

Composite Family (Compositae)

Karen Legasy

General: Perennial; up to 100 cm tall; stem stout, densely hairy, branchless or sometimes branched.

Leaves: Alternate; simple; lower leaves on winged stalks, oval with pointed to blunt tips, 5–12.5 cm long and 2.5–5 cm wide, hairy on both sides, margins usually toothed; upper leaves stalkless, oblong with pointed tips, smaller, hairy, margins slightly toothed or toothless.

Flowerheads: Yellow; strap-like (ray) florets white to pale cream-coloured, 3.5–4 mm long, about 1 mm wide; 9–12 tubular (disc) florets, 3–3.5 mm long; sepal-like bracts (involucre) overlapping, 3–5 mm high, margins white, midrib green and conspicuous; densely crowded in somewhat narrow elongated clusters toward top of stem; on short stalks; August–September.

Fruit: Small, dry, hard, single-seeded (achene); hairless or with a few flattened hairs; tuft of soft, white hairs at tip.

Habitat: Dry, sandy and rocky areas; sandy jack pine forests; spreading along sides of trails and roads; common.

Notes: Hairy goldenrod is almost identical to silverrod (*Solidago bicolor*) except that silverrod's flowers are white to pale cream while hairy goldenrod's are yellow; however, hairy goldenrod's yellow flowers sometimes fade, making it difficult to distinguish between the 2 plants. Silverrod is known to exist in parts of southern Ontario, but is not known to occur in northeastern Ontario.

]1 cm

Composite Family (Compositae)

General: Annual; 30–90 cm tall; stems hairless to softly bristly, usually erect and branching.

Leaves: Opposite; stalkless; simple; lance-shaped or narrowly oblong, taper to slender point at tip; 7.5–15 cm long, 0.5–2.5 cm wide; hairless; margins coarsely toothed to toothless.

Flowerheads: Yellow; nodding; 6–8 petal-like (ray) florets up to 1.5 cm long; darker-yellow central disc rounded (globe-like), 1.2–2.5 cm wide.

Fruit: Dry, hard, single-seeded (achene); narrowly triangular with narrow end toward base; 4 (rarely 2) sharp, barbed, stiff bristles.

Karen Legasy

Habitat: Wet areas and swamps; common along wet shores and in marshes; forms large colonies.

Notes: Ducks will sometimes eat the seeds. • Bur-marigold is also commonly known as 'beggar's ticks' because its hooked fruit sticks to clothing and animal fur.

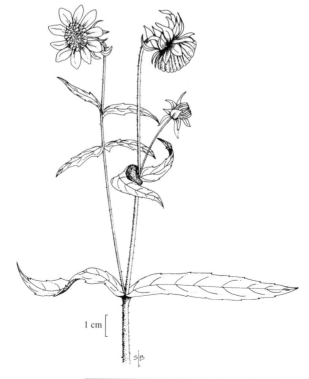

1 cm

GRAMINOIDS

To assist in the identification of graminoids (grasses, sedges and rushes), illustrations are provided below which highlight the main identifying features of these often difficult-to-identify plants.

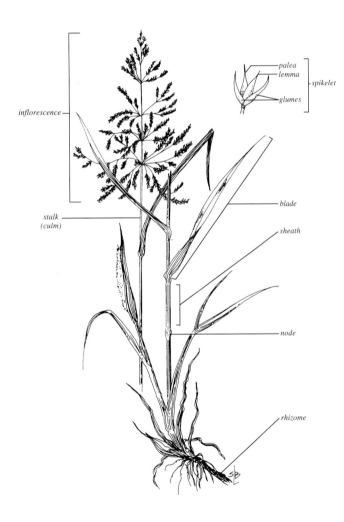

inflorescence

palea
lemma
spikelet
glumes

stalk (culm)

blade

sheath

node

rhizome

Agrostis gigantea

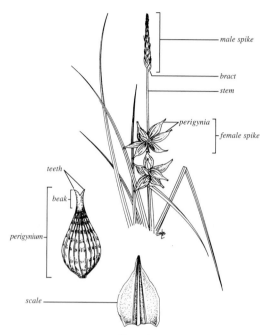

Carex intumescens

WHITE-GRAINED MOUNTAIN RICE ♦ *Oryzopsis asperifolia*
ORYZOPSIS À FEUILLES RUDES

Grass Family (Gramineae)

Bill Crins

General: Perennial; flowering stems erect or abruptly bent at lowest node, smooth or rough; 25–50 cm tall.

Leaves: Basal leaves dark, evergreen, erect, rough on surface and edges, 40 cm long, 4–10 mm wide, often equalling or exceeding flowering stem, tapering gradually to tip and to base, flat or curved inward on margins; sheath purple; stem leaves shorter, blades usually less than 1 cm long and sheaths tubular.

Inflorescence: Narrow, short-branched cluster (panicle); 5–12 cm long; spikelets sometimes paired on stem, 6–8 mm long (excluding 6–14 mm long hair-like awn); 2 large, translucent outer scales (glumes) remain after seeds are shed; May–June.

Habitat: Dry to moist sites, all soil textures, conifer and hardwood mixedwood stands; frequent.

Notes: The genus name *Oryzopsis* combines words for 'rice' and 'appearance.' White-grained mountain rice is not related to cultivated rice and does not even look like it, but its grains vaguely resemble those of rice and are about the same size.

] 1 cm

Grass Family (Gramineae)

General: Perennial; green; erect; 30–120 cm tall; from tough, extensively creeping, whitish or yellowish underground stems (rhizomes).

Leaves: Flat, green, somewhat soft, rough-hairy on edges, sparsely hairy on upper surface, underside hairless and with fine, white lines with small, slender teeth at upper edge; 7.5–30.5 cm long, 5–10 mm wide; sheaths usually shorter than internodes.

Karen Legasy

Inflorescence: Spike; 5–25 cm long; spikelets flattened, 0.6–2.2 cm long, 2- to 9-flowered; scales (glumes and lemmas) oblong to lance-shaped with a sharp point or bristle (awn) at tip, hairless, herbaceous, with 5–7 prominent, slender nerves; July–September.

Habitat: Roadsides, infrequently spreading to sandy shores; fields, a troublesome weed in gardens; common.

Notes: Also called *Agropyron repens*. • Quack grass has been used for grazing and hay production, but it is also a troublesome weed. It persists in ploughed areas and spreads very rapidly.

 ] 1 cm

TIMOTHY ♦ *Phleum pratense*
PHÉOLE DES PRÉS

Grass Family (Gramineae)

Karen Legasy

General:
Perennial; flowering stems stiffly erect, hairless; 30–100 cm tall; base bulb-like with fibrous roots; in clumps.

Leaves: Wide, flat; tapering to tip; hairless, rough-margined; 8–22 cm long, 5–10 mm wide.

Inflorescence: Narrow, cylindrical, very dense cluster (panicle) of spikelets; green, becomes drab; 1–22 cm long, 7–10 mm thick; stiff, harsh and rough-textured; 2 outer scales (glumes) of each spikelet have short, stiff bristle-tips (awns); July–August.

Habitat: Fields, clearings, roadsides and into the forest; common where horses were used in logging operations.

Notes: Timothy is an important hay grass. Older plants are too rough to be eaten by livestock, but they make a good winter food when dried.

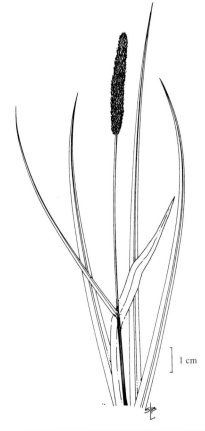

] 1 cm

Grass Family (Gramineae)

General: Perennial; stems erect or abruptly bent at base; up to 1.5 m tall; from numerous prolonged, scaly, underground stems; basal shoots sterile, reclining and often form creeping stems above (stolons); forms large colonies.

Leaves: Deep green; 5–9 mm wide.

Inflorescence: Loose, irregular and open pyramid-shaped cluster (panicle) 15–30 cm long; purple to green or reddish; branches spread when in fruit; spikelets 2–3.5 mm long, scales (glumes) rough on midvein only.

Habitat: Common along roadsides, in meadows, clearings and on disturbed ground; occasional in thickets and along damp shores.

Notes: Redtop was introduced from Europe. You can recognize it by its often reddish-tinged inflorescence. • Songbirds eat the seeds, as do the small mammals who use the grass as cover.

Karen Legasy

] 1 cm

Grass Family (Gramineae)

Bill Crins

General: Perennial; flowering stems erect, tall, hairless, slender, 60–120 cm tall, pale green; from creeping underground stems (rhizomes); solitary or in loose tufts.

Leaves: Flat, thin and wide; 10–25 cm long, 7–15 mm wide; margins rough; spreading at right angles to stem.

Inflorescence: Drooping, loosely flowered panicle; spikelets 2–4.5 mm long, with rough scales and 1 flower; clusters loose, open, pale green, shiny and 12.5–25 cm long; flower scale (lemma) with short, straight bristle-tip (awn); branches hair-like, usually spreading and often drooping, lowest branches 3.8–12.5 cm long; August–September.

Habitat: Wet organic to fresh, coarse-loamy upland sites; conifer and hardwood mixedwoods, moderately rich sites, disturbed areas; occasional.

Notes: The species name *latifolia* means 'broad-leaved.'

1 cm

Grass Family (Gramineae)

General: Large, robust perennial; flowering stems erect, smooth or somewhat rough, not hairy, often bluish to purplish around joints; 5–15 cm tall; from numerous creeping underground stems (rhizomes); in dense clumps or patches.

Leaves: Flat, numerous, gradually tapering to a long, pointed tip; 15–30 cm long, 4–8 mm wide; sheaths shorter than internodes; rough, especially on edges and upper surface.

Karen Legasy

Inflorescence: Loose, irregular, open cluster (panicle), widely lance- to egg-shaped, occasionally drooping; 10–20 cm long, 2–10 cm wide, purplish to greenish or straw-coloured; spikelets 2–6 mm long, 1-flowered; flower scale (lemma) with a slender hair (awn) on back and a dense tuft of long hairs at base; outer scales (glumes) lance-shaped to narrowly egg-shaped; July–September.

Habitat: All moisture regimes, soil and stand types; characteristic grass of open, low shores; also occurs in open, damp forests, ditches and wet clearings; common.

Notes: This grass spreads quickly in disturbed areas. • Canada blue joint provides cover and food for small mammals, songbirds eat its seeds and moose occasionally browse it.

] 1 cm

FALSE MELIC GRASS ♦ *Schizachne purpurascens*
SCHIZACHNÉ POURPRÉ

Grass Family (Gramineae)

Bill Crins

General: Perennial; flowering stems erect from reclining base, 0.3–1 m tall, slender, hairless; loosely tufted; from underground stems (rhizomes).

Leaves: Flat, upright, narrowed at base; 1–5 mm wide; sheaths purplish at base of stem, closed at first, splitting with maturity; shorter than flowering stem.

Inflorescence: Loose, lax cluster (panicle) 5–15 cm long, slender with a few drooping branches; spikelets bronze to purplish, 1.3–2.3 cm long, 1–3 per branch, 3- to 5-flowered; each flower scale (lemma) has an 8–15 mm long, hair-like bristle (awn) from its tip and a dense tuft of short hairs at its base; mid-May to August.

Habitat: Moist to dry, fine-loamy to sandy sites, rich conifer and hardwood mixedwoods; frequent.

Notes: The species name *purpurascens* means 'becoming purple.'

]1 cm

Grass Family (Gramineae)

General: Perennial; flowering stems erect, softly hairy, up to 60 cm tall; solitary or in tufts from fibrous roots.

Leaves: Narrow, stiff, flat to folded; 2.5–10 cm long, up to 5 mm wide; hairless or hairy; rough to touch, especially on edges.

Inflorescence: Shiny, dense, spike-like panicle, 2.5–12.5 cm long, often interrupted near base, shaggy with many protruding awns; spikelets 2-flowered, with a long, hair-like bristle (awn) from back of each flower scale (lemma); August–September.

Habitat: Dry, rocky or gravelly open areas; locally abundant on these sites.

Notes: The species name *spicatum* means 'with spikes' and refers to the spike-like panicle.

Anna Roberts

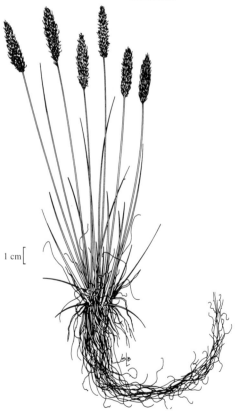

1 cm

DANTHONIA ♦ *Danthonia spicata*
DANTHONIE À ÉPI

Grass Family (Gramineae)

Karen Legasy

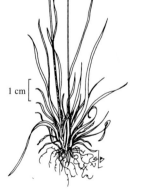

1 cm

General: Medium-sized perennial; flowering stems erect, wiry, smooth, hairless, rounded in cross-section, leafless for much of their length, 10–60 cm tall, 0.5–1.5 mm thick at base; in clumps; from shallow, fibrous roots.

Leaves: Basal leaves in tufts, rolled inward or flat and slender, often curved or twisted, much shorter than stems; stem leaves few, 3–18 cm long, upper leaves smaller, remote from long-stalked flower cluster; sheaths shorter than internodes, usually long, soft-hairy and with a tuft of long hairs at upper edge.

Inflorescence: Stiff, erect cluster (panicle) 2.5–5 cm long with 2–13 spikelets, short branches with usually 1 spikelet, scales (lemmas) hairy on the back, 3.4–5.2 mm long; bristle (awn) 4–7 mm long; July–September.

Habitat: Dry, open jack pine and deciduous forests; frequent.

Notes: Also known as 'poverty oat grass.' • Danthonia is not palatable to livestock, possibly because the plants pull up by their roots so easily.

Grass Family (Gramineae)

General: Perennial; erect flowering stems strongly flattened, abruptly bent at base to upward-growing, smooth, stiff and wiry; often bluish-green; 10–70 cm tall; grows in clumps from long, horizontal underground stems (rhizomes).

Karen Legasy

Leaves: Shorter than flowering stem; ending in a boat-shaped tip; 2.5–10 cm long, 2–4 mm wide; upper surface rough, underside smooth; sheaths loose, flattened and sharply ridged (keeled), shorter than internodes.

Inflorescence: Long, narrow, stiff cluster (panicle) 2–8 cm long; branches short, stiff, usually in 2s and bearing spikelets nearly to base; spikelets 3–6 flowered, crowded, almost stalkless, 3–8 mm long; May–September.

Habitat: Dry soil; waste places, cultivated areas, roadsides and sandy clearings; frequent.

Notes: You can recognize wire-grass by its bluish-green colour, flat stem and narrow, stiff, short-branched inflorescence. Wire-grass is sometimes called 'Canada blue-grass.'

 1 cm

FOWL MANNA GRASS ♦ *Glyceria striata*
GYLCÉRIE STRIÉE

Grass Family (Gramineae)

Brenda Chambers

General: Medium-sized, slender perennial; pale green; 0.3–1.5 m tall; often in large clumps from long, creeping underground stems (rhizomes).

Leaves: Flat, firm, narrow with tiny, pointed tip and rough surface; 2–10 mm wide, uppermost leaves 10–20 cm long; sheaths smooth or slightly rough, closed nearly to the top, finely nerved and cross-veined.

Inflorescence: Small, drooping clusters (panicles) 10–20 cm long; spikelets crowded near branch tips; greenish to purplish, 2–4 mm long, oblong to egg-shaped, 4- to 7-flowered; overlapping flower scales (lemmas) distinctly nerved; June–September.

Habitat: Wet organic to moist silty sites; black spruce and conifer mixedwood stands; common in wet places and abundant in wet fields.

Notes: Fowl manna grass's distinguishing features are its small, usually purplish flower clusters, distinctly nerved scales, drooping branches and slender stems.

1 cm

Grass Family (Gramineae)

General: Perennial; flowering stems erect, hairless or soft-hairy; 0.3–1.2 m tall; often grows in tufts.

Leaves: Flat, lax; taper to long tip; 10–20 cm long, 5–10 mm wide; upper surface hairless or sparsely hairy and rough, underside smooth with white midrib; sheaths often softly hairy and shorter than internodes.

Inflorescence: Open cluster at top of stem with branches drooping to 1 side; 10–20 cm long; spikelets 5- to 10-flowered, 1.5–3 cm long, 4–10 mm wide; greenish to bronze or purplish-tinged; flower scales (lemmas) overlapping, rounded on back, lance-shaped with a 3–4 mm bristle-tip (awn), slender-nerved, long-hairy along margins; July–August.

Habitat: Shorelines, roadsides; banks; clearings and waste areas around settlements; common.

Notes: Fringed brome grass is Ontario's most common native brome grass.

Karen Legasy

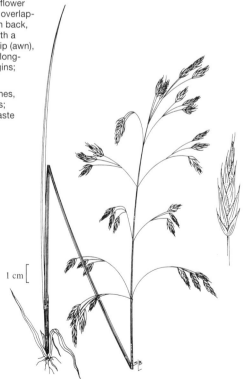

1 cm

Sedge Family (Cyperaceae)

Karen Legasy

General: Perennial; flowering stems triangular in cross-section and solid (i.e., filled with pith rather than hollow); from underground stems (rhizomes) with fibrous roots.

Leaves: Along stem's 3 angles in 3 vertical rows (3-ranked); sheaths closed, usually unclear exactly where leaves attach to stem (i.e., no distinct joints).

Flowers: Male or female, borne in spikes; female flowers produce single, minute, hard fruits (achenes) in tiny sacs called perigynia; perigynia inflated and easy to see on some species, such as bladder sedge (*Carex intumescens*), flat or thin on others; fruits angled (2- or 3-sided).

Notes: You can usually distinguish sedges by their triangular stems ('sedges have edges'). • Songbirds, small mammals, spruce grouse and ruffed grouse eat the seeds, the southern bog lemming eats the leaves and bases, and sedges provide browse for moose and small mammals.

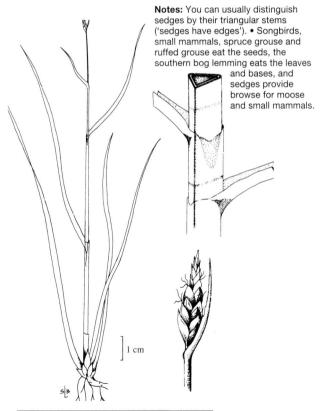

] 1 cm

Sedge Family (Cyperaceae)

General: Perennial; stems almost thread-like, rough, often reclining, 5–60 cm long; light green; from long, slender underground stems (rhizomes); solitary or in loose tufts.

Leaves: Flat, soft and weak; usually shorter than flowering stem; 1–2 mm wide; margins usually rough to base; drooping or weakly upward-growing.

Inflorescence: Slender, interrupted linear cluster of 1–5 small, stalkless spikes; with 1–5 (typically 1–2) female flowers (seed sacs) at base and 1–2 male flowers at tip, distantly spaced or upper few close together on main stalk; seed sacs (perigynia) egg-shaped or elliptic, 2–2.8 mm long, hard, with minute beak and many fine nerves, green, ripen to dark brown or black; small bract at base of inflorescence is either very short or missing; June–August.

Bill Crins

Habitat: Usually on organic soils; moist to wet areas such as lowland cedar and black spruce stands; forests, bogs and shorelines; spreads into wet clearings; common.

Notes: The very short bract at the base of soft-leaved sedge's inflorescence distinguishes it from the similar-looking three-fruited sedge (*Carex trisperma*), which has a long, bristle-like bract that overtops the flowers.

1 cm

THREE-FRUITED SEDGE ♦ *Carex trisperma*
CAREX TRISPERME

Sedge Family (Cyperaceae)

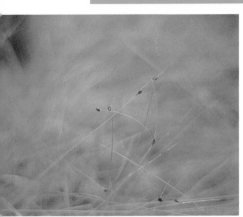

Karen Legasy

General: Perennial; flowering stems thread-like, weak, slightly roughened and usually reclining or spreading, 20–70 cm long; bright green; from slender, often elongated underground stems (rhizomes); solitary or in loose tufts.

Leaves: Soft, flat, narrow, 1–2 mm wide, shorter than flowering stem; margins rough to base; usually drooping; numerous dead leaves at base of plant.

Inflorescence: Slender, interrupted linear cluster of 1–3 (usually 3), stalkless spikes, spaced about 1–4 cm apart; spikes have 1–5 (usually 2–3) female flowers (seed sacs) at tip and male flower(s) at base; seeds sacs (perigynia) greenish, 2–4 mm long, flattened on 1 side, short-beaked and finely and many-nerved; leaf-like bract at base of inflorescence is bristle-like and overtops upper spikes, 2–4 cm long; June–August.

Habitat: Common on organic soils; in moist to wet areas; abundant.

Notes: Three-fruited sedge may be confused with soft-leaved sedge (*Carex disperma*). See notes on soft-leaved sedge for ways to distinguish these 2 species.

1 cm

Sedge Family (Cyperaceae)

General: Small perennial; flowering stems usually less than 10–50 cm tall; thread-like, hairless, erect or spreading; light green; from thread-like, creeping underground stems; densely tufted.

Leaves: Very narrow, about 1 mm wide, slightly shorter than flowering stem, upright, thin, wiry and soft; margins smooth except near top.

Anna Roberts

Inflorescence: Solitary terminal spike; narrowly oblong; 4–16 mm long; male portion at tip, short, female flowers below, overlapping; seed sacs (perigynia) green to yellowish-green, 2.4–6.2 mm long, oblong or elliptic, rounded and beakless at tip and tapered at base, finely nerved; bract at base is rough-margined and abruptly pointed, but sometimes with a long bristle-tip (awn) about length of spike; scales membranous, much shorter than seed sacs, lower scales tipped with sharp, firm point; June–August.

Habitat: Usually on organic soils; swamps, ditches and wet openings in black spruce stands; frequent.

Notes: Deer mice and other small mammals eat sedge seeds.

1 cm

Sedge Family (Cyperaceae)

General: Perennial; flowering stem thread-like, weak, hairless; 7–40 cm high; pale green; from slender, creeping underground stems (rhizomes); in dense tufts.

Leaves: Thread-like (less than 1 mm wide), shorter than flowering stem, flat or with edges rolled inward.

Inflorescence: Cluster with 2–4 long-stalked female spikes at base and 1 stalkless male spike at tip; male spike 4–8 mm long, usually overtopped by female spike; female spikes egg-shaped, 3–6 mm long, erect, on slender stalks, loosely 2–6 flowered, lower spike sometimes distant; seed sacs (perigynia) egg-shaped, 1.5–2 mm long, light green to dark brown, very faintly few-nerved; scales egg-shaped, usually blunt, shorter than seed sacs, whitish to pale brown, thin and transparent; bladeless sheaths at base of spikes are 5–12.5 cm long, colourless, with pale-green nerves; May–July.

Habitat: Dry, sandy to rocky soils; occasional on shores or open slopes of limestone areas, rare elsewhere.

Notes: The species name *eburnea* means 'ivory-white.'

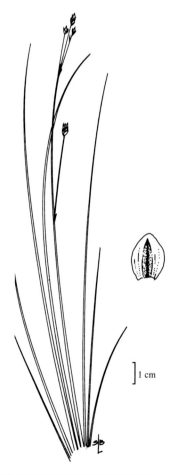

] 1 cm

Sedge Family (Cyperaceae)

General: Erect, slender, hairless perennial; flowering stems 10–30 cm high; light- to pale-green, growing in loose tufts; from long, slender underground stems (rhizomes).

Leaves: Usually near base, flat, often taller than flowering stem; 1–3 mm wide.

Inflorescence: Dense to elongated cluster of 3–5 female spike below and a male spike at tip; male spike short-stalked, narrow, sometimes a few female flowers at tip; 3–5 female spikes oblong, 5–15 mm long, loose to compact, 4- to 20-flowered,

Bill Crins

erect, stalked; seed sacs (perigynia) widely and inversely egg-shaped, plump, 2–3 mm long, white or almost white when young, orange to golden-yellow (dry brown) and fleshy when mature, several-nerved, beakless; scales highly variable, egg-shaped with blunt or pointed tip and membranous; bract at base of lowest spike has 3–12 mm sheath and blade often overtops spikes; summer.

Habitat: Wet areas; fields, damp shorelines, wet rocks; occasional but locally abundant in sedge meadows and along wet clay banks.

Notes: You can recognize golden-fruited sedge by its rounded, orange to golden-yellow, fleshy perigynia.

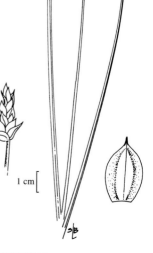

1 cm

SLENDER SEDGE ♦ *Carex lasiocarpa*
CAREX À FRUITS TOMENTEUX

Sedge Family (Cyperaceae)

Bill Crins

General: Perennial; flowering stems slender, 30–120 cm tall, stiff, smooth and hairless, bluntly angled, reddish at base; light green; 0.3–1.2 m high; loosely tufted from long, horizontal underground stems (rhizomes); in large colonies.

Leaves: Very narrow and slenderly tapering; 0.5–2 mm wide, typically do not overtop stem; basal leaves reduced to scales (aphyllopodic); margins inrolled and rough.

Inflorescence: Elongate, linear cluster 6–35 cm long with 1–3 stalkless female spikes in lower part and 1–3 male spikes at tip; male spikes linear-cylindric, on rough stalk, 1–7 cm long; female spikes cylindrical to elliptical, stalkless or nearly so, erect, 1–3 cm long; seed sacs (perigynia) oblong-egg-shaped, 3–4.5 mm long, densely hairy, with beak 1/4 to 1/3 as long as body bearing 2 sharp, 1 mm long teeth; scales pointed, reddish- or purplish-brown with wide, green centres; June–August.

Habitat: Wet fields and swamps; edges of streams and lakes; common and locally abundant in boggy sedge marshes.

Notes: The species name *lasiocarpa* means 'rough' and refers to the hairy fruit.

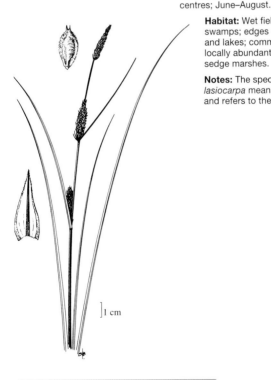

]1 cm

Sedge Family (Cyperaceae)

General: Perennial; flowering stems slender, smooth or strongly roughened, hairless, sharply angled and erect; pale green; 10–80 cm high; roots yellowish-woolly; usually in small clumps; from short or long underground stems (rhizomes).

Leaves: Flat; 2–4 mm wide and usually shorter than stem; light brown to pinkish-tinged sheaths at base of plant; margins slightly rolled under.

Inflorescence: Slender, 5–12 cm long cluster of 1–4 long-stalked, nodding female spikes with 1 male spike at tip; male spike 4–12 mm long, long-stalked; female spikes short-cylindric, 8–20 mm long, nodding or spreading on thread-like stalks 1–4 cm long; seed sacs (perigynia) green with a bluish-white tinge, brown at maturity, elliptic, 3–4 mm long, somewhat flattened, short-stalked and nearly beakless; scales lance-shaped with long, narrow point, brown, often with green midrib, longer but narrower than seed sac; lowermost bract usually overtops inflorescence; July–August.

Habitat: Poor fens, conifer swamps or peaty, wet areas; occasional.

Notes: Few-flowered sedge is also known as *Carex paupercula*.

Bill Crins

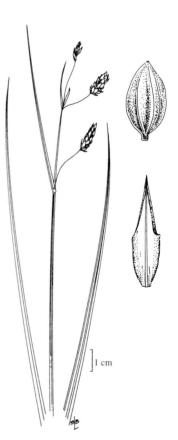

1 cm

RETRORSE SEDGE ♦ *Carex retrorsa*
CAREX RÉFLÉCHI

Sedge Family (Cyperaceae)

Karen Legasy

General: Perennial; flowering stem 0.3–1 m tall, erect, stout, smooth or slightly rough above, hairless; dark green; in large, dense clumps, from short underground stems (rhizomes).

Leaves: Flat, thin, soft, 30–40 cm long, 4–10 mm wide; margins rough.

Inflorescence: Relatively dense, 5–15 cm long, linear clusters of 3–8 large, short-stalked female spikes, with 1–4 smaller, nearly stalkless male spikes at tip; male spikes 1–3 cm long, linear, often with a few seed sacs at or below middle; female spikes upward-growing or spreading, cylindrical and thick, 1.5–8 cm long, 1.2–2 cm thick, become yellowish-green to tawny, closely crowded or lower ones are more distant; seed sacs (perigynia) dense, spreading to backward-pointing, egg-shaped, 7–10 mm long, with about 10 coarse nerves; tapering to smooth, slender beak about 1/2 as long as body, with 2 small, stiff teeth at tip; scales lance-shaped, pointed, smooth, 1/3 to 1/2 as long as perigynia; most leaf-like bracts at base of spikes are much longer than inflorescence; August–September.

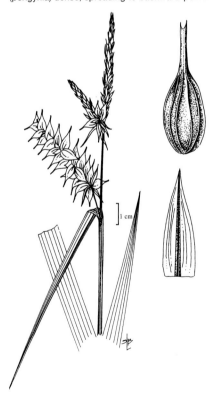

1 cm

Habitat: Rich low areas, swamps and wet fields; shorelines and thickets; occasional.

Notes: You can recognize retrorse sedge by its distinctive, spreading to backward-pointing seed sacs (perigynia).

Sedge Family (Cyperaceae)

General: Medium to large, smooth, hairless perennial; flowering stems slender and erect, up to 80 cm tall; dark green; flowering stems up to 80 cm high; some shoots have red bases; clumped; with or without short underground stems (rhizomes).

Leaves: Soft and drooping, flat or folded; up to 80 cm long, 4–8 mm wide, equal to or shorter than flowering stem; margins rough to base.

Karen Legasy

Inflorescence: 3–5 cm long cluster of 1–3 crowded, stalkless female spikes and a terminal male spike; male spike narrow 15–25 mm long, long-stalked; female spikes essentially stalkless, globe-like, 10–20 mm across, 5- to 10-flowered; seed sacs (perigynia) crowded, spreading, bladder-like, shiny, many-nerved, rounded at base, taper to rough beak; scales narrowly lance-shaped, 1/2 as long as seed sacs; leaf-like bracts at spike bases overtop inflorescence; May–October.

Habitat: Mineral soils, swamps, wet woods and bogs; frequent in shore thickets and wet forest openings.

Notes: You can recognize bladder sedge by its large, roundish female spikes with their inflated, bladder-like sacs.

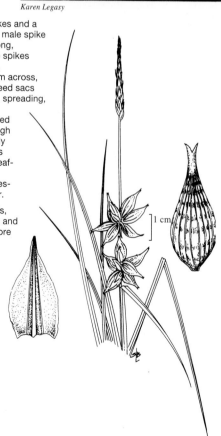

1 cm

COTTONGRASS ♦ *Eriophorum vaginatum*
LINAIGRETTE DENSE ssp. *spissum*

Sedge Family (Cyperaceae)

Bill Crins

General: Perennial; flowering stems stiff, 3-angled and rough at tip; 15–70 cm high; densely tufted.

Leaves: Basal leaves stiff, thread-like, 1 mm wide; basal sheaths brown, long and persistent, with fine fibres; stem leaves bladeless, consist of a conspicuously inflated sheath, with network of veins and dark, membranous tip.

Inflorescence: Single, erect spike, usually silky-white, cottony head; inversely egg-shaped to slightly roundish; 0.8–1.5 cm high; scales lead-coloured to blackish with whitish margins; fruit tiny, black, 3-sided, dry, hard, single-seeded (achene), surrounded (and hidden) by long, white bristles; April to mid–July.

Habitat: Acidic bogs and wet soils; open sphagnum bogs and low boggy thickets; frequent.

Notes: The genus name *Eriophorum* means 'wool-bearing.' The bright-white bristles of the seeds look like cotton.

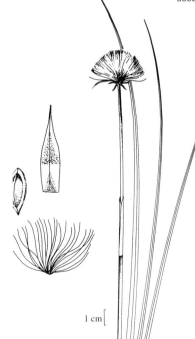

1 cm

Sedge Family (Cyperaceae)

General: Upright perennial; flowering stems triangular, slender and leafy, 0.3–1.8 m high, 1 to few from leafy crown; dark green; tufted, from stout, spreading underground stems (rhizomes).

Leaves: 0.5–2 cm wide; mainly on lower stem; sheath greenish, with V-shaped opening.

Inflorescence: Crowded, flat-topped, 3–20 cm high cluster of 4–8 primary stalks, each tipped with a dense head (glomerule) of spikelets; spikelets

Karen Legasy

greenish-brown (dark brown to blackish at maturity), egg-shaped to almost cylindrical, 2–8 mm long; scales egg-shaped to oblong, greenish-brown, midvein goes to beyond tip (excurrent) in a prominent bristle-tip (awn); fruit dry, hard, single-seeded (achenes), pale to white, flattened, wider above middle, 0.8–1.2 mm long, with or without bristles; 2 or more spreading bracts at base of inflorescence; June–August.

Habitat: Swamps, wet meadows; marshy shores.

Notes: Also called *Scirpus pallidus*.
• The species name *atrovirens* means 'dark green.'

1 cm

WOOL-GRASS ♦ *Scirpus cyperinus*
SCIRPE SOUCHET

Sedge Family (Cyperaceae)

Karen Legasy

General: Perennial; flowering stems thick or slender, smooth, obscurely triangular or nearly rounded in cross-section; leafy; 1–1.5 m high; in dense tufts with many curving basal leaves; from fibrous roots.

Leaves: Long, flat and rigid, 3–10 mm wide; margins rough.

Inflorescence: Dense to loose, reddish-brown cluster 3–10 cm long, upward-growing to drooping branches, each tipped with a loose cluster of slender-stalked spikelets; spikelets numerous, egg-shaped, 3–6 mm long, soft white-hairy with long, protruding bristles at maturity; bracts at base leaf-like, spreading and usually drooping at tips, often longer than inflorescence; August–October.

Habitat: Shorelines, marshes, ditches, swamps, bogs or wet clearings; common.

Notes: Wool-grass is a native perennial.

] 1 cm

TOAD RUSH ◆ *Juncus bufonius*
JONC DES CRAPAUDS

Rush Family (Juncaceae)

General: Annual; flowering stem low and slender, erect to spreading, unbranched or branching at base; 3–20 cm high; tufted; from fibrous roots.

Leaves: Thread-like and rolled inward, 1 mm wide; few; sheaths gradually taper to blade; usually shorter than flowering stem.

Inflorescence: Open, branching, wide, appears laterally flattened, clusters with remote flowers scattered along branches; about 1/2 as high as plant; flowers whitish, greenish or pale brown, 3–7 mm long, with 6 lance-shaped, scale-like petals and sepals; June–November.

Linda Kershaw

Habitat: Wet sandy areas; occasional but vigorously spreads along roadsides and in clearings.

Notes: The scientific species name *bufonius* means 'pertaining to the toad.'
• Toad rush grows in almost every country of the world.

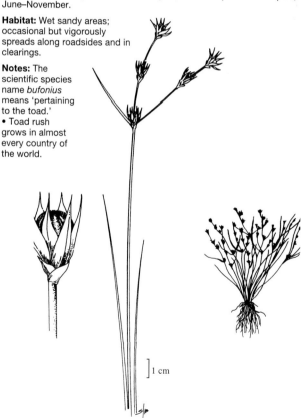

1 cm

WOOD RUSH ♦ *Luzula acuminata*
LUZULE ACUMINÉE

Rush Family (Juncaceae)

Brenda Chambers

General: Perennial; flowering stems erect, 10–35 cm high; loosely tufted from spreading underground stems (rhizomes).

Leaves: Basal leaves flat, up to 30 cm or more long, 1 cm wide, with white, cobwebby hairs; 2–4 stem leaves shorter and narrower with swollen, solid tips and widely separated, long, coarse hairs.

Inflorescence: Flat-topped clusters of spreading to drooping, 3–6 cm long branches bearing 1–few flowers; flowers 3–6 mm long; pale brown to straw-coloured; fruit a plump, cone- or egg-shaped, shiny capsule 3.2–4.5 mm long containing 1.5–2 mm long seeds; April–May.

Habitat: Moist clayey to medium-loamy sites; hardwood mixedwoods.

Notes: The species name *acuminata* means 'long-pointed' or 'tapering.'

1 cm

Rush Family (Juncaceae)

General: Perennial; flowering stems many, erect, up to 50 cm high; pale green; loosely to densely tufted.

Leaves: Basal leaves several, 1–7 mm wide, margins have sparse or abundant cobwebby hairs; 2–3 stem leaves flat with swollen tips.

Inflorescence: Open or dense cluster of short to elongated, slender stalks, each bearing a dense, egg-shaped to cylindrical cluster (glomerule) of flowers; 4–11 mm long and 6–9 mm thick; flowers pale, 2–3.7 mm long; fruit an egg-shaped capsule containing 1–1.3 mm long seeds with small, triangular basal appendages; flowers early in spring before leaves come out.

Habitat: Woods, fields; roadsides; scarce.

Notes: *Multiflora* means 'many-flowered.'

Brenda Chambers

]1 cm

FERNS & ALLIES

Illustrations of two common ferns are included to highlight features that will aid in identification. In addition, a simple pictorial key is provided to illustrate differences between ferns and their allies (the horsetails and club-mosses).

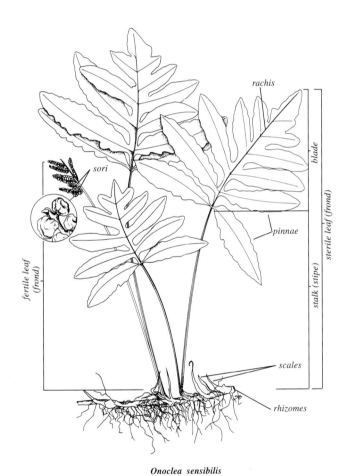

Onoclea sensibilis

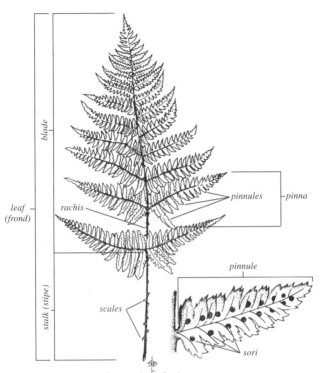

blade

leaf (frond)

rachis

pinnules — *pinna*

stalk (stipe)

scales

pinnule

sori

Dryopteris carthusiana

Simple Pictorial Key to Ferns and Allies

Sporophytes
vascular plants reproducing by spores

Leaves divided into branches or lobes with blades; feather- or fan-shaped

Leaves simple or branch-like

Branches and leaves whorled; stem ribbed

Branches and leaves alternate or opposite; stem not ribbed

Ferns
(Onoclea sensibilis)

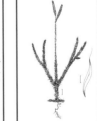

Horsetails (Equisetum)
(E. arvense)

Club-mosses (Lycopodium)
(L. clavatum)

SWAMP HORSETAIL ♦ *Equisetum fluviatile*
PRÊLE FLUVIATILE

Horsetail Family (Equisetaceae)

General: Highly variable; up to 90 cm tall; from a hollow, shiny, creeping underground stem (rhizome).

Stems: Usually solitary; erect; 3–8 mm thick with 5–10 grooves; fertile and sterile stems similar; stem sheaths have about 18 dark brown to blackish teeth that have narrow, white margins and are short, pointed and rigid; central stem cavity large (about 4/5 of diameter); branches none or in irregular to regular whorls, upright to spreading, 2–20 cm or more long, nearly smooth, 4–6-ridged, greenish, slender, hollow, unbranched.

Fruiting Structure: Terminal, spore-bearing cones, 9–35 mm long, on 5–32 mm long stalks.

Habitat: Frequently forms large colonies on silted riverside and lakeshore marshes; occasionally occurs in thickets, very wet black spruce forests and bogs.

Jim Pojar

Notes: One of swamp horsetail's distinguishing features is the large central cavity of its hollow stem. • The species name *fluviatile* means 'relating to or occurring in a river.' • Caribou eat dried horsetails in winter and moose occasionally eat them in summer.

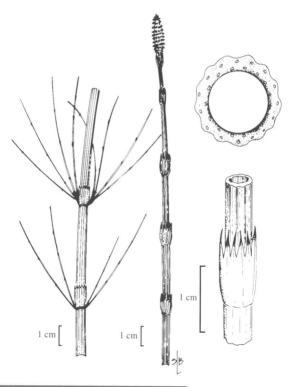

1 cm

1 cm

1 cm

1 cm

Horsetail Family (Equisetaceae)

General: Small or medium-large perennial; usually erect, commonly up to 25 cm tall, occasionally up to 40 cm; from extensively creeping underground stems (rhizomes).

Stems: Single or clustered; 4–14 ridged; fertile stems light brown, unbranched, appear in early spring before sterile stems and soon wither away; sheaths whitish, 14–20 mm long, with large, dark, clasping, lance-shaped teeth, each 5–9 mm long; sterile stems slender, green with bushy, upward-growing to spreading, simple branches in whorls; sheaths green, with 4 brown to blackish teeth; first branch segment is equal to or longer than nearest stem sheath.

Karen Legasy

Fruiting Structure: Terminal spore-bearing cones, 1.7–4 cm long, on 2.2–5.5 cm long stalks.

Habitat: Wet organic to moist upland sites, black spruce and conifer and hardwood mixedwood stands; frequent on low, wooded shores and forest clearings and openings; common on road embankments and railways; forms large colonies on clay riverbanks affected by high spring flood waters.

Notes: Aboriginal peoples used field horsetail for smoothing and polishing surfaces and as an indicator of where to find water. They also used the plant in a remedy for bladder and kidney ailments. See caution in Introduction.
• Horsetail species have apparently been used as indicators of gold deposits. See notes on meadow horsetail (*Equisetum pratense*).

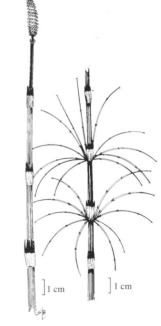

Horsetail Family (Equisetaceae)

NWO FEC Photo

General: Slender, erect, feathery perennial; 20–40 cm tall; from slender, solid, black, creeping underground stems (rhizomes); branches spread outward in whorls.

Stems: Usually single; fertile stems unbranched at first, appear in spring before sterile stems, eventually develop branches and resemble sterile stems; sterile stems slender and greenish with whorls of short, straight, spreading branches; sheaths have short, dark, sharp-pointed, white-margined, brown teeth; branches unbranched, very slender, 3-angled and 4–15 cm long; first segment on branch is shorter than nearest stem sheath.

Fruiting Structure: Terminal spore-bearing cones, 2–2.5 cm long, on 2–4.8 cm long stalks.

Habitat: Wet organic to moist spruce, and conifer and hardwood mixedwood stands; riverbanks and ravines; frequent.

Notes: You can distinguish meadow horsetail from the similar-looking field horsetail (*Equisetum arvense*) by their branches and sheaths. The first segment of each branch of meadow horsetail is shorter than the stem sheath near it, whereas the first sheath on each branch of field horsetail is equal to or longer than the stem sheath near it. Meadow horsetail is usually more delicate-looking than field horsetail and has conspicuous white-margined teeth in the stem sheaths.

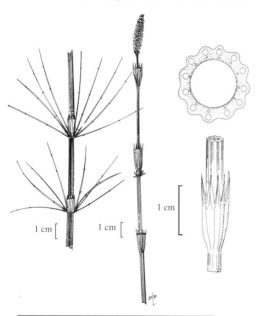

1 cm

1 cm

1 cm

Horsetail Family (Equisetaceae)

General: Delicate, lacy perennial; erect, up to 50 cm tall; from deep, creeping underground stems (rhizomes).

Stems: Mainly solitary, hollow with central cavity almost 1/2 diameter of stem; fertile stems brownish and unbranched at first, appear in early spring before sterile stems, sheaths relatively long, eventually become green and branched like sterile stems; sterile stems green with whorls of feathery branches; branches branched, thin, delicate, solid, upward-growing to spreading or drooping; sheaths green at base, chestnut brown at top, 4–5-toothed.

Fruiting Structure: Terminal spore-bearing cones, 1.5–3 cm long, on 2–6.5 cm long stalks; soon wither away.

NWO FEC Photo

Habitat: Wet organic to fresh upland sites, black spruce and rich conifer and hardwood mixedwoods; occurs in large patches in wet openings and thickets; common in damp forests.

Notes: Woodland horsetail differs from field horsetail (*Equisetum arvense*) and meadow horsetail (*E. pratense*) in the way its branches are further branched; those of field and meadow horsetail are not.

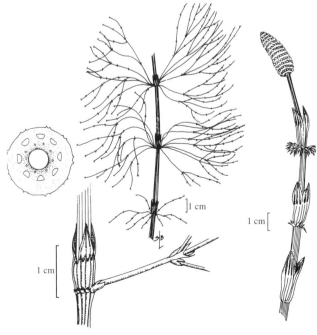

Horsetail Family (Equisetaceae)

Bill Crins

General: Smallest of the horsetails, grows in a curling, matted form much like horsehair; up to 20 cm tall; from shallow, slender, creeping and branching underground stems (rhizomes); often forms dense tufts or mats.

Stems: Clustered, prostrate, upward-growing and arched to recurving or zigzag; sterile and fertile stems similar, but fertile stems usually more erect; solid, dark green, 3-ridged, deeply grooved, slender, 0.5–1 mm thick, 3–20 cm long; unbranched, sometimes with small, irregular branches; sheaths have 3 (sometimes 4) sharp-pointed, triangular teeth with dark centres and light edges.

Fruiting Structure: Short, black, terminal, spore-bearing cones, 2–3 mm long, with a short, pointed tip, stalkless.

Habitat: Wet organic to moist upland sites, black spruce and conifer mixedwoods; humus of wet coniferous and deciduous forests, hazel thickets and around springs; occasional.

Notes: You can recognize dwarf scouring rush in the field by its slender, zigzag stems that often form dense tufts.

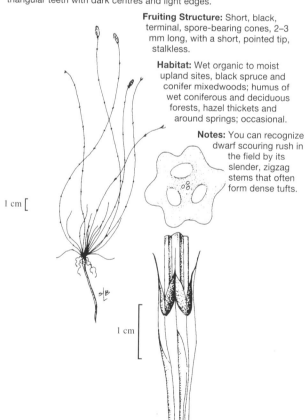

1 cm

1 cm

Club-moss Family (Lycopodiaceae)

General: Low, trailing, prostrate perennial; stems creeping, up to 2 m long, forked, often slightly covered by thin layer of humus; branches erect, stiff, unbranched or forked 1–2 times, 6–30 cm tall.

Leaves: Needle-like, stiff, narrowly lance-shaped, widest near middle or above, sharp-pointed tip, narrowed base, dark green and shiny; margins slightly to coarsely toothed toward top; 2.5–11 mm long; spreading to sometimes bent downward.

Fruiting Structure: Oblong to cylindrical, spore-bearing cones, 0.6–4.5 cm long, solitary, terminal and stalkless.

Habitat: All moisture regimes, soil textures and stand types; common.

MNR Photo

Notes: The annual growth of this club-moss is indicated by interruptions or indentations in the leaf pattern of its branches. • Interrupted club-moss has been used to make Christmas decorations. Aboriginal peoples used the spore powder as a drying agent for wounds, diaper rash and nosebleeds. See caution in Introduction.

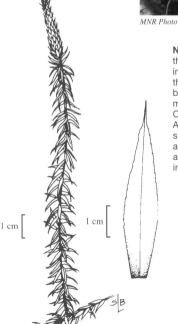

1 cm

1 cm

RUNNING CLUB-MOSS ♦ *Lycopodium clavatum*
LYCOPODE CLAVIFORME

Club-moss Family (Lycopodiaceae)

Karen Legasy

General: Low, trailing, prostrate perennial; up to 25 cm tall; stems extensively creeping on ground, branching, rooting at intervals; branches erect, widely forked or branched 1–4 times; stems and branches densely covered with spreading leaves; evergreen.

Leaves: Needle-like; lance-shaped or linear; 3.5–7 mm long, 0.5–0.8 mm wide; bright green; crowded, upright-growing to spreading; hair-like tip; margins untoothed to minutely toothed.

Fruiting Structure: Terminal, linear to cylindrical, spore-bearing cones, single or in groups of 2–3; long stalked.

Habitat: Dry to moist, rocky to medium-loamy sites, all stand types; common.

Notes: You can recognize running club-moss in the field by its widely forking, erect stems that often resemble a wolf's claw and give this plant its other common name, 'wolf's claw club-moss.' • The spore powder is flammable and has historically been used in fireworks and for flash explosions in photography. The powder was also used to treat skin disorders. See caution in Introduction.

1 cm

1 cm

Club-moss Family (Lycopodiaceae)

General: Perennial; 10–25 cm tall; stems horizontal, creeping, 10–40 cm long, often covered with humus and rooting, bearing many withered brown leaves; upward-growing to erect at tips; erect stems densely covered in leaves, forked or branched 1–3 times.

Leaves: Needle-like; lance-shaped with widest part usually toward tip; dark green, shiny; 0.6–1.5 cm long, 0.8–2.6 mm wide; margins sparsely toothed at tip; widely spreading to irregularly bent downward; dead leaves remain on plant.

Brenda Chambers

Fruiting Structure: Kidney-shaped, orangish-yellow spore cases (sporangia) in the axils of upper leaves.

Habitat: Fresh to moist, silty to sandy sites, transition-tolerant hardwood and hardwood mixedwoods; frequent.

Notes: Also known as *Huperzia lucidula*. • Shining club-moss may be confused with interrupted club-moss (*L. annotinum*) in the field, but shining club-moss does not have cones at its branch tips as does interrupted club-moss. Also, the erect portion of shining club-moss's creeping stem is at the stem tip, whereas the erect stems of interrupted club-moss are branches, produced at intervals along the main creeping stem.

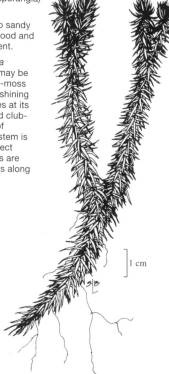

1 cm

GROUND PINE ♦ *Lycopodium dendroideum*
LYCOPODE FONCÉ

Club-moss Family (Lycopodiaceae)

Karen Legasy

General: Erect, bushy, 'tree-like' perennial; normally less than 25 cm tall; branchless near base, heavily branched above; branches upright and irregular; from deep, creeping underground stems (rhizomes).

Leaves: Needle-like; densely cover branches; lance-shaped, tapering to a sharp point at tip, base narrowed; about 5 mm long; dark green and shiny; margins smooth.

Fruiting Structure: Yellow, cylindrical, spore-bearing cones, 3.5 cm long at branch tips; stalkless; erect.

Habitat: Dry to moist, rocky to clayey sites, transition-tolerant hardwood and conifer and hardwood mixedwood stands; common.

Notes: Ground pine's distinguishing features are its distinctive, tree-like shape and needle-like leaves. • Aboriginal peoples used ground pine in a medicine for stiff joints. See caution in Introduction.

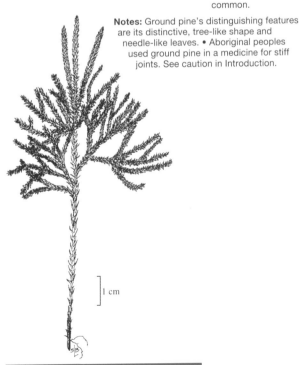

1 cm

Club-moss Family (Lycopodiaceae)

General: Erect, bushy, 'tree-like' perennial; 3–40 cm tall; main stems creeping on ground or slightly below surface; branches erect, irregularly forked 3–4 times, flattened.

Leaves: Scale-like (resemble cedar leaves); tiny, less than 1 mm long; in 4 rows; overlapping with bases extending downward and fused to the stem (except for the lower leaves); upper leaves narrow and curved inward; side leaves wider with spreading tips; lower leaves minute and triangular.

Karen Legasy

Fruiting Structure: Cylindrical, spore-bearing cones, 1–3 cm long, on 3–6 cm long stalks at branch tips; solitary or in groups of 2–5 on forked stalks.

Habitat: Dry to fresh, rocky to sandy conifer stands and conifer and hardwood mixedwoods; frequent.

Notes: Also known as *Lycopodium digitatum.*
• You can recognize ground cedar by its flat branches, which resemble the branches of white cedar (*Thuja occidentalis*).

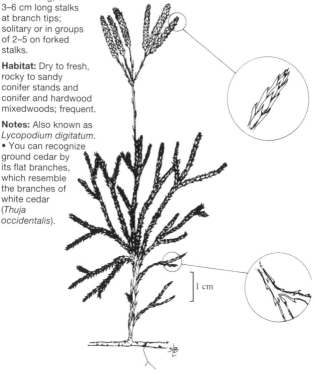

1 cm

RATTLESNAKE FERN ♦ *Botrychium virginianum*
BOTRYCHE DE VIRGINIE

Adder's Tongue Family (Ophioglossaceae)

NWO FEC Photo

General: Erect perennial; fruiting stem 5–45 cm tall, smooth, fleshy and pink at base, with single leaf.

Leaves: Single; terminal or near middle of fruiting stem; compound, lacy, 2–3 times divided (bi- to tripinnate); triangular, 5–40 cm wide and nearly as long; bright green, thin; leaflets lance-shaped to oblong, short-stalked, pinnate–bipinnate; sub-leaflets divided 1–2 times into small, oblong segments; margins sharp-toothed.

Fruiting Structure: Long-stalked fertile leaf with double rows of round spore cases (sporangia); blade 2–3 times divided, 2–20 cm long; stalk 3–30 cm long, from axis of sterile leaf; spore cases 0.5–1 mm in diameter, stalkless.

Habitat: Moist medium-loamy to clayey upland sites, to wet organic sites; rich conifer and hardwood mixedwoods and transition-tolerant hardwood stands; frequent.

Notes: Rattlesnake fern was probably named for the way the fertile spike resembles a rattlesnake's rattle.

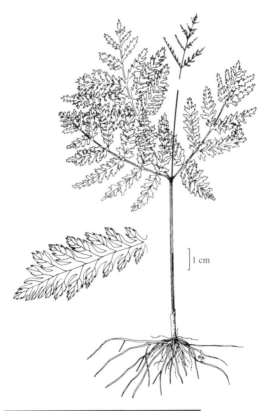

1 cm

Royal Fern Family (Osmundaceae)

General: Coarse, arching, large, often over 1 m tall; from a stout, creeping underground stem (rhizome) covered with bases of old leafstalks.

Leaves: Clustered, erect, greenish, spreading from a central point; compound, almost twice-divided with leaflets deeply cut into blunt lobes; oblong, widest near middle, tapering at tip and base; woolly when young, becomes hairless; outer leaves usually sterile and spreading, inner leaves usually fertile and erect; sterile leaves up to 1 m long, 30 cm wide and distinctly arching outward; fertile leaves usually taller, with relatively small leaflets that are greenish at first but later become blackish.

Fruiting Structure: Dense, dark clusters of spore cases (sporangia) on 2–4 pairs of fertile leaflets near middle of fertile leaves.

Karen Legasy

Habitat: Fresh to moist, coarse-loamy to silty sites; transition-tolerant hardwood and hardwood/conifer mixedwood stands; locally abundant in wet clearings and roadside ditches.

Notes: The common name refers to the fertile leaves, which are 'interrupted' in the middle by the small fertile leaflets.

1 cm

ROYAL FERN ♦ *Osmunda regalis*
OSMUNDE ROYALE

Royal Fern Family (Osmundaceae)

Karen Legasy

General: Large, delicate perennial; 0.6–1.8 m tall; large crowns of leaves (fronds) from thick, long-lived underground stems (rhizomes).

Leaves: Clustered from a central point, erect; compound, twice-divided (bipinnate) into 5–7 pairs of sub-opposite leaflets (pinnae); blade egg-shaped to widely so, dull green, 30–130 cm long, 10–55 cm wide; leaflets oblong-oval to lance-oblong, short-stalked, up to 30 cm long and 14 cm wide; sub-leaflets (pinnules) alternate, 7–10 to a side, narrow and oblong, taper slightly at tip, rounded and oblique at base, hairless and very short-stalked; stalks (stipes) pinkish, hairless, 20–50 cm long.

Fruiting Structures: Brown, erect, spore-bearing (fertile) leaflets, in branched, terminal clusters on sterile blades.

Habitat: Usually in acidic and wet soil; shorelines, particularly where boulders occur, forms extensive colonies in front of shore thickets; occasional.

Notes: The roots were historically used in a remedy for jaundice and in an ointment for wounds, bruises and dislocation. See caution in Introduction.

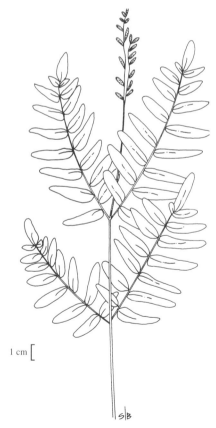

1 cm

s/b

Wood Fern Family (Dryopteridaceae)

General: Medium to large perennial, somewhat coarse; usually 50–70 cm tall; forms loose patches; from stout, brown, extensively creeping underground stems (rhizomes).

Leaves: Loosely clustered; compound, once-divided (pinnate); sterile leaves widely triangular with 5–11 pairs of deeply cut, lance-shaped to oblong leaflets 3–18 cm long and 1–5 cm wide; margins wavy; wing along central axis progressively wider toward leaf tip; stalks stiff, brittle and naked or have a few scattered scales near the base.

Karen Legasy

Fruiting Structure: Dark brown, spore-bearing (fertile) leaves, less than 40 cm long, often not developed, lance-shaped to oblong, compound, twice-divided (bipinnate); leaflets (pinnae) erect; sub-leaflets (pinnules) rolled into tight, bead-like balls around spore clusters.

Habitat: Shore thickets, wet woods and clearings, ditches; common.

Notes: The sterile leaves are very sensitive to cold and usually turn black after the first frost. The fertile leaves often persist over winter. Sensitive fern can be cultivated in moist garden soil in partial sun, but its creeping underground stems tend to make it a bit weedy for a garden.
• Sensitive fern is considered **poisonous to horses**.

1 cm

OAK FERN ♦ *Gymnocarpium dryopteris*
DRYOPTÉRIDE DISJOINTE

Wood Fern Family (Dryopteridaceae)

John Seyler

General: Small and delicate; up to 35 cm tall; solitary leaves or extensive patches from blackish underground stems (rhizomes) that bear scattered leafstalks (stipes).

Leaves: Single; compound, divided 2–3 times (bi- to tripinnate); widely triangular, thin and lacy; yellowish-green; up to 18 cm long and 25 cm wide; leaflets triangular, on stalks, 2 lowest leaflets are opposite and top 1 is longer, leaflets further divided into sub-leaflets; smallest segments of leaf have round teeth; stalks scaly at base, shiny and straw-coloured.

Fruiting Structure: Spores; on underside of leaflets in small circular or dot-like clusters near margins.

Habitat: Wet organic to moist, fresh upland sites, rich conifer and hardwood mixedwoods and transition-tolerant hardwood stands; common.

Notes: Oak fern can be cultivated in potting or rich garden soil and makes a nice addition to woodland gardens.

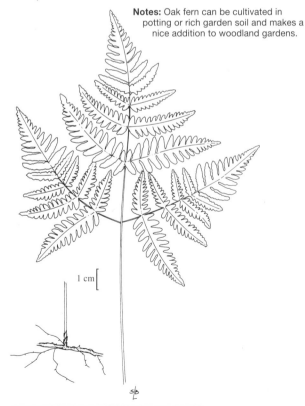

1 cm

s/b

Wood Fern Family (Dryopteridaceae)

General: Medium to large, delicate perennial; 30–70 cm tall, but sometimes up to 1 m; circular cluster of leaves from scaly underground stem (rhizome).

Leaves: Clustered, erect to spreading; compound, divided 2 to almost 3 times (bi- to tripinnate); blade dark green, 10–50 cm long, 5–30 cm wide; blade and leaflets lance- or egg-shaped to triangular; leaflets (pinnae) in 17–33 pairs, progressively smaller upward on leaf; sub-leaflets (pinnules) oblong, blunt; margins have sharp, pointed teeth; stalk densely scaly below leaflets, scattered scales above.

Brenda Chambers

Fruiting Structure: Round to kidney-shaped, dot-like spore clusters on underside of sub-leaflets near mid-vein.

Habitat: All moisture regimes, soil textures and stand types.

Notes: Historically, the fresh pulp from the underground stems (rhizomes) was applied to cuts and the leaves were soaked for several days to make a liquid used for washing hair. See caution in Introduction. • See notes on lady fern (*Athyrium filix-femina* ssp. *angustum*).

]1 cm

Marsh Fern Family (Thelypteridaceae)

Karen Legasy

General: Small and somewhat coarse perennial; up to 40 cm tall; from a long, slender, creeping underground stem (rhizome).

Leaves: Single, erect; compound, once- to nearly twice-divided (pinnate to nearly bipinnate); narrowly triangular; blade 6–25 cm long, 4–15 cm wide; leaflets long, narrow, pointed, in 10–25 opposite pairs, spreading at right angles to axis except for lowest pair, which bend sharply downward; margins deeply lobed so there appear to be sub-leaflets; lobes rounded; needle-like hairs, 0.5–1 mm long, on veins and margins of central axis; stalk brown and slightly scaly toward base, straw-coloured above, hairy, up to twice as long as blade.

Fruiting Structure: Small, circular spore clusters near margins on underside of lower leaflets.

Habitat: Acidic soils; moist woods, rich forest sites; shaded banks of creeks or streams; occasional.

Notes: Also known as *Thelypteris phegopteris*.
• Northern beech fern's distinguishing feature is its 2 bottom leaflets, which are distinctly separate from the others and bend downward and outward.

1 cm

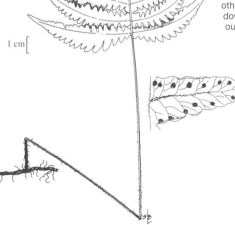

Marsh Fern Family (Thelypteridaceae)

General: Medium-sized, delicate, thin perennial; 10–70 cm tall; from a slender, black, long, creeping underground stem (rhizome).

Leaves: Single; compound, once to nearly twice-divided (pinnate to nearly bipinnate); blade oblong to lance-shaped, pointed, widest near base, green or yellowish-green, up to 45 cm long and 15 cm wide; leaflets in 17–40 pairs, all spreading at right angles to axis, lance-shaped, pointed, deeply lobed; lobes oblong, blunt-tipped, almost form sub-leaflets; young leaves minutely hairy on both surfaces; stalk of sterile leaf 9–35 cm long, pale green above, black at base, smooth or with a few scattered scales, shorter or longer than blade; stalk of fertile leaf up to 70 cm long, longer than blade.

Bill Crins

Fruiting Structure: Round spore clusters on underside of upper leaflets of fertile leaves.

Habitat: Wet areas; swamps, bogs, marshes and low forest areas.

1 cm

Notes: You can cultivate marsh fern in potting or garden soil for a woodland garden, but you may find this plant difficult to control because of its spreading and weedy growth habit.

LADY FERN ♦ *Athyrium filix-femina* ssp. *angustum*
ATHYRIUM FOUGÈRE-FEMELLE

Wood Fern Family (Dryopteridaceae)

Brenda Chambers

General: Medium to large perennial; up to 1 m tall; circular clusters of leaves from a creeping to erect, scaly underground stem (rhizome).

Leaves: Erect; compound, twice-divided (bipinnate) to almost 3-times-divided (sub-tripinnate); blade narrowly to widely lance-shaped, tapered at both ends, 40–90 cm long, 10–35 cm wide, pale green; leaflets (pinnae) lance-shaped, pointed, short-stalked to stalkless; sub-leaflets (pinnules) oblong to lance-shaped, toothed, those near leaflet tips merge; stalks (stipes) straw-coloured to brownish or reddish, fragile, grooved and scaly near base, shorter than blade.

Fruiting Structure: Slightly arching to kidney- or almost horseshoe-shaped spore clusters on underside of leaflets.

Habitat: Moist to rich sites, medium-loamy to clayey upland soils; conifer and hardwood mixedwoods and transition tolerant hardwood stands; frequent and locally abundant in wet openings and alder thickets.

Notes: Lady fern may be confused with spinulose shield fern (*Dryopteris carthusiana*) in the field. Lady fern can be distinguished by the way its leaves taper, with smaller leaflets near the base. On spinulose shield fern, the leaflets near the base are longer than the leaflets near the middle. The spore clusters are also different. On lady fern, the clusters are almost horseshoe-shaped, while on spinulose shield fern they are round. • Aboriginal peoples used the leaves to cover food. The fresh fiddleheads were eaten in early spring. See caution in Introduction.

1 cm[

Polypody Family (Polypodiaceae)

General: Large, coarse perennial; up to 1 m tall; often forms large patches from deep, spreading, branching underground stems (rhizomes).

Leaves: Single; compound, divided 2–3 times (bi- to tripinnate); blade widely triangular, up to 90 cm long and wide, held horizontally at the top of erect stalks; leaflets (pinnae) opposite, oblong, with narrowed and blunt tips; lowest leaflet pair much larger and twice-divided (bipinnate); upper leaflets once- to twice-divided (pinnate to bipinnate); sub-leaflets (pinnules) oblong to lance-shaped; underside hairless to hairy; margins rolled under; stalks hairless, straw-coloured to brownish, rigid, swollen at base.

Karen Legasy

Fruiting Structure: Strips of spore clusters on underside of leaves, along edges; often hidden by curled margins.

Habitat: Fresh to moist, sandy to clayey upland sites, conifer to hardwood mixedwoods and transition tolerant hardwood stands; common in sandy openings and along roadsides.

Notes: Recent research has discovered a carcinogenic compound in bracken fern that may be harmful to humans and live-stock. If cattle eat mature bracken fern leaves, the hazardous compounds can be passed on to humans through milk. • Aboriginal peoples used the underground stems and fiddleheads for food. See caution in Introduction. • Bracken fern is a minor food source for white-tailed deer and snowshoe hare.

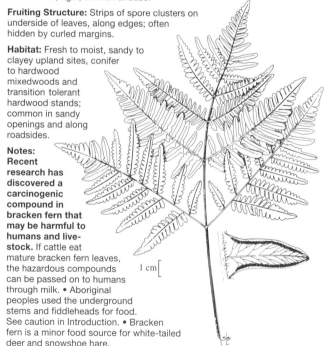

1 cm

COMMON POLYPODY ♦ *Polypodium virginianum*
POLYPODE DE VIRGINIE

Polypody Family (Polypodiaceae)

Brenda Chambers

General: Small, evergreen perennial; 8–30 cm tall; forms mat from spongy, rope-like, scaly, shallow, 2–7 mm thick underground stems (rhizomes).

Leaves: Loosely clustered, erect to spreading; deeply cut into 10–20 alternate to nearly opposite pairs of leaflets; leathery, deep green, often golden above; blade lance-shaped to almost oblong with pointed tip and squared (truncate) base, 5–25 cm long, 3–6 cm wide; leaflets (pinnae) 3–5 mm wide, 3–5 times longer than wide, rounded to pointed at tip, smaller toward leaf tip; stalk smooth and slender.

Fruiting Structures: Large, round, reddish-brown spore clusters, in 2 rows on underside of leaflets.

Habitat: Dry rocks and rarely on soil; shade or semi-shade; cool, damp, rocky shade along shores; common.

Notes: Common polypody can be cultivated in moist, subacidic potting soil in a sunny location, but it is difficult to establish in woodland gardens.

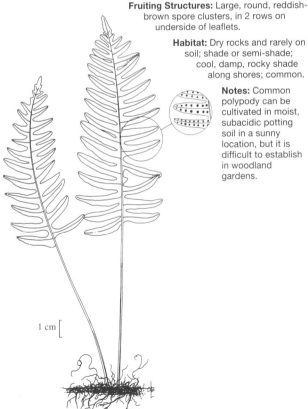

1 cm

MOSSES AND LIVERWORTS

To aid in the identification of mosses and liverworts, diagrams are provided which highlight the identifying features of these groups of plants. A pictorial key is also provided.

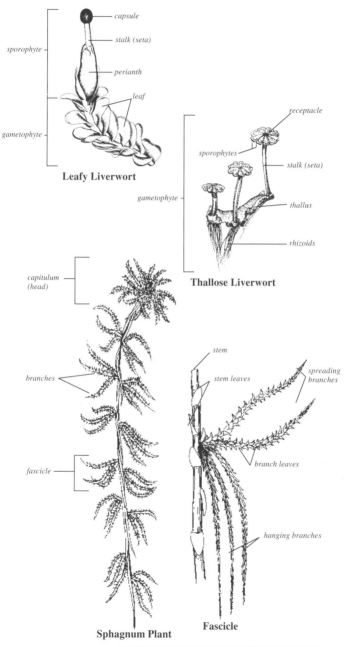

Leafy Liverwort

Thallose Liverwort

Sphagnum Plant

Fascicle

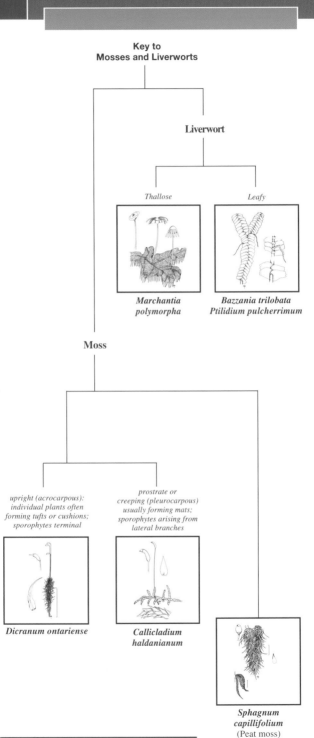

**Key to
Mosses and Liverworts**

Liverwort

Thallose

Leafy

***Marchantia
polymorpha***

***Bazzania trilobata
Ptilidium pulcherrimum***

Moss

*upright (acrocarpous):
individual plants often
forming tufts or cushions;
sporophytes terminal*

*prostrate or
creeping (pleurocarpous)
usually forming mats;
sporophytes arising from
lateral branches*

Dicranum ontariense

***Callicladium
haldanianum***

***Sphagnum
capillifolium***
(Peat moss)

Marchantiaceae

General: Large, leaf-like (thalose) growth; pale- to dark-green; about 2–10 cm long and 1–2 cm wide with wavy lobes along edges; upper surface flattened with barrel-shaped pores and (usually) a dark line down the centre, underside purplish and has numerous yellowish, thin filaments (rhizoids) that help anchor the plant; tiny, round, bowl-like bodies of vegetative reproduction cells (gemmae); umbrella-like male and female stalked fruiting bodies often present.

Dale Vitt

Habitat: Rock or moist soil; moist to wet areas; stream edges; ditches, burned areas; common.

Notes: Common liverwort's distinguishing features are its umbrella-like stalked fruiting bodies (gemmae cups), back midrib and smooth surface. Common liverwort has no fragrance, even when crushed.

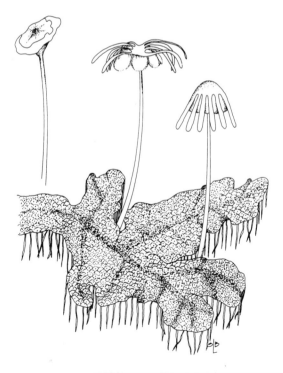

Ptilidiaceae

General: Prostrate; deep green or reddish-brown; in low, flat, dense, fuzzy and often circular tufts; stems prostrate, leafy and with upward-growing tips.

Leaves: Midrib absent; hand-shaped with roundish central area and 3–4 narrow lobes; margins have long, thread-like hairs; in 2 rows along upper side of stem; cells visible with a 10x hand lens.

Capsules: Cylindrical to pear-shaped, inflated; produce spores; at stem tips.

Robin Bovey

Habitat: All moisture regimes and soil textures, jack pine, black spruce and conifer and hardwood mixedwoods; on bark, rotting wood and rock, rarely on soil; very common.

Notes: *Ptilidium ciliare* is a similar species that appears to be larger and is much more upright. Unlike *P. ciliare*, *P. pulcherrimum* does not grow on soil and it is more firmly attached to its substrate.

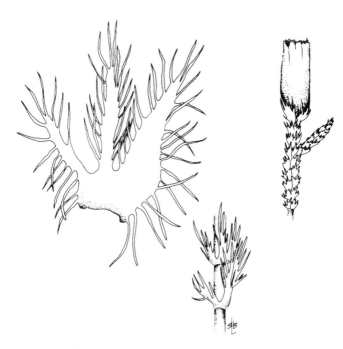

THREE-LOBED LIVERWORT ♦ *Bazzania trilobata*
BAZZANIE TRILOBÉE

Lepidoziaceae

Lepidoziaceae

General: Large, robust and leafy; dark green; usually 3–6 mm wide; leaves in 2 rows, drape down sides of stem and overlap upward so leaf at base of branch overlaps next leaf above it and so on to branch tip, giving a shingle-like appearance; leaves have 3-toothed tips; forms thick mats.

Habitat: Moist to wet areas; decaying logs and stumps, humus, tree bases and rock; shaded, moist or swampy forest areas.

Notes: Three-lobed liverwort's distinguishing feature is the

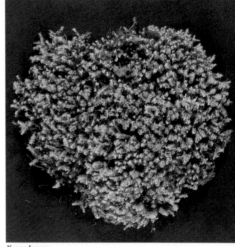

Karen Legasy

reversed shingle-like appearance of its leaves (think of looking at the arrangement of shingles on a roof, where the base of the stem would be the peak of the roof). In most other liverworts, the leaves overlap from the tip downward. The 3 small lobes or teeth at its leaf tips are another identifying feature.

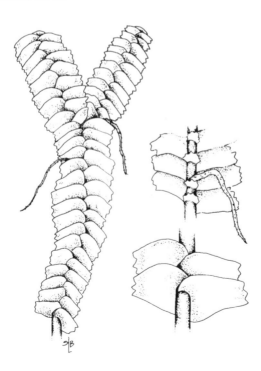

PEAT MOSS

**No Large
Terminal Buds**

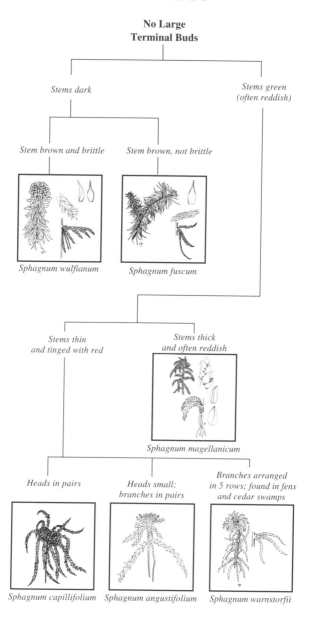

Stems dark

*Stems green
(often reddish)*

Stem brown and brittle

Stem brown, not brittle

Sphagnum wulfianum

Sphagnum fuscum

*Stems thin
and tinged with red*

*Stems thick
and often reddish*

Sphagnum magellanicum

Heads in pairs

*Heads small;
branches in pairs*

*Branches arranged
in 5 rows; found in fens
and cedar swamps*

Sphagnum capillifolium

Sphagnum angustifolium

Sphagnum warnstorfii

Peat moss (continued)

Large
Terminal Buds

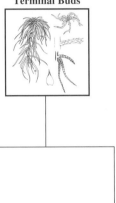

*Thick branches
with spreading tips*

Sphagnum squarrosum

*Thin branches; star-
shaped heads (5 rays)*

terminal
bud

Sphagnum girgensohnii

Sphagnaceae

Karen Legasy

General: Small to moderate, slender; head small, flat or rounded with a slightly star-like appearance; greenish to yellowish or brownish; forms dense mats and small hummocks; stems upright, usually distinctly pinkish but can range from pale green to yellowish, about 9 cm high; hanging branches normally thread-like, almost white, up to 10 mm long, loosely spaced and in distinctive pairs (note hanging branches just below the head).

Leaves: Midrib absent; stem leaves triangular with blunt tip, tiny and less than 0.8 mm long, margins occasionally have minute teeth; branch leaves egg- to lance-shaped, tiny and up to 1 mm long, occasionally wavy and curved toward underside on dry branches.

Capsules: Uncommon; rounded, dark brown or black; 1–2 mm in diameter; on short, erect stalks from the head.

Habitat: Wet organic to moist upland soils, black spruce and mixed conifer stands, open bog depressions above water level; on sides of hummocks formed by other *Sphagnum* spp. such as *S. fuscum* and *S. magellanicum*; open and treed fens, swamps and on damp humus; common.

Notes: You can recognize poor-fen sphagnum by its slender shape, its often pinkish stem and its distinctive pairs of hanging branches. It has one of the widest habitat ranges of the peat mosses.

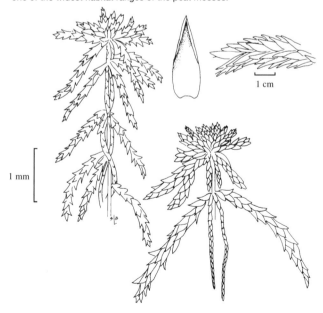

1 cm

1 mm

Sphagnaceae

General: Small, slender, delicate and wiry; normally dark-to rust-brown, occasionally greenish; head small and compact; forms dense, brown to brownish-green, rounded, cushion-like patches (hummocks); stems small, upright, dark reddish-brown, about 10 cm high, slender branches in clusters of 3–5.

Leaves: Midrib absent; stem leaves tongue-shaped with widely rounded tip, 0.8–1.3 mm long; branch leaves egg- to lance-shaped, tapering to point at tip, 0.9–1.3 mm long; margins curved toward surface and finely toothed at tip (use hand lens).

Karen Legasy

Capsules: Uncommon; round; dark brown to black; 1–1.5 mm in diameter on erect, short stalks from the head.

Habitat: Wet organic sites, black spruce stands; on top of larger hummocks; nutrient-poor areas; common.

Notes: Common brown sphagnum usually grows at the top of old, dry hummocks. Its brownish colour, compact growth, thread-like branches and brown stems help to distinguish this moss in the field.

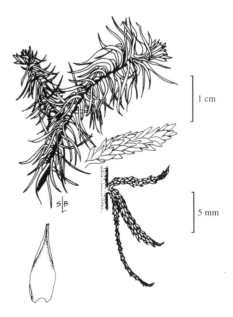

Karen Legasy

S | B

1 cm

5 mm

Sphagnaceae

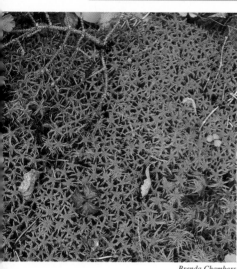

Brenda Chambers

General: Moderate to robust, slender and wiry; green to slightly yellow, never red; flat, star-shaped head has 5 radiating points and a distinct, shiny terminal bud in the centre; forms large, loose carpets or mounds; stems erect, stiff, woody, snap crisply in 2, green to pale green or yellow, about 8 cm high; branches in groups of 3–5 droop downward to be almost perpendicular to stem.

Leaves: Midrib absent; stem leaves widely tongue-shaped, only slightly longer than wide, tips blunt or flat with a ragged or toothed edge, 1.0–1.3 mm long, tightly pressed against stem; branch leaves egg- to lance-shaped, tapering to pointed tip, margins toothless (except at tip) and strongly rolled inward near tip, 1.0–1.4 mm long and closely overlapping.

Capsules: Uncommon; rounded; 1–2 mm in diameter; dark brown to black; on erect short stalks from the head.

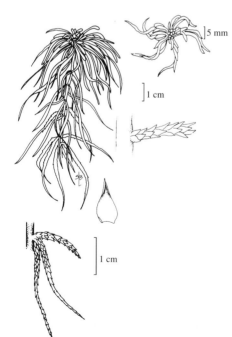

Habitat: Wet organic to moist upland sites, black spruce and mixed conifer stands, swamps and fens with black spruce and white cedar, poor to rich sites; common.

Notes: Common green sphagnum is one of the most common peat mosses. It can be recognized by its flat, star-shaped top, spreading branches that hang almost perpendicular to the stem and squarish stem leaves with a toothed, flat tip.
• The yellow-bellied flycatcher builds its nest well hidden in sphagnum moss.

Sphagnaceae

General: Large and robust; green to pinkish, red, or purplish-red; forms hummocks; stems erect, red when scraped and 8–20 cm high; branches in groups of 4–5, short, plump and appear thick and swollen.

Leaves: Midrib absent; stem leaves tongue- or spoon-shaped with widely rounded or minutely fringed tip, up to 2 mm long; branch leaves widely egg-shaped, curved inward (concave or hood-shaped), margins minutely toothed at tip, 1.5–2.0 mm long.

Capsules: Uncommon; round; dark brown to black; 1–2 mm in diameter; on short, erect stalks at top of plant.

Habitat: Wet organic to moist upland sites, black spruce and mixed conifer stands; sides of hummocks; poor to moderately rich sites; common.

Notes: Midway peat moss can be distinguished by its robust size, thick or swollen branches and its stem, which is red when scraped. It is usually green when growing in shaded areas and red when in the open.
• Sphagnum moss bogs provide habitat for the pygmy shrew.

Brenda Chambers

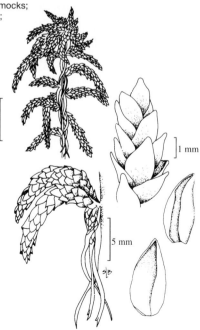

1 cm

1 mm

5 mm

Sphagnaceae

Rob Arnup

General: Small to medium, slender and usually short; pale or brownish-green to pinkish-red; forms tight, carpet-like mounds; head small and rounded; stems erect, stiff, occasionally forked with a double head, 5–8 cm high; branches in groups of 3–5, long, sweeping and outward-curving.

Leaves: Midrib absent; stem leaves tongue-shaped to oblong with bluntly pointed tip that is slightly notched or fringed and curved inward (use hand lens), 1.0–1.8 mm long; branch leaves egg- to lance-shaped with pointed tip, margins curved slightly inward at tip (use hand lens), about 1.2 mm long and closely overlapping.

Capsules: Uncommon; round; dark brown to black; 1–2 mm in diameter; on short, erect stalks at top of plant.

Habitat: All moisture regimes and soil textures, black spruce and mixed conifer stands; usually on sides or tops of existing mounds; open or shady acidic conditions; common.

Notes: Also known as *Sphagnum nemoreum*. • Common red sphagnum can be recognized by its sweeping, outward-curving branches that resemble long hair or tresses. • When dry, *Sphagnum* spp. are capable of absorbing a large amount of liquid. They have historically been used for personal hygiene, in diapers and to dress wounds (some *Sphagnum* spp. have antibiotic properties). See caution in Introduction.

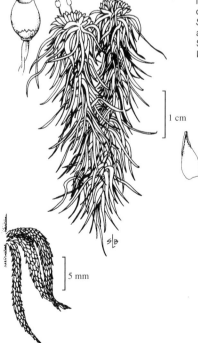

1 cm

5 mm

Sphagnaceae

General: Robust, tall and stiff; bright-to pale-green or yellowish; terminal bud prominent and surrounded by short, loosely clustered branches; forms loose mats; stems thick and green to reddish-brown; branches in groups of 5, loosely clustered; hanging branches closely cover stem.

Karen Legasy

Leaves: Midrib absent; stem leaves oblong to tongue-shaped with wide, rounded, slightly jagged tip, margins indistinctly bordered, large, 1.5–2.5 mm long, curved slightly inward; branch leaves egg- to arrowhead-shaped, abruptly narrowing to pointed and toothed tip that is distinctly rolled inward, large, 2–2.8 mm long, wide-spreading or spreading at right angles and erect at base, margins toothless (except at tips).

Capsules: Round; dark brown to black; on short stalks from the top or head.

Habitat: Moist areas, coniferous forests or rich fens with alder and willow, shaded areas, boggy depressions, rich cedar swamps; found with *Sphagnum girgensohnii*; common.

Notes: After you identify shaggy sphagnum once, you'll find it easy to recognize in the field by its branch leaves that spread at right angles, its bright-green colour, large size and large terminal bud.

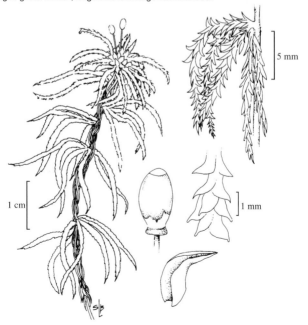

5 mm

1 cm

1 mm

Sphagnaceae

General: Delicate and slender, small to medium-sized, green in shade or red in sun, forms loose carpets and low hummocks; stems soft, weak and slender, usually reddish but sometimes brown, branches in clusters of 3–5 with 2 of them spreading, slender and strongly diverging.

Leaves: Midrib absent; stem leaves tongue-shaped with wide, rounded tip and shallow notch, margins toothless with a strong border strongly widened at base, 0.8–1.3 mm long; branch

Robin Bovey

leaves egg- to lance-shaped, recurved near tip on dry branches and straight on moist branches, 0.6–1.4 mm long and usually spirally arranged in 5 distinct rows; margins toothless and with a border.

Capsules: Uncommon; round; dark brown or black; on short, erect stalks from the head.

Habitat: Wet organic to moist, fine-loamy upland sites, black spruce stands, open, rich fens, swamps and bog forests.

Notes: Warnstorf's peat moss is usually red, and even in green shade forms, the red branch axis is visible through the leaves. This axis usually indicates calcium and, therefore, an enhanced wetland nutrient status.

1 cm

5 mm

Sphagnaceae

General: Medium to large; dark- to brownish-green, occasionally with pink to light-red tinge near top; rounded heads appear woolly or shaggy with densely crowded branches that resemble a clover head; forms loose carpets; stems erect, wiry, thick, stiff and brittle (snap when broken), dark brown to blackish and about 9 cm high; 6–12 branches in each branch cluster.

Leaves: Midrib absent; stem leaves triangular to tongue-shaped with pointed or slightly rounded tip that may be fringed; less than 0.8 mm long; branch leaves narrowly egg- to lance-shaped,

Karen Legasy

tapering to long, pointed, toothed tip, spreading when dry, margins toothless, 1.0–1.2 mm long.

Capsules: Uncommon; rounded; dark brown to black; 1–2 mm in diameter; on short, erect stalks from top of plant.

Habitat: Wet organic to moist upland sites, black spruce and mixed conifer stands; common.

Notes: You can recognize *Sphagnum wulfianum* in the field by its large, distinctive clover-like head and the 6 or more branches in every branch cluster along the dark, wiry main stem. See notes on *S. angustifolium*.

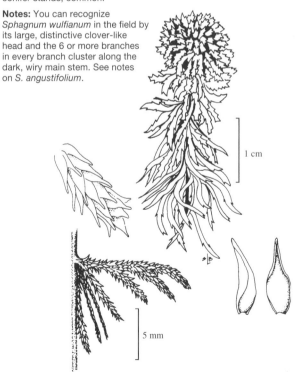

1 cm

5 mm

Polytrichaceae

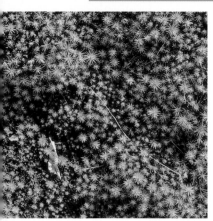

Brenda Chambers

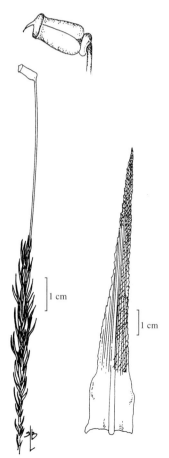

1 cm

1 cm

General: Small, robust; green, bluish-green to reddish-brown; often forms extensive, loose mats or tufts; stems stiff and coarse, upward-growing, 1–13 cm high and unbranched.

Leaves: Midrib single and extends along middle to tip; lance-shaped with pointed tip ending in a brown, short to long, toothed, bristle-like point; margins toothless and folded inward on leaves toward top of stem to give them a needle-like appearance; 4–8 mm long; straight or curved, erect and moderately spreading when moist, pressed to stem when dry; sheathing leaf base 1–2.5 mm long.

Capsules: Longer than wide, 4-angled (squarish); dark brown, covered with a pale, hairy cap; 2.5–5 mm long; slightly erect to horizontal on stalks 2–6 cm long.

Habitat: All moisture regimes, soil textures and stand types; mainly on mineral soils, sometimes on humus or decaying stumps; usually in dry, open or partially shaded areas; open forests or disturbed areas; common.

Notes: Both juniper moss and common hair cap moss can be recognized by the 'hairy cap' on their capsules. Juniper moss can be distinguished from common hair cap moss (*Polytrichum commune*) in that it is usually smaller (1–13 cm high whereas common hair cap moss is 4–45 cm high), its leaves have a brown, bristle-like point at their tips, the upper leaves are inrolled, giving them a needle-like appearance and its margins are toothless while common hair cap moss's margins are distinctly toothed (use hand lens).

Polytrichaceae

General: Robust; dark green to brownish; in loose to somewhat dense mats or tufts; stems stiff and coarse, 4–45 cm high, usually erect from a prostrate and slightly twisted base, unbranched.

Leaves: Midrib extends beyond tip and is sometimes toothed at back; lance-shaped with pointed tip and sheathing, yellowish-brown, shiny base; about 2–3 mm long; margins sharply toothed nearly to base; 6–10 mm long; erect to spreading, usually near tips; rolled and pressed to stem when dry, spreading and curved downward when moist.

Brenda Chambers

Capsules: 4-angled (slightly cubed) and covered by a hairy cap; reddish-brown; 3–5 mm long; on stalks 5–9 cm long.

Habitat: All moisture regimes, soil and stand types; predominantly on mineral soils in conifer forests, may also grow on decaying logs, rocks covered with moss, in sphagnum hummocks and on edges of swampy coniferous stands; common.

Notes: Common hair cap moss was used for bedding, to stuff pillows and to make small brooms for dusting. • See notes on juniper moss (*Polytrichum juniperinum*) for distinguishing features.

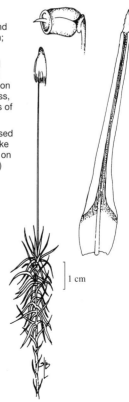

1 cm

Robin Bovey

General: Rather small; green to reddish-brown, dull; in tufts or growing close together; stem erect, leafy, resembles *Mnium* spp. and often ends in a bowl-like terminal rosette, 8–15 mm high and unbranched.

Leaves: Midrib narrow, single and strong, ending below tip in lower leaves, almost to tip in upper leaves; lower leaves egg-shaped with pointed tip; upper leaves gradually longer and narrower; margins flat and toothless or reflexed when attached to stems; upper leaves about 1–2 mm long, lower leaves up to 3 mm long.

Capsules: Narrowly cylindric, smooth; red or brown at mouth with 4 teeth inside mouth; 2–3 mm long; on erect stalks 6–14 mm long.

Habitat: Usually on rotten stumps or logs in advanced decay (in forest conditions), rarely on soil or rock; very common.

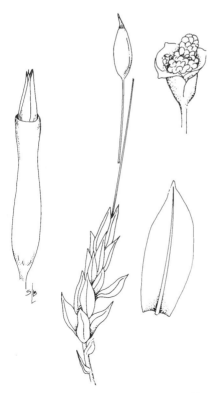

Notes: You can recognize *Tetraphis pellucida* by its *Mnium*-like leaves, the way its stem often ends in a bowl-like rosette of leaves and by the capsule with 4 teeth inside its mouth. The sterile stems of this moss frequently end in a cluster of gemmae cups (small bodies of a few cells which serve in vegetative reproduction). If you kick a rotten, moss-covered stump and it collapses, chances are you will find *Tetraphis pellucida* there.

Fissidentaceae

General: Minute to fairly large; growing close together or tufted; stems mainly erect and unbranched or sparsely branched.

Leaves: Midrib single and usually well-developed, rarely absent, ends below tip or extends shortly beyond; leaves narrow, tongue- to lance-shaped, in 2 rows and flattened together, usually crowded or overlapping.

Capsules: Symmetrical or curved, often abruptly narrowed below mouth, smooth, erect to bent or inclined; 16 red to reddish-brown teeth at or near mouth (peristome teeth); stalks terminal or lateral, elongated, erect or wavy and often abruptly bent at base.

Karen Legasy

Habitat: Soil, trees or rocks; submerged in running water.

Notes: There are approximately 15 species of the *Fissidens* genus in Ontario. This genus is very difficult to identify to the species level in the field. • *Fissidens* means 'split tooth' and refers to the usually forked teeth at or near the capsule mouth.

Dicranaceae

General: Small; dirty green to yellowish-brown or reddish; often in dense, dull tufts or mats; stems unbranched, often forked and 0.5–2.5 cm high.

Leaves: Midrib extends to tip or beyond; lance-shaped with sharply pointed tip; margins strongly bent backward from base and nearly to tip where they are irregularly notched or minutely toothed; 1.8–2 mm long.

Capsules: Cylindrical and deeply furrowed when dry; 1.25–2 mm long; leaning to horizontal on dark purplish-red stalks 8–30 mm long.

Dale Vitt

Habitat: Dry areas, exposed mineral or sterile soil, open and disturbed areas (often appear after fire); occasional on rock or rotting wood; roadsides; very common.

Notes: Fire moss can be difficult to identify in the field. One distinguishing feature is its deeply furrowed capsules with dark purplish-red stalks, and another is that fire moss will grow in a lot of different places, like cracks in the sidewalk or on old roofs. This moss is considered a weed and is often an early invader of disturbed sites such as burned areas, but it is eventually replaced by other species.

Dicranaceae

General: Large and showy; light- to yellow-green or golden; forms dense, woolly mats or tufts; usually shiny; stems erect, covered with thick, whitish fuzz or wool, 2–15 cm high and unbranched.

Leaves: Midrib very narrow, disappears below tip and has 2 toothed ridges at the back; lance-shaped with long, slender, pointed tip; margins sharply toothed to about halfway down leaf and widely curved downward below the middle; 8–10 mm long; spreading and slightly twisted or wavy (undulate).

Brenda Chambers

Capsules: Urn-shaped, strongly curved; 2.5–4 mm long; grooved when empty and dry; horizontal to slightly erect on stalks 2–3.7 cm long; usually a cluster of 1–5 stalks bearing capsules at top of each stem.

Habitat: All moisture regimes, soil textures and stand types.

Notes: Wavy-leaved moss can be distinguished by the whitish wool or fuzz on its stem and its cluster of 1–5 capsule-bearing stalks (most *Dicranum* spp. have only 1 stalk at the top). It is the largest and showiest of the *Dicranum* spp. See notes on *Dicranum scoparium*.

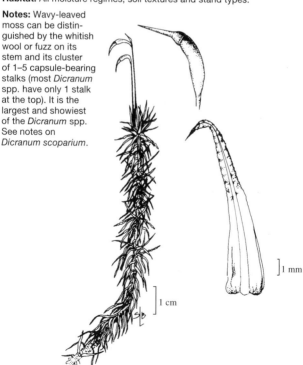

1 cm

1 mm

Dicranaceae

Karen Legasy

General: Fairly robust and usually coarse; green to dirty green or yellowish to brownish; forms shiny (sometimes dull) tufts or mats; stems densely woolly and 2–8 cm high.

Leaves: Midrib extends to tip or slightly beyond and usually has 4 ridges on the back; narrowly to widely lance-shaped with long, slender to broad point; margins usually strongly toothed in upper 1/3; 3.5–8 mm long; mainly folded and curved to 1 side or erect and spreading, occasionally pressed together; sometimes wavy (undulate); highly variable.

Capsules: Urn-shaped, curved; 2.3–5 mm long; smooth to grooved when old; horizontal to almost erect; on stalks 18–35 mm long; capsule lid (operculum) is often longer than capsule.

Habitat: Usually on soil; dry to moist forest areas.

Notes: Broom moss's distinguishing features are its leaves, which are strongly curved toward 1 side and its 1 (rarely 2) stalks with a capsule at the top of each stem.

Dicranaceae

General: Fairly large; dull-green or yellowish-brown tufts; unbranched; in compact tufts; stems erect, covered with thick, orange or yellowish 'wool,' about 4–8 cm high and unbranched.

Leaves: Midrib narrow and well-developed; lance-shaped, folded above, sometimes wavy, spreading or curved to 1 side, taper to long, pointed tip, crisped and curled when dry, dull; margins toothed in upper 1/2 or 1/3; 5–9 mm long.

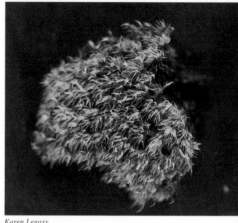

Karen Legasy

Capsules: Urn-shaped; 2–2.5 mm long; horizontal, strongly curved, grooved; on stalks 20–27 mm long; usually clustered in 3s.

Habitat: Coniferous woods on humus, dry habitats; rare along bog margins.

Notes: You can recognize *Dicranum ontariense* by its clustered capsules, its very wide-spreading leaves with their contorted, curled leaf tips and by its woolly stems.

1 cm

Dicranaceae

Karen Legasy

General: Very small to moderate; dark green to brownish or yellow-brown; forms dense, dull and woolly mats or tufts; stems erect, 0.5–3 cm high and unbranched.

Leaves: Midrib extends to tip or slightly beyond; narrowly lance-shaped with long, pointed tip; margins minutely toothed to about halfway down the leaf; 2–3.5 mm long; very wavy when dry; curved inward but usually not tubular above.

Capsules: Urn-shaped; 1.5–1.75 mm long; erect but usually slightly curved; slightly grooved when dry; on smooth, erect, yellow to reddish-brown stalks 6–14 mm long; solitary or in clusters at stem tips.

Habitat: Decaying logs and stumps, bark at tree bases or exposed roots; common.

Notes: *Dicranum montanum* is smaller than most *Dicranum* spp. It forms dull, dense, woolly mats that look like a small green lawn, and can be found on the bark at the base of trees or on rotting wood.

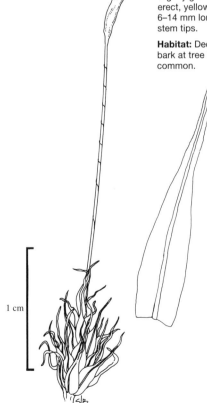

1 cm

General: In small compact tufts; dull green to brownish; usually has clusters of stout, stiff, rounded branchlets with minute, pressed-together leaves in axils of upper leaves; stems about 1–3 cm high and woolly below.

Leaves: Midrib extends to tip or beyond; leaves curved and turned to 1 side or spreading; lance-shaped with slenderly tapered tip or lance-egg-shaped with blunt to pointed tip; margins minutely toothed; 2–3 mm long; nearly tubular with margins strongly curved inward toward surface.

Capsules: Urn-shaped, irregularly furrowed when dry; 2–3 mm long; erect or almost so; on stalks 10–20 mm long.

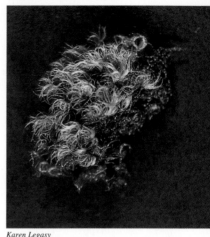

Karen Legasy

Habitat: Rotten logs and stumps; very common.

Notes: Spiky dicranum has almost tubular leaves and branchlets in the axils of its upper leaves. The leaves and branchlets will rub off in the palm of your hand because they are very brittle and break off easily.

Bryaceae

Karen Legasy

General: Robust; dark green, commonly reddish-tinged; in loose tufts or mats; main stems underground; secondary stems erect, 1–5 cm high and unbranched.

Leaves: Midrib ends at tip or shortly above; oblong to egg-shaped, with abrupt, rigid and stout point at tip; margins rolled downward on lower 2/3 of leaf, toothed on upper 1/3 to 1/2; 5–10 mm long; upper leaves crowded near top of stem to form a rosette up to 1.5 cm wide, lower leaves smaller, scale-like and remote; wide-spreading when moist, erect and irregularly twisted when dry.

Capsules: Oblong or cylindrical, short-necked and curved; 4–7 mm long; horizontal to hanging or drooping; smooth; on stalks 2.5–4 cm long and curved or hooked at the top; 1–8 stalks from each rosette.

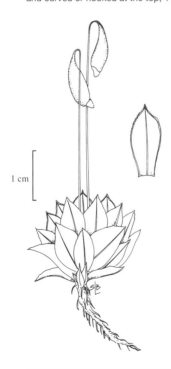

1 cm

Habitat: Wet organic to moist, fine-loamy upland sites, black spruce to rich conifer mixedwoods; occasionally on decaying logs or on bark at base of trees; uncommon.

Notes: In the field, rose moss and *Mnium* spp. appear very similar. The microscopic difference is in the leaf margins.

Mniaceae

General: Medium sized to fairly robust; light- to dark-green, yellowish, brown or reddish; in tufts and often densely matted with hairs below; stems erect, unbranched or forked.

Leaves: Midrib ends well below tip or extends almost to tip or slightly beyond; leaves oblong to egg-shaped or inversely egg-shaped to almost round, rounded to widely pointed tip often ends in a short, abrupt point (mucronate); margins toothless to strongly toothed and often bordered.

Karen Legasy

Capsules: Oblong-cylindrical from a short, usually inconspicuous neck; yellow or yellow-brown; sub-erect to inclined or hanging.

Habitat: Wet organic to moist upland sites, rich conifer and hardwood mixedwood stands; soil, humus, decaying logs and rocks; along edges of creeks or springs.

Notes: There are a number of *Mnium* spp., and they can usually be distinguished by looking at the leaves with a hand lens. Three of the most common *Mnium* spp. in our region are *M. cuspidatum*, *M. punctatum* and *M. pseudopunctatum*.

M. cuspidatum

M. punctatum

M. pseudopunctatum

Aulacomniaceae

General: Robust; yellowish-green to yellowish-brown; shiny; in loose to dense tufts or clusters; stems erect; green with a dense woolly or fuzzy reddish-brown to creamy covering; 3–9 cm high; unbranched or forked.

Leaves: Midrib prominent and extends almost to tip; egg- to lance-shaped with blunt to pointed tip; margins toothless or minutely toothed (use hand lens); 2–4 mm long; folded and usually twisted and crisp when dry; erect and spreading; usually grow together to form point at top of stem.

Brenda Chambers

Capsules: Cylindrical, curved and leaning or horizontal to almost erect; reddish-brown; 2.5–4 mm long; solitary at tip of an erect, 2.5–4.5 cm long stalk that grows from stem tip; have distinct ribs when dry.

Habitat: Wet to moist sites, organic to fine-loamy upland soils, moist microsites over rock, black spruce and conifer mixedwood stands.

Notes: Ribbed bog moss may appear greenish or brownish, but it always has a yellowish tinge.

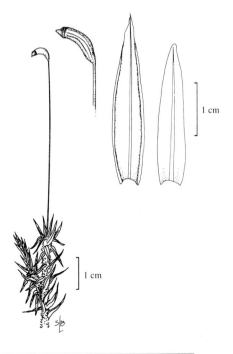

1 cm

1 cm

Hedwigiaceae

General: Coarse and mainly robust; olive-green, yellow or brown; usually greyish and very brittle when dry, softer and greener when moist; forms dull, loose to dense mats; immature stems upward-growing and curved or at an angle of 45° or more, irregularly branched.

Leaves: Midrib absent; widely oblong to egg-shaped with short to long, usually whitish, pointed tip; margins rolled downward in lower 2/3 or sometimes nearly to tip, irregularly and minutely toothed at tip; 1.3–2.3 mm long; erect or pressed to stem with tips spreading when moist and sometimes widely spreading when dry.

Capsules: Rounded; pale brown near base, rim reddish-brown; smooth, shiny when dry; erect; deeply immersed in leaves at stem top; on a very short stalk.

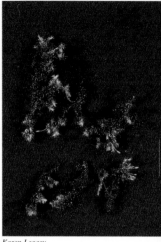

Karen Legasy

Habitat: Dry rock (granite); open or partially shaded areas, open forests; roadsides; common.

Notes: You can recognize witch's hair in the field by the following characteristics: it has transparent, whitish leaf tips, it is rigid and greyish when dry, but becomes softer and olive-green with spreading leaves when moist and its capsules are immersed in the leaves. It grows like hair hanging down on rock.

Neckeraceae

General: Medium to fairly large; light- to yellow-green; soft, shiny; forms mats.

Stem: Stems creeping, 5–10 cm long; secondary stems horizontal or somewhat hanging, with numerous flat and spreading branches on 2 sides, like a feather (sub-pinnate).

Leaves: Midrib short and double or lacking; oblong-lance-shaped to oblong-egg-shaped with pointed tip; margins minutely toothed at tip and indistinctly wavy and minutely toothed to middle or below; 2–2.5 mm long; soft, shiny.

Capsules: Oblong-egg-shaped; brown; about 1.5 mm long; immersed or completely covered; on stalks about 1 mm long (shorter than capsule).

Habitat: Usually on tree trunks in moist coniferous forests, sometimes on logs or rocks; common.

Notes: You can recognize *Neckera pennata* by its flat, outward-spreading branches and its soft, shiny, wavy leaves. It eventually becomes faded and shaggy.

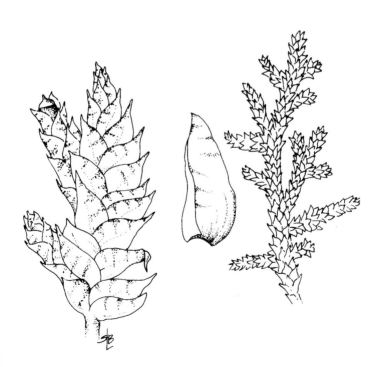

Thuidiaceae

General: Robust and fern- or lace-like; green to yellowish; forms mats; stems spreading or upward-growing and arched, 3–8 cm long and branched 2–3 times with branches on both sides of axis (bi- to tripinnate), resembling a fern frond or leaf.

Leaves: Midrib 1/2 to 2/3 leaf length; stem leaves triangular to egg-shaped with pointed tips, margins minutely toothed and rolled downward, 0.6–1.4 mm long, folded or pleated; branch leaves of primary branches are egg-shaped with pointed tips,

Karen Legasy

tiny, less than 0.5 mm long, erect and spreading; leaves of secondary branches are smaller.

Capsules: Cylindrical, curved; 1.8–4 mm long; slightly erect to horizontal on smooth, reddish stalks 1.5–4.5 cm long.

Habitat: Wet organic to moist, coarse-loamy to clayey upland sites, rich conifer and hardwood mixedwoods and transition tolerant hardwood stands.

Notes: You may encounter a similar species, *Thuidium recognitum*, in our region, and it is difficult to distinguish the 2 in the field. You can recognize common fern moss by its lace-like appearance. Common fern moss may be confused with stair-step moss (*Hylocomium splendens*), but common fern moss's vertical stem does not give the image of steps as does stair-step moss.

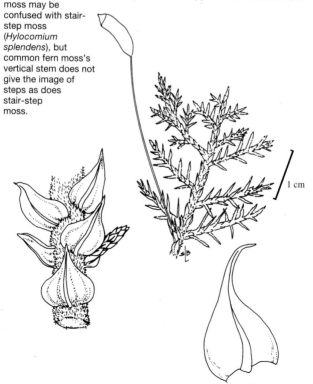

1 cm

Amblystegiaceae

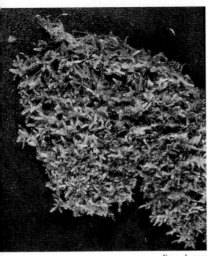

Karen Legasy

General: Slender to medium-sized; green, yellowish or brownish; forms loose, slightly shiny mats or tufts; stems creeping to crowded and upward-growing or erect; branches irregularly located on both sides of stem (pinnate).

Leaves: Midrib single and extends to tip; lance-shaped with long, pointed tip; margins remotely and minutely toothed toward tip; 2.5–4 mm long; strongly curved toward same side of branch or stem which appears hooked at the end (sickle-shaped); slightly to strongly folded or pleated, especially when dry.

Capsules: Oblong to cylindrical, curved and usually horizontal at tips of stalks, brown, 1.7–3 mm long; stalks 1.5–3.2 cm long.

Habitat: All moisture regimes, soil textures and stand types; decaying wood, humus, bark at tree bases and rocks.

Notes: You can recognize sickle moss by the way its hooked leaves curve or curl toward 1 side of the stem or branch. Sickle moss was named for its curled leaves, which are are said to resemble a sickle (a tool with a curved blade used for cutting tall grass, etc.).

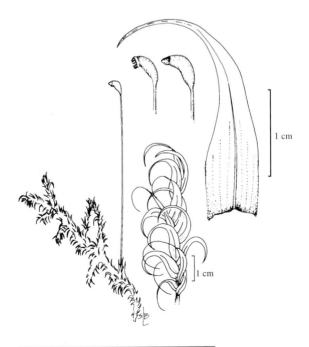

1 cm

1 cm

Bracytheciaceae

General: Robust and rigid or stiff; yellowish-green to golden-brown; in dense to loose mats or tufts; usually glossy or shiny when dry; stems upward-growing, brown and woolly or felt-like, 5–15 cm high, once-branched on each side (pinnate); branches normally straight and horizontal-growing.

Leaves: Midrib slender, difficult to see and extends to 3/4 or more of leaf; stem leaves slenderly triangular, tapering to long, pointed tip; margins toothless; 3–4 mm long; stiff; erect and spreading, occasionally turned toward 1 side; strongly folded or pleated lengthwise; branch leaves similar.

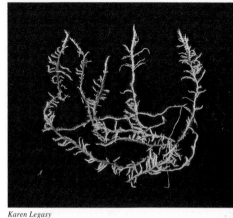

Karen Legasy

Capsules: Oblong to cylindrical and curved; orangish-brown; 2–3 mm long; horizontal or slightly erect; on smooth, reddish stalks 2.7–4.7 cm long.

Habitat: Wet organic to silty, moist upland sites, black spruce and conifer mixedwood stands, calcium-rich sites, fens and swamps; characteristic of rich, open bogs.

Notes: Fuzzy brown moss can be recognized by its yellowish-golden colour, its erect stem with a brown, felt-like or woolly covering and its erect, pleated leaves which are usually shiny when dry.

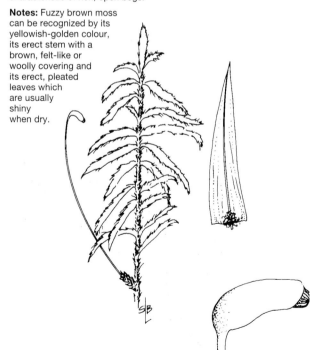

Brachytheciaceae

Karen Legasy

General: Slender to somewhat robust; green to whitish-green or yellowish-golden; usually in flat, small to large and slightly shiny mats; stems curved or creeping with upward-growing tips; irregularly branched; often have runners at ends.

Leaves: Midrib extends to top of leaf but rarely to tip; stem leaves egg- to lance-shaped with long, pointed tips; margins usually flat and finely toothed, usually curved inward and pleated, erect or angled and occasionally slightly turned to 1 side, crowded; branch leaves similar but usually shorter and narrower.

Capsules: Oblong to egg-shaped with wider end toward top, relatively short and thick; curved; leaning to horizontal on elongated stalks, smooth.

Habitat: Rock, soil, decaying wood and tree bases; dry to moist forest areas; light or shade.

Notes: *Brachythecium* spp. are difficult to distinguish in the field. You can recognize them by their greenish to yellowish colour, strong midrib and the flat, slightly shiny mats they form.

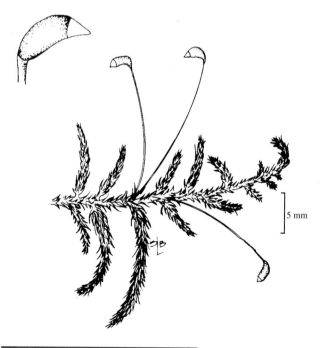

5 mm

Hypnaceae

General: Bright green to yellowish or brownish; forms extensive flat, shiny and often large mats; stems creeping with short, unequal, tapered, flat and straight or curved branches.

Leaves: Midrib very short and double or absent; stem leaves egg-shaped, narrow to a short or long, pointed tip, margins toothless, 1–1.7 mm long, their appearance does not change much when dry, often arranged slightly toward 1 side, especially near branch ends (appear flat at branch ends), erect and spreading; branch leaves similar.

Brenda Chambers

Capsules: Narrowly cylindrical, curved, erect to inclined; 1.7–3 mm long; individuals at tips of slender, erect, reddish to brownish stalks 16–32 mm long.

Habitat: Dry to moist, sandy to fine-loamy upland sites, conifer and hardwood mixedwoods; usually on logs or stumps and in partial shade, sometimes on bark at base of tree trunks; rocks.

Notes: *Callicladium haldanianum* can be recognized by its short, flattened branches that often resemble small swords and by its erect, curved capsules.

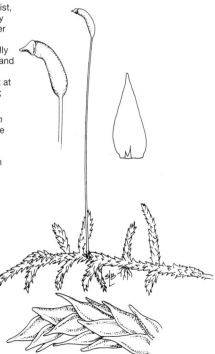

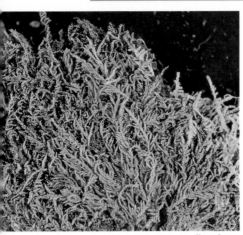

General: Small; dark- to yellow-green; forms dense, slightly shiny mats; stems creeping with branches arranged along 2 sides, resembling a feather (pinnate).

Leaves: Midrib short and double; oblong to egg-shaped with pointed tip; margins minutely toothed; 0.6–1 mm long; crowded, erect and spreading, folded and bent to 1 side, very tiny.

Capsules: Cylindrical and curved; about 1.5–2 mm long; partially erect; on stalks 6–13 mm long.

Karen Legasy

Habitat: Dry to moist upland sites, rich hardwood-dominated and conifer mixedwood stands; usually grows on bark at tree bases (mainly hardwoods), may also grow on logs and humus; common.

Notes: You can distinguish *Hypnum pallescens* by its very small size (which makes it a difficult genus to identify in the field) and by the way it usually grows on the bark at the base of hardwoods.

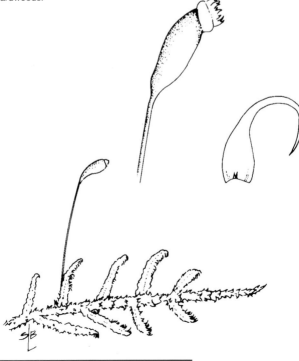

General: Robust and striking feathermoss; bright green to goldish; flat, feather-like; densely overlapping in patches to form shiny mats; stems semi-erect, greenish, 3.5–11 cm high, branches taper to become shorter toward base and tip of stem, stem and branch tips curved.

Leaves: Midrib short and double or absent; stem leaves egg-shaped to triangular with long, pointed tips prominently curved and turned to 1 side, concave with folds or pleats; margins flat and minutely toothed toward tip, 2–3 mm long; branch leaves similar but slightly smaller, 1.2–2 mm long.

Brenda Chambers

Capsules: Oblong to cylindrical, curved and tapered at base; reddish-brown, dull; 2–3 mm long; horizontal on a glossy, reddish-brown stalk 25–45 mm long.

Habitat: All moisture regimes, soil textures and stand types; logs, stumps, stones, humus and mineral soil; grows with Schreber's moss.

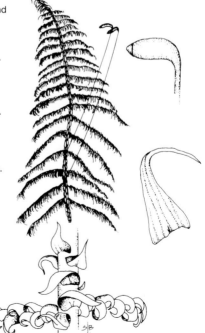

1 cm

Notes: Its distinctive feather- or plume-like appearance gives this moss its common name.

SCHREBER'S MOSS ♦ *Pleurozium schreberi*
HYPNE DE SCHREBER

Hylocomiaceae

Karen Legasy

General: Bright, glossy and robust feathermoss; light green to yellowish; forms large, shiny mats; stems upward-growing to erect from a prostrate base, red, 7–16 cm high, branches give a feather-like appearance (pinnately branched).

Leaves: Midrib very short, double, near base and not always apparent; stem leaves egg-shaped to widely oval with pointed to blunt or rounded tips; margins curved inward to give a spoon-like appearance, may have tiny teeth at tip (use hand lens) and are about 1.5 mm long; branch leaves similar, slightly smaller, and about 1.3 mm long.

Capsules: Cylindrical and curved; brown to reddish-brown; 2–2.5 mm long; on a glossy, reddish-brown stalk 20–43 cm long; scattered along stem.

Habitat: A wide range of forest habitat soil and site conditions, shady to open areas; very common.

Notes: Schreber's moss is the most common feathermoss in the boreal forest of Northern Ontario. • Schreber's moss has commonly been called 'big red stem moss' because of its red stem.

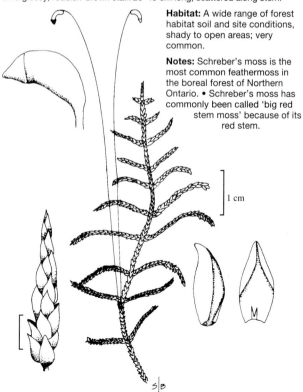

1 cm

Hylocomiaceae

General: Delicate feathermoss; yellowish to brownish-green; forms loose, silk-like mats; stems arched and wiry, reddish to brownish and covered with green scales; up to 15 cm long, branches further branched 2–3 times to give a lacy appearance and new growth starts near centre of previous year's shoot to give a step-like appearance, step-like layers or fronds somewhat triangular.

Leaves: Midrib double and less than 1/3 to nearly 1/2 of leaf length; stem leaves egg-shaped with sharply pointed tips, margins curled inward in a spoon-like fashion and have tiny

Karen Legasy

teeth (use hand lens), about 3 mm long and loosely overlapping with curled tips; branch leaves about 1.2 mm long, similar but tightly overlapping, tips not curled.

Capsules: Egg-shaped with long, beaked lid (operculum); brown to reddish-brown; 1.5–2.7 mm long; horizontal on smooth, reddish stalks 12–30 mm long; scattered along stem.

Habitat: All moisture regimes, soil textures and stand types; normally grows with Schreber's moss and plume moss; common.

Notes: You can recognize stair-step moss by its distinctive, step-like appearance.

Hylocomiaceae

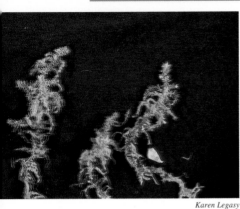

Karen Legasy

General: Coarse and robust; dark- to bright-green or yellowish-green; forms loose mats or tufts; stems reclining to erect, orange-red, up to 20 cm long, branches irregular and unequal, orange-red, on all sides of stem, horizontal and usually tapered and curved downward at tips.

Leaves: 2 prominent midribs extend from base to almost 2/3 of leaf length; stem leaves egg- to heart-shaped with a wide, long, tapered and pointed tip and clasping base; margins densely toothed in upper 1/2, remotely and minutely toothed toward base; 3.5–5 mm long; erect and spreading; irregularly wrinkled or pleated; branch leaves oblong to egg-shaped with long, pointed tip and clasping base; margins usually distantly and minutely toothed all around but sometimes densely toothed near tip; 1.5–3 mm long; erect or erect and spreading.

Capsules: Cylindrical, curved and horizontal to drooping; reddish-brown; 1.5–3 mm long; on glossy, reddish-brown stalks 1.5–4.5 cm long that become somewhat twisted when dry.

Habitat: All moisture regimes and soil textures (except very dry rocky sites), often in herb-rich conifer and hardwood mixedwood stands; common.

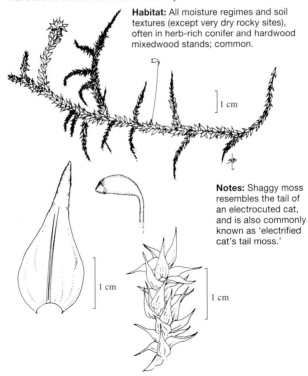

1 cm

1 cm

1 cm

Notes: Shaggy moss resembles the tail of an electrocuted cat, and is also commonly known as 'electrified cat's tail moss.'

Climaceaceae

General: Tree-like; yellowish-green or dark green; dull, but shiny when dry; soft; stems upward-growing, branched and usually 3–9 cm but sometimes up to 13 cm high.

Leaves: Midrib extends almost to tip; egg- to slightly lance-shaped with blunt to short, pointed tip; margins coarsely toothed near top; 2–3 mm long.

Capsules: Oblong to cylindrical; 1.5–3 mm long; erect; on stalks 1.8–4.5 cm long; capsule lid (operculum) beaked.

Karen Legasy

Habitat: Wet organic and moist clayey to fine-loamy upland sites, rich conifer and hardwood mixedwoods; common.

Notes: You can recognize tree moss by its small, tree-like shape. • Some people tried to use *Climacium* spp. to decorate women's hats, without success.

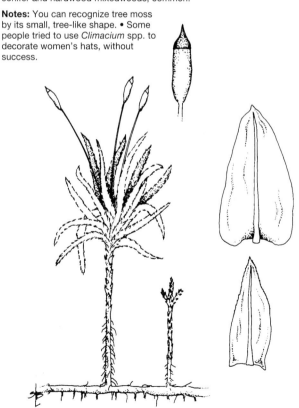

LICHENS

This group has been divided into 4 subgroups based on differences in life form. These are leaf, club/cup, shrub and hair (pendant) lichens. A pictorial key to these subgroups follows illustrations which highlight identifying features of common lichens.

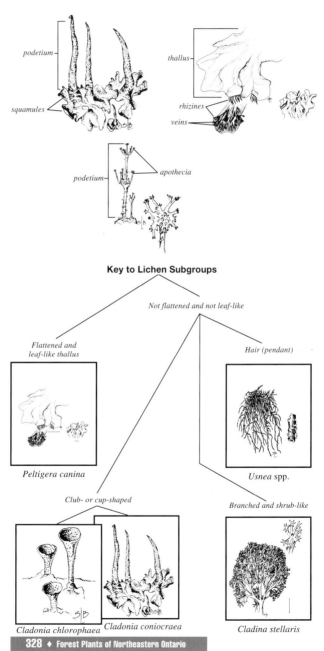

Key to Lichen Subgroups

Not flattened and not leaf-like

Flattened and leaf-like thallus

Peltigera canina

Hair (pendant)

Usnea spp.

Club- or cup-shaped

Cladonia chlorophaea *Cladonia coniocraea*

Branched and shrub-like

Cladina stellaris

Peltigeraceae

General: Loosely growing on the ground to sub-erect, leaf-like, ranges in appearance from wide, shallowly lobed and flat to numerous small and semi-erect lobes; upper surface green to greyish- or bright-green when moist and has scattered, dark-green to dark-brown wart-like markings, underside greyish-brown to dirty white near margins, veins indistinct, densely covered with matted, wool-like or cottony hairs.

Habitat: All moisture regimes, soil textures and stand types; among feathermosses such as Schreber's moss and stair-step moss; common.

Notes: Spotted dog lichen can be recognized by its greenish colour and wart-like markings.

Linda Kershaw

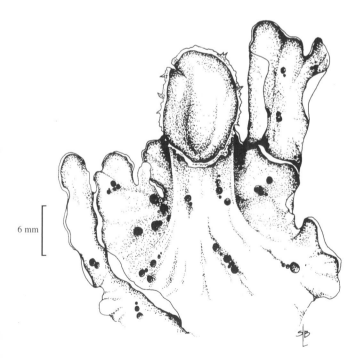

6 mm

Peltigeraceae

General: Lobed leaf lichen, pressed to ground; upper surface light brown with whitish tinge when dry, darker brown when wet, has fine hairs, underside tan to whitish with long, slender, horizontal, root-like stems (rhizomes); up to 30 cm or more across, lobes up to 8 cm across; margins wavy and usually turned downward.

Karen Legasy

Habitat: All moisture regimes, soil textures and stand types; on rocks, rotten wood and tree bases; very common.

Notes: Dog's tooth lichen was once believed to be a cure for rabies, and that is how it got its common name. See caution in Introduction.

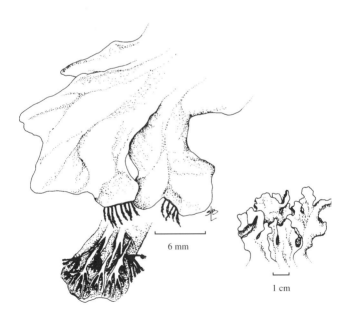

6 mm

1 cm

General: Variable cup formation with sieve-like openings to the cup interiors; greenish to brownish mineral-grey with dark-brown markings (apothecia); 3–5 cm high; leaf-like lobes at base (squamules) are medium-sized at 1–4 mm long and up to 0.5 mm wide; upper surface olive-green or brownish, underside white and darkens toward base, upward-growing and flat to curved inward; margins often have secondary ranks of cups.

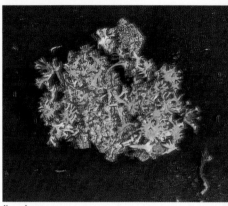

Karen Legasy

Habitat: Soils; roadsides; among mosses and on rotting logs in moist areas; fairly common.

Notes: You can recognize perforated cladonia by the sieve-like openings to its cup interiors.

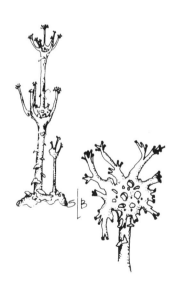

Cladoniaceae

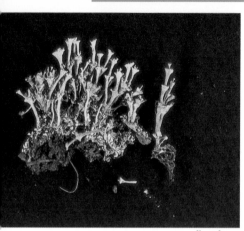

General: Upright, ladder-like, quickly flaring into short, wide, deep cups up to 9 mm wide, with small, pointed or secondary cups from centres of closed cups; greenish mineral-grey; 2–8 cm high; margins smooth or with rounded, brown to reddish-brown fruiting bodies (apothecia) that are stalkless or on short stalks; often with several layers of cups; leaf-like lobes at base (squamules) persist or disappear, up to 8 mm long and 4 mm wide; upper surface olive-green, brownish or slate-green, underside white or black toward base, irregularly wedge-shaped or lobed, margins round-toothed, flat or rolled inward and often upward-growing.

Karen Legasy

Habitat: Mineral soils, thin layers of soil over rock outcrops and rarely on rotting wood; common.

Notes: You can recognize ladder lichen by its ladder-like appearance, which is created by the way several tiers of cups originate from the centres of other cups.

Cladoniaceae

General: Upright, goblet-shaped cups; greenish mineral-grey with brown markings (apothecia); 0.5–1.5 cm high; unbranched; margins round-toothed, upward-facing and more or less curled inward; leaf-like lobes at base (squamules) persist or disappear, 4–7 mm long and almost as wide, upper surface whitish or olive-whitish and dull to rarely shiny, underside white and darkens toward base, upward-growing, margins scalloped.

Habitat: Soil, rocks, tree bases, rotting wood and mosses on roadbanks; rarely on thick humus; very common.

Karen Legasy

Notes: False pixie cup can be recognized by its goblet-shaped cups. It is the most commonly collected of the cup lichens.

Cladoniaceae

Karen Legasy

General: Usually has pointed tips or, occasionally, small, narrow, irregular cups; whitish-green, occasionally with brown markings (apothecia) at tips or cup margins; 0.5–2 cm high; unbranched; leaf-like lobes at base (squamules) are mid-sized to very long, thick, dense; upper surface olive-green or powdery-white to brownish and rounded or hollowed, underside white; margins toothless or round-toothed.

Habitat: Humus, rotting wood, tree bases; over rocks in moist areas; very common.

Notes: Powder horn lichen forms a fine, whitish to yellowish or greenish powder.

Cladoniaceae

General: Erect, narrow, with hollow, cup-like projections (podetia) lacerated at the tips; whitish mineral-grey with small brownish markings (apothecia) on cup margins or tips; 1–4 cm high; sparingly branched in upper parts; margins inrolled and often bear secondary cups; leaf-like lobes at base (squamules) are 1–3 mm long, 1 mm thick, upper surface pale- to olive-green or brownish, underside white, lobes irregularly divided, upward-growing, flat or curved inward, scattered or in tufts, margins scalloped.

Karen Legasy

Habitat: Soil or humus, rotten stumps and wood; open areas; fairly common.

Notes: You can recognize powdered funnel cladonia in the field by the inrolled margins of its cups.

Cladoniaceae

Karen Legasy

General: Short, wide, goblet-shaped cups; greenish with deep-red markings (apothecia) on proliferations or growths on margins; 1–2 cm high; cup margins regular and smooth or toothed to multiplying (proliferating) and rarely bearing small cups; leaf-like lobes at base (squamules) are small to large at 1–7 mm long and up to 5 mm wide, persist or disappear; margins irregularly toothed or lobed.

Habitat: Clayey soils and rocks with a thin layer of soil; common.

Notes: You can recognize *Cladonia pleurota* by the deep-red markings (apothecia) on the proliferations of its margins and by its short, wide cups.

Cladoniaceae

General: Upright, slightly cylindrical, brittle and cupless; light-green or pale- to deep-yellowish with brown tips; 20–80 mm high, 1–1.5 mm in diameter; irregularly and repeatedly branched, ultimate branchlets spine-like and in small whorls around open perforations; leaf-like lobes at base (squamules) are absent; forms dense mats or tufts.

Habitat: Sandy soil; among mosses in bogs or on rock; open areas; common.

Notes: *Cladonia uncialis* is similar to *Cladina* spp. and often grows with them; you can distinguish it by its smooth, shiny outer layer.

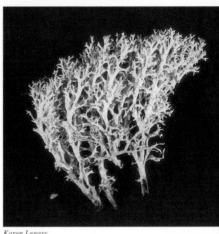

Karen Legasy

CORAL LICHEN ◆ *Cladina stellaris*
CLADINE ÉTOILÉE

Cladoniaceae

Brenda Chambers

General: Upright, distinctive coral- or cauliflower-like compact heads separate or loosely grouped, lacks a distinctive main stem; pale greenish or yellowish-grey; 6–10 cm high; branches tangled; grows in separate or loosely clumped colonies.

Habitat: Dry to fresh, rocky to sandy upland and wet organic sites, jack pine, black spruce and mixed conifer stands; common.

Notes: Coral lichen is often used to make trees and shrubs in model train-set layouts. • Coral lichen's coral- or cauliflower-like head distinguishes it from yellow-green lichen (*Cladina mitis*) and reindeer lichen (*C. rangiferina*). Yellow-green and reindeer lichen each have a distinctive main stem, which coral lichen lacks. Coral lichen can also be recognized by the way its branch tips end in a star-shaped whorl of 4–5 tiny branches surrounding a central hole. • Moose and caribou graze lichens, and the northern flying squirrel uses them to build nests.

1 cm

Cladoniaceae

General: Upward-growing with a distinct round, fibrous and dull stem with numerous branches; ash-grey colour; 6–10 cm high; branching pattern mostly in 4s; fruiting bodies (apothecia) dark brown and very rare; scattered but often forms extensive colonies of entangled masses.

Habitat: All moisture regimes, soil textures and stand types; common.

Notes: Yellow-green lichen (*Cladina mitis*) is very similar-looking,

Karen Legasy

but it is greenish-yellow in colour while reindeer lichen is distinctively ash-grey. Reindeer lichen may also be confused with coral lichen (*Cladina stellaris*), but coral lichen does not form a distinctive roundish, coral- or cauliflower-like head as does coral lichen.

1 cm

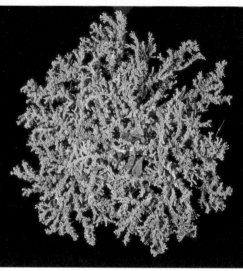

General: Prostrate to slightly erect; whitish mineral-grey; 4–8 cm high; few branches at base, upper section has many recurved, short branches; fruiting bodies (apothecia) are dark-brown discs at branch ends; in loose patches.

Habitat: Common on soil over rocks, on humus and in open places.

Notes: Foam lichen can be recognized by its foam-like appearance.
• Lichens are a large component of the caribou's diet. Since lichens

Karen Legasy

grow continuously, have no leaves to drop, are extremely long-lived and receive their nourishment from the air, they store large amounts of radioactive fallout from atomic weapons testing conducted in the North. When caribou feed on these lichens, the toxic, radioactive by-products enter their systems and contaminate their meat. Eskimo and Lapp people eat the meat, and their systems are contaminated in turn.

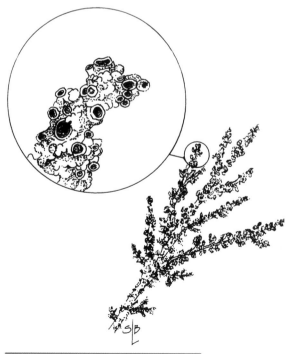

General: Erect or hanging hair lichen, usually attached to a branch; 4–40 cm long, depending on species; sometimes in 2 parts, more commonly has a central axis with longer or shorter side branches projecting; main axis often dark at base, smooth, with minute, wart-like markings, small knobby markings or powdery; side branches often differ from main axis; main branches sometimes pitted with grooves or depressions and have a distinct outer layer.

Karen Legasy

Habitat: Arboreal (grows on trees [conifer or deciduous] and shrubs).

Notes: The northern parula bird builds its nest in *Usnea* spp. *Usnea* spp. can usually be seen dangling from branches and can be recognized by their central axis or stem.

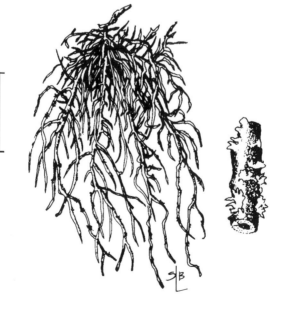

1 cm

APPENDIX
Species Dependent on Forest Plants in Our Region

Birds†

Northern Harrier (*Circus cyaneus*)
Sharp-shinned hawk
    (*Accipiter striatus*)
Cooper's hawk (*Accipiter cooperii*)
Goshawk (*Accipiter gentilis*)
Red-shouldered hawk (*Buteo lineatus*)
Broad-winged hawk
    (*Buteo platypterus*)
Red-tailed hawk (*Buteo jamaicensis*)
American kestrel (*Falco sparverius*)
Merlin (*Falco columbarius*)
Spruce grouse
    (*Dendragapus canadensis*)
Ruffed grouse (*Bonasa umbellus*)
Sharp-tailed grouse
    (*Tympanuchus phasianellus*)
Killdeer (*Charadrius vociferus*)
Common snipe (*Gallinago gallinago*)
American woodcock (*Scolopax minor*)
Black-billed cuckoo
    (*Coccyzus erythropthalmus*)
Great horned owl (*Bubo virginianus*)
Northern hawk-owl (*Surnia ulula*)
Barred owl (*Strix varia*)
Great gray owl (*Strix nebulosa*)
Long-eared owl (*Asio otus*)
Boreal owl (*Aegolius funereus*)
Northern saw-whet owl
    (*Aegolius acadicus*)
Common nighthawk
    (*Chordeiles minor*)
Whip-poor-will
    (*Caprimulgus vociferus*)
Ruby-throated hummingbird
    (*Archilochus colubris*)
Yellow-bellied sapsucker
    (*Sphyrapicus varius*)
Downy woodpecker
    (*Picoides pubescens*)
Hairy woodpecker (*Picoides villosus*)
Three-toed woodpecker
    (*Picoides tridactylus*)
Black-backed woodpecker
    (*Picoides arcticus*)
Northern flicker (*Colaptes auratus*)
Pileated woodpecker
    (*Dryocopus pileatus*)
Olive-sided flycatcher
    (*Contopus borealis*)
Eastern wood-pewee
    (*Contopus virens*)
Yellow-bellied flycatcher
    (*Empidonax flaviventris*)
Least flycatcher
    (*Empidonax minimus*)
Alder flycatcher
    (*Empidonax alnorum*)
Great crested flycatcher
    (*Myiarchus crinitus*)

Gray jay (*Perisoreus canadensis*)
Blue jay (*Cyanocitta cristata*)
American crow
    (*Corvus brachyrhynchos*)
Common raven (*Corvus corax*)
Black-capped chickadee
    (*Parus atricapillus*)
Boreal chickadee (*Parus hudsonicus*)
Red-breasted nuthatch
    (*Sitta canadensis*)
White-breasted nuthatch
    (*Sitta carolinensis*)
Brown creeper (*Certhia americana*)
House wren (*Troglodytes aedon*)
Winter wren
    (*Troglodytes troglodytes*)
Golden-crowned kinglet
    (*Regulus satrapa*)
Ruby-crowned kinglet
    (*Regulus calendula*)
Eastern bluebird (*Sialia sialis*)
Veery (*Catharus fuscescens*)
Swainson's thrush
    (*Catharus ustulatus*)
Hermit thrush (*Catharus guttatus*)
Wood thrush (*Hylocichla mustelina*)
American robin (*Turdus migratorius*)
Gray catbird
    (*Dumetella carolinensis*)
Brown thrasher (*Toxostoma rufum*)
Cedar waxwing
    (*Bombycilla cedrorum*)
European starling (*Sturnus vulgaris*)
Solitary vireo (*Vireo solitarius*)
Warbling vireo (*Vireo gilvus*)
Philadelphia vireo
    (*Vireo philadelphicus*)
Red-eyed vireo (*Vireo olivaceus*)
Tennessee warbler (*Vermivora peregrina*)
Orange-crowned warbler
    (*Vermivora celata*)
Nashville warbler
    (*Vermivora ruficapilla*)
Northern parula warbler
    (*Parula americana*)
Yellow warbler (*Dendroica petechia*)
Chestnut-sided warbler
    (*Dendroica pensylvanica*)
Magnolia warbler
    (*Dendroica magnolia*)
Cape May warbler
    (*Dendroica tigrina*)
Black-throated blue warber
    (*Dendroica caerulescens*)
Yellow-rumped warbler
    (*Dendroica coronata*)
Black-throated green warbler
    (*Dendroica virens*)
Blackburnian warbler
    (*Dendroica fusca*)

Pine warbler *(Dendroica pinus)*
Palm warbler *(Dendroica palmarum)*
Bay-breasted warbler
  (Dendroica castanea)
Blackpoll warbler *(Dendroica striata)*
Black-and-white warbler
  (Mniotilta varia)
American redstart
  (Setophaga ruticilla)
Ovenbird *(Seiurus aurocapillus)*
Northern waterthrush
  (Seiurus noveboracensis)
Connecticut warbler
  (Oporornis agilis)
Mourning warbler
  (Oporornis philadelphia)
Common yellowthroat
  (Geothlypis trichas)
Wilson's warbler *(Wilsonia pusilla)*
Canada warbler
  (Wilsonia canadensis)
Scarlet tanager *(Piranga olivacea)*
Rose-breasted grosbeak
  (Pheucticus ludovicianus)

Indigo bunting *(Passerina cyanea)*
Chipping sparrow
  (Spizella passerina)
Song sparrow *(Melospiza melodia)*
Lincoln's sparrow
  (Melospiza lincolnii)
White-throated sparrow
  (Zonotrichia albicollis)
Dark-eyed junco *(Junco hyemalis)*
Brown-headed cowbird
  (Molothrus ater)
Northern oriole *(Icterus galbula)*
Pine grosbeak *(Pinicola enucleator)*
Purple finch *(Carpodacus purpureus)*
Red crossbill *(Loxia curvirostra)*
White-winged crossbill
  (Loxia leucoptera)
Pine siskin *(Carduelis pinus)*
American goldfinch
  (Carduelis tristis)
Evening grosbeak
  (Coccothraustes vespertinus)
[†]Order follows American
Ornithologist's Union (1983)

Herpetiles[†]

Blue-spotted salamander
  (Ambystoma laterale)
Eastern red-backed salamander
  (Plethodon cinereus)
American toad *(Bufo americanus)*
Northern spring peeper
  (Hyla crucifer)

Boreal chorus frog
  (Pseudacris triseriata)
Wood frog *(Rana sylvatica)*
Mink frog *(Rana septentrionalis)*
Eastern garter snake
  (Thamnophis sirtalis)
[†]Order follows Cook (1984).

Mammals[†]

Masked shrew *(Sorex cinereus)*
Smokey shrew *(Sorex fumeus)*
Arctic shrew *(Sorex arcticus)*
Pygmy shrew *(Microsorex hoyi)*
Short-tailed shrew
  (Blarina brevicauda)
Star-nosed mole *(Condylura cristata)*
Snowshoe hare *(Lepus americanus)*
Eastern chipmunk *(Tamias striatus)*
Least chipmunk *(Eutamias minimus)*
Woodchuck *(Marmota monax)*
Red squirrel
  (Tamiasciurus hudsonicus)
Northern flying squirrel
  (Glaucomys sabrinus)
Deer mouse
  (Peromyscus maniculatus)
Boreal red-backed vole
  (Clethrionomys gapperi)
Southern bog lemming
  (Synaptomys cooperi)
Northern bog lemming
  (Synaptomys borealis)
Heather vole
  (Phenacomys intermedius)

Meadow vole
  (Microtus pennsylvanicus)
Rock vole *(Microtus chrotorrhinus)*
Meadow jumping mouse
  (Zapus hudsonius)
Woodland jumping mouse
  (Napaeozapus insignis)
Porcupine *(Erethizon dorsatum)*
Coyote *(Canis latrans)*
Wolf *(Canis lupus)*
Red Fox *(Vulpes vulpes)*
Black bear *(Ursus americanus)*
Raccoon *(Procyon lotor)*
Pine marten *(Martes americana)*
Fisher *(Martes pennanti)*
Ermine *(Mustela erminea)*
Long-tailed weasel *(Mustela frenata)*
Least weasel *(Mustela nivalis)*
Striped skunk *(Mephitis mephitis)*
Lynx *(Felis lynx)*
Woodland caribou *(Rangifer tarandus)*
White-tailed deer
  (Odocoileus virginianus)
Moose *(Alces alces)*
[†]Order follows Simpson (1945).

GLOSSARY

achene: a small, dry, hard, single-seeded fruit that does not open

annual: having a life cycle (from seed to maturity to seed) of 1 year

apothecia: a cup-shaped structure in most lichens in which the disc-shaped or elongated fruiting body is found

ascending: growing on an upward slant

awn: a slender, terminal bristle

berry: a fleshy fruit with a pulpy interior, usually containing several seeds

biennial: having a life cycle (from seed to maturity to seed) of 2 years

blade: the flat, expanded part of a leaf

bloom: a whitish, powdery coating that is often waxy

bog: an open or sparsely treed wetland habitat; poor in mineral nutrients (supplied primarily by precipitation); characteristically acidic

bract: a reduced or modified leaf, usually at the base of a flower or inflorescence

branchlet: a small branch, usually referring to the most recent year's growth

callus: a hard swelling or bulging from the surrounding surface

calyx: the leaves (sepals) enclosing a flower bud

capsule: a dry fruit, usually containing 2 or more seeds, that splits into sections at maturity; also the spore-bearing structure of a moss sporophyte

catkin: a dense spike of small male or female flowers without petals

clasping: usually referring to leaves which partially surround a stem

conifer mixedwoods: mixedwood stands dominated by conifer species, including black spruce, white spruce, balsam fir, larch, eastern white cedar or jack pine

corolla: a whorl of petals

cuspidate: with a sharp and firm point at the tip

cutover: an area that has been logged

deciduous: leaves shed at maturity or the end of the growing season; not evergreen or persistent

decurrent: extending down the stem, i.e., the base of a leaf extending down the stem so that the stem appears winged

detrital material: debris produced by the action of erosion

disc: an enlargement of the end of the flower stalk to which the flower parts are attached

disc flower: a flower with a tubular corolla

drupe: a fleshy or pulpy, 1-seeded fruit in which the seed has a hard, stone-like covering

ephemeral: short-lived

esker: a ridge of sand and gravel, formed within tunnels in glacial ice, and deposited when the ice melts

evergreen: needles or green leaves that stay on the plant throughout the year

fen: an open or sparsely treed wetland habitat which is more mineral-rich than a bog due to groundwater and surface input of nutrients; ranging from acidic to alkaline

fibrous: made up of or looking like fibres

free end: the unattached end of a berry

frond: the leaf of a fern; in mosses, a stem which is closely and regularly branched in 1 plane, thus resembling a fern leaf

gemmae: small, asexual reproductive structures in mosses and liverworts that become detached from their parents and develop into new individuals

glaciofluvial: referring to a type of landform developed from the action of meltwater in a glacial environment

gland: a small structure or surface that secretes substances such as oil or nectar

glume: a bract at the base of a spikelet in the grass family

habit: the general appearance of a plant

hardwood mixedwoods: mixedwood stands dominated by trembling aspen, white birch, balsam poplar or black ash

herb: a plant without woody above-ground parts, the stems dying back to the ground each year

herbaceous: herb-like

hummock: an elevated, dry, wooded area in a swamp

humus: dark-brown to black, decomposed plant remains in the organic layer of a soil profile; origin or structure of original plants, for the most part, impossible to identify

inflorescence: the flowering part of a plant, in various arrangements, e.g., spike or panicle

internode: the section of stem between 2 adjacent nodes

involucre: a set of bracts beneath an inflorescence; (liverworts) a protective covering around the hood of a capsule

kame: a cone-shaped hill made up of sediments deposited by meltwaters falling from the edge of a glacier

lateral: on or from the side of an organ

leaflet: one of the divisions of a compound leaf

lemma: the lower of the 2 bracts immediately enclosing an individual grass flower

lens-shaped: rounded and convex

lenticel: raised, cork-like markings or spots on young bark

ligule: in grasses, the thin outgrowth from the inner surface of a leaf at the junction of the sheath and blade

lip: a projection or expansion of something, such as the lower petal of an orchid or violet flower

litter: the top layer of organic matter (e.g., leaves and twigs) on a forest floor

lobe: a partial division of an organ such as a leaf

marsh: an open wetland habitat with submerged and floating grass-like vegetation, with up to 2 m of water (fluctuates seasonally), typically neutral with high oxygen levels

membranous: thin, soft, pliable and somewhat semitransparent

mucro: a small, short, slender, abrupt tip

node: the point on a stem at which a leaf, bud or branch arises; in grasses there is a noticeable swelling or 'joint' at each node

nutlet: a small nut

obscurely toothed: having teeth which are difficult to see without magnification

operculum: the lid of a capsule on a moss

ovary: a structure that encloses young, undeveloped seeds

ovoid: shaped like a chicken's egg

overtop: to be taller than

panicle: a branched inflorescence

papillae: minute, wart-like swellings or bulges

perennial: growing for 3 or more years, usually flowering and producing fruit each year

perianth: (flowers) the sepals and petals of a flower, collectively; (liverworts) a tube, apparently of 2–3 fused leaves, surrounding a developing sporophyte

peristome: the fringe of teeth at the opening of a moss capsule

perigynium: a membranous sac that encloses the seeds of sedges

persist: to remain attached after normal function has been completed

petal: a member of the inside ring of modified flower leaves, usually white or brightly coloured

pinna: the primary division of a pinnate compound leaf (see pictorial glossary)

pinnate: divided, as with a compound leaf, such that the segments are arranged on 2 sides of a central axis; feather-like (see pictorial glossary)

pinnule: the secondary or ultimate leaflet or division of a pinnately compound leaf (see pictorial glossary)

pistil: the female organ of a flower, usually differentiated into a stigma, style and an ovary

pith: the central part of a stem

pod: a dry fruit, especially of the pea family

podetia: a stalk-like, hollow structure that supports apothecia in lichens

pome: a fruit with a core, such as an apple

prickle: a small, slender and sharp outgrowth

proliferations: small outgrowths or offshoots in lichens

reticulate: having a network of veins

rhizoid: a thread-like, branched or unbranched growth on mosses and liverworts that serves as an anchor or is used for absorption

rhizome: a horizontal underground stem, distinguished from a root by the presence of nodes, buds or scale-like leaves

rootstalk: see rhizome

rosette: a circular cluster of leaves, usually at the base of a plant

runner: a very slender, wiry stolon

samara: a winged fruit that does not open

saprophyte: a plant, usually without green colour, which derives its food from dead organic matter

scabrous: rough

scale: any small, thin or flat structure; in cones of conifer tree species the scales are woody and enclose the seeds

scape: a leafless flower stem

scarious: having a thin, dry, membranous texture

sepal: a member of the outside ring of modified flower leaves (the calyx), usually green sheath: a tubular envelope surrounding another organ, as the lower part of the leaf of grasses and sedges which surrounds the stem

sinus: the space or cleft between 2 lobes

spike: an elongated flower cluster with the flowers being stalkless or nearly so

spikelet: a small or secondary spike; the smallest flower cluster in grasses and sedges

spindle-shaped: long and thin

sporangia: sacs or containers in which spores are produced

sporophyte: the spore-bearing part or phase of a plant

spur: a slender, tubular or sac-like and usually hollow projection from some part of a flower

squamule: a small, scale-like lobe on lichens

stigma: the tip of the female organ in plants, where the pollen lands

stipe: a stalk-like support; the stalk of a fern leaf from the base of the leaf to the point of attachment to the rhizome

stipule: a small, leaf-like growth at the base of a leafstalk

stolon: from the base of a plant, a creeping, horizontal branch or stem which produces new shoots

style: the stalk of the pistil, connecting the ovary and the stigma

swamp: thicket or wooded wetland habitat with standing to gently flowing water (seasonally fluctuating) with strong sub-surface flow; rich in mineral nutrients; neutral to moderately acidic; little development of peat

taproot: a primary, downward-growing root

tendril: a slender, twining outgrowth from a stem or leaf; used for climbing or support

thallose: having a thallus

thallus: a main plant body, not differentiated into stem and leaves, in lichens and some liverworts

thicket: a dense patch of shrubs or small trees

transition tolerant hardwood stands: stands dominated by sugar maple and/or yellow birch, and red maple mixedwoods, typical of the Great Lakes–St. Lawrence region; at the northern limit of their range in the northeast region, these stands are typically restricted to warm ecoclimates or ridges, plateaus or hilltops.

transitional Great Lakes–St. Lawrence forest stands: see transition tolerant hardwood stands

truncate: having a blunt end or ending abruptly, with the base nearly straight across

tuber: a short, thickened underground stem

tubercle: a small swelling or projection on an organ

unarmed: without thorns or prickles

understorey: vegetation underneath forest tree canopy layers

undulate: having a wavy appearance

varved: having repeating, annually deposited layers of clays, silts or sands in a sediment deposited in a lake environment; clay (dark, thin layers) indicating deposition in winter months, silts or sands (thick, light layers) indicating deposits in summer

whorl: a group of 3 or more similar organs radiating around a node (see pictorial glossary)

PICTORIAL GLOSSARY

Leaf Arrangement

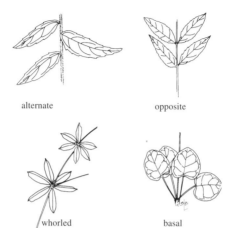

alternate

opposite

whorled

basal

Leaf Margin

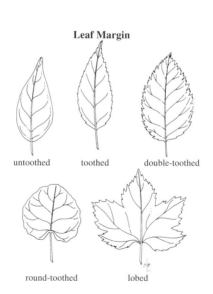

untoothed

toothed

double-toothed

round-toothed

lobed

Leaf Shape

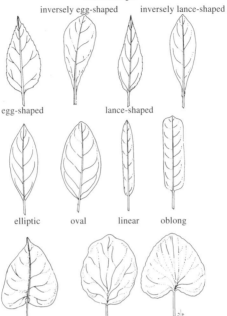

inversely egg-shaped   inversely lance-shaped

egg-shaped   lance-shaped

elliptic   oval   linear   oblong

heart-shaped   round   kidney-shaped

Leaf Structure

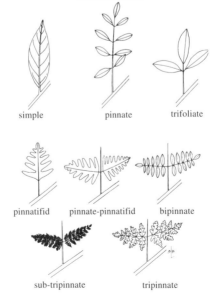

simple   pinnate   trifoliate

pinnatifid   pinnate-pinnatifid   bipinnate

sub-tripinnate   tripinnate

INDEX